EVERYMAN, I will go with thee,
and be thy guide,
In thy most need to go by thy side

JOHN CLARE

Born at Helpston, Northamptonshire, 13 July 1793. Died in St Andrew's County Asylum at Northampton, 20 May 1864.

JOHN CLARE

Selected Poems

Edited by
J. W. Tibble

Formerly Professor of Education in the University of Leicester

and
Anne Tibble

Dent: London and Melbourne
EVERYMAN'S LIBRARY

All rights reserved
Made in Great Britain by
Guernsey Press Co. Ltd, Guernsey, C.I.
for
J. M. Dent & Sons Ltd
Aldine House, 33 Welbeck Street, London W1M 8LX

This edition was first published in
Everyman's Library in 1965
Last reprinted 1984

No 563 Hardback ISBN 0 460 00563 4
No 1563 Paperback ISBN 0 460 11563 4

INTRODUCTION

Hope, love, joy are poesy.

CLARE: The Progress of Rhyme

Real excellence must be its own creation—it must be the over-flowings of its own mind and must make its admirers willing converts from its own powerful conceptions and not yield to win them by giving way to their opinions.

CLARE: Essay on Landscape

JOHN CLARE was born, he himself tells us, on 'July 13, 1793, at Helpstone,[1] a gloomy village in Northamptonshire, on the brink of the Lincolnshire fens'. His father, Parker Clare, was 'one of fate's chancelings'; and his mother, Ann Stimson, was a daughter of the 'town shepherd' of the neighbouring village of Castor. His paternal grandfather, John Donald Parker, was 'a Scotchman by birth and a schoolmaster by profession', who fled the village on the appearance of his illegitimate son. Parker Clare became a flail-thresher, a whopstraw; but in his spare time he was in great demand as a rustic wrestler and a ballad singer.

The Clares were no poorer if no richer than most other villagers. At the time of Clare's birth Helpston was unenclosed. Before enclosure and its bid for more economic agriculture, rural England was probably less under actual rigours of poverty, as poverty was then understood. Cut off by lack of roads, lack of transport, lack of drainage, areas such as the Fens and Fen-verge remained self-contained and slow to change. Cecil Sharp notes how, up to a generation before the end even of the nineteenth century, folk-song in Britain's rural areas was a still unbroken tradition. Up to that time, Sharp wrote, labourer, thresher, cowherd, ploughman, pinder, goosewoman, wood-cutter, shepherd, cress-gatherer and bird-scaring boys 'sang

[1] 'Helpston' now.

in the fields, and they trudged home in the evenings to the accompaniment of song'. Clare says that his father knew by heart 'over a hundred ballads'. These Parker Clare sang at village fair and feast. Clare's mother's ballads too, and his frequent mention of villagers 'singing at their toil', lend substance to what might otherwise tend to be dismissed as a romantic overstatement of Sharp's.

Clare was a twin and when young was of 'waukly constitution':

> so much so that my mother often told me she never could have dreamt I should live to make a man, while the sister that was born with me . . . was . . . a fine lively bonny wench, whose turn it was to die first; she lived but a few weeks, proving the old saying for once mistaken, 'that the weakest always goeth to the wall'. As my parents had the good fate to have but a small family, I being the eldest of 4, two of whom died in their Infancy, my mother's hopeful ambition ran high of being able to make me a good scholar, as she said she experienced enough in her own case to avoid bringing up her children in ignorance; but God help her, her hopeful and tender kindness was often crossed with difficulty, for there was often enough to do to keep cart upon wheels, as the saying is . . .[1]

The small, frail child, with startling blue eyes and fair hair, was self-contained and solitary. When he was five he wandered off alone one morning over the flat, mole-hilly common called Emmonsales Heath. 'I wanted', he tells later in his 'Notes for my Life', to find 'the brink of the world: to

> look down like looking into a large pit & see into its secrets the same as I believed I coud see heaven by looking into the water. So I eagerly wanderd on & rambled along the furze the whole day till I got out of my knowledge . . . the very sun seemed to be a new one & shining in a different quarter of the sky still I felt no fear my wonder-seeking happiness had no room for it . . . but . . . The sky still touched the ground in the distance & my childish wisdom was puzzled . . . when I got home I found my parents in the greatest distress & half the village about hunting me . . .[1]

[1] *Sketches in the Life of John Clare by Himself*, ed. Edmund Blunden, 1931, p. 46. The original was sent to London to John Taylor in 1825.

He went to school three months of each year until he was twelve. The few pence needed for schooling he himself earned, usually by helping his father to thresh—with a light flail his father made to his size:

> I resigned myself willingly to the hardest toils . . . and tho' one of the weakest, was stubborn and stomachful, and never flinched from the roughest labour; by that means I always secured the favour of my masters, and escaped the ignominy that brands the name of idleness; my character was always 'weak but willing'. . . . Winter was generally my season of imprisonment in the dusty barn, Spring and Summer my assistance was wanted elsewhere, in tending sheep or horses in the fields, or scaring birds from the grain, or weeding it; which was a delightful employment, as the old women's memories never failed of tales to smoothen our labour.[1]

The school he attended from the age of five years to seven was a dame-school in his own village. His next school, to which he walked two miles along the Fen road with the towering arc of sky over it, was held in the vestry above the gravestones and beneath the tall spire of the village church of Glinton.

The boy had one of those rare memories of a kind now rarer still: he could 'get the whole of the book of Job by heart'. At home he read, 'beside the Bible and the Prayer-Book', sixpenny chapbooks—*Cinderella*, *Little Red Riding Hood*, *Jack and the Beanstalk*, *Zig Zag*, *Prince Cherry*, *Robin Hood's Garland* and *Robinson Crusoe*. These were a great advance on his father's reading of 'the superstitious tales that are hawked about the street for a penny—old Nixon's Prophesies and Mother Shipton's Legacy'. The Clares' cottage table,

> which, old as it was, doubtless never was honoured with higher employment all its days than the convenience of bearing at meal times the luxury of a barley loaf, or dish of potatoes, was now covered with the rude beggings of scientific requisitions, pens, ink, and paper—one hour hobbling the pen at sheephooks and tarbottles, and another, trying on a slate a knotty question in

[1] Ibid., p. 48.

Numeration, or Pounds, shillings and Pence; at which times my parents' triumphant anxiety was pleasingly experienced; for my mother woud often stop her wheel, or look off from her work, to urge with a smile of the warmest rapture in my father's face her prophesy of my success, saying 'she'd be bound I shoud one day be able to reward them with my pen for the trouble they had taken in giving me schooling'.[1]

At Glinton he had one of those childish friendships, 'not found[ed] like bargains on matters of interest, nor broken for selfish ends'.[2] This was with Richard Turnill. When Richard died of typhus his elder, boarding-schooled brother John appalled Clare by showing him the night sky through a tele-scope. The fragmentary 'memoirs' or 'Notes for my Life' among Clare's manuscripts, more detailed than the *Sketches*, tell also:

> I was a lover very early in life—my first attachment . . . being a schoolboy affection was for Mary—who . . . was beloved with a romantic or Platonic sort of feeling If I coud but gaze on her face or fancy a smile on her countenance it was sufficient I went away satisfied we played with each other but named nothing of love yet I fancyd her eyes told me her affections. We walked together as school-companions in leisure hours but our talk was of play & our actions the wanton nonsense of children yet young as my heart was it woud turn chill when I touchd her hand & tremble & I fancyd her feelings were the same for as I gazed earnestly in her face a tear woud hang in her smiling eye . . . her heart was as tender as a birds. . . . I cannot forget her little play-ful fairy form & witching smile even now.[2]

This girl, Mary Joyce, was the child of a well-to-do Glinton farmer. She, or Clare's memory of her, was to exert a deep influence, both conscious and unconscious, on his poetry and all his life.

By the age of twelve the boy was already imposing on himself an apprenticeship in the writing of verse. He was inspired to

[1] Ibid., p. 49.
[2] *John Clare. A Life*, 1932, pp. 33–4. These fragmentary 'memoirs' are pieced together in *The Prose of John Clare*, 1950.

try his hand by his father's and mother's 'trash of Ballad Singing':

> . . . I cannot say . . . at what age I began to write it but my first feelings & attempts at poetry were imitations of my father's songs. . . . I made a great many things before I venturd to comit them to writing for I felt ashamed to expose them on paper & after I venturd to write them down my second thoughts blushd over them & burnt them for a long time but as my feelings grew into song I felt a desire to preserve some & usd to correct them over & over until the last copy had lost all kindred to the first even in the title   I went on for some years in this way wearing it in my memory as a secret to all tho my parents usd to know that my leisure was occupyd in writing yet they had no knowledge of what I coud be doing for they never dreamd of me writing poetry   at length I venturd to divulge the secret a little by reading imitations of some popular songs floating among the vulgar at the markets & fairs till they were common to all   but these imitations they only laughd at & told me I need never hope to make songs like them   this mortified me often & almost made me desist for I knew that the excelling such doggerel woud be but a poor fame if I coud do nothing better   but I hit upon a harmless deception by repeating my poems over a book as tho I was reading it   this had the desird effect   they often praised them & said if I coud write as good I shoud do   I hugd myself over this deception & often repeated it & those which they praised as superior to others I tryd to preserve in a hole in the wall but my mother found out the hoard & unconsciously took them for kettle-holders & fire-lighters . . .[1]

His father had recited Pomfret's 'Love Triumphant over Reason' to him before he himself could read. This 'vision' of Pomfret's, as Clare called it, was 'more known among the lower orders than anything else of poetry at least with us'. His mother brought him Chatterton's 'verses on resignation' printed on a handkerchief from Deeping May Fair. One of his mother's unlettered brothers gave him a penny broadside edition of John Cunningham's poems. A weaver in that 'illiterate' village, much older than Clare, lent him Thomson's *The Seasons*. The opening of 'Spring'—'Come gentle Spring,

---

[1] See ibid., pp. 41–2; also *The Prose of John Clare*, 1950, p. 30.

ethereal mildness come'—Clare writes, 'made my heart twitter with joy'.

He 'teazed' the necessary one and sixpence out of his father. Next day he gave another boy a penny to use his clappers, bird-scaring for him. Walking five miles to Stamford town to buy a copy of The Seasons for himself, he thus began his collecting of the library of poetry that graced his cottage all his life. For the next four or five years, he records, 'I scribbled on unceasing' while 'my Judgement began to expand and improve'.

But by the end of schooldays one of those known and accepted Fenland misfortunes had fallen on the family. His father—'a very tender father to his children' Clare has emphasized more than once—became disabled by the Fen scourge, rheumatism. It was necessary that the boy should earn a living as soon as possible. He became horse-boy for a year for the fatherly landlord of the Blue Bell Inn next door to the Clares' cottage. One of his duties at Francis Gregory's of the Blue Bell was to bring a bag of flour once a week from the mill at Maxey, a village two miles from Helpston.

> The traditional Registers of the village was uncommonly super-stitious (Gossips and Grannys); and I had one or two haunted spots to pass. . . . Therefore I must in such extremities seize the best remedy to keep such things out of my head, as well as I could; so on these journeys I muttered over tales of my own fancy, contriving them into rhymes as well as my abilities was able; . . . and tho', however romantic my story might be, I had always cautions fearful enough, no doubt, to keep ghosts and hobgoblins out of the question . . . for as I passed those haunted places, tho' I dare not look boldly up, my eye was warily on the watch, gleg-ging under my hat at every stir of a leaf or murmur of the wind, and a quaking thistle was able to make me swoon with terror.[1]

Next he took the job of ploughboy at Woodcroft Castle; and some time then, through seeing a loader fall from his wagon and break his neck, Clare became subject to actual swooning fits. These fits, he says, were 'stopt by a Mr Arnold, M.D.', of Stamford. He left Woodcroft after about a year, and his parents, disappointed, feared he would stick at nothing long.

[1] Sketches in the Life of John Clare by Himself, pp. 56-7.

He grew more and more solitary: 'I hunted curious flowers in rapture & mutterd thoughts in their praise.' After some negotiations, first for being a shoemaker's apprentice, and then for being a solicitor's clerk, wanting to be more than a ploughman he became gardener at Burghley House; but this, too, from the incredibly unsatisfactory quarters allotted to the men, proved unsatisfactory. Clare and another, older gardener left by night and tramped to Newark.

By this time he was nineteen. At Newark he volunteered for the Militia, in order to get the bounty of two guineas—rather than be 'forced' and 'go for nothing'. The Militia was the home force hastily called together to repel Napoleon. In 1812, he tells us, 'the country was chin-deep in the fears of invasion'. The raw recruit, five feet two, a rhymer whose 'thoughts were often absent when the word of command was given' and 'never wonderful clean' in his dress, soon encountered the persistent sneering of 'a little louse-looking corporal'. Taunted beyond endurance one morning on parade, the awkward private seized the scurrilous corporal by the throat and hurled him down. For this breach of discipline Clare was threatened with the 'Black Hole , with tying to the halberd and with the whip. But a friendly captain saved him more than an additional 'guard'.

On his return home some eighteen months later Clare renewed his hopes of Mary Joyce. It is possible they had a short idyllic courtship. No one knows quite what happened: whether Mary herself grew 'haughty' and 'felt her station above mine', as Clare says, or whether her father intervened. She was a daughter of a prosperous farmer. Clare was a labourer earning nine shillings a week by no means regularly, a crippled thresher's son. Mary died unmarried at the age of forty-one in 1838. After a number of attachments that came to nothing, he went lime-burning at Pickworth, Ryhall and Casterton. At Bridge Casterton he met Martha Turner, 'Patty of the Vale', the black-haired daughter of the small holder of Walkherd Lodge Farm. Patty joined the Clare family at Helpston just before the birth of the first of their eight children. Of these seven lived to reach maturity.

On 16th January, two months before his marriage, and

after long and determined effort on his part, Clare's first book of poems was published by John Taylor. Taylor was Keats's valiant publisher, then in the brief heyday of his enterprise. Clare's book bore the clumsy title *Poems Descriptive of Rural Life and Scenery*; but it caught the tail-end of one of the recurrent vogues in British 'pastoral' poetry.

It brought him fame. Lionized in London's literary circle, henceforward Charles Lamb's 'princely Clare' could list among his friends Admiral Lord Radstock, Tom Hood, Allan Cunningham, George Darley, H. F. Cary, Mrs E. L. Emmerson, Charles Wentworth Dilke, Charles Abraham Elton, William Hone, James Montgomery and contributors to the important *London Magazine*. Letters and messages from people such as John Keats and visits to London helped Clare to endure the isolation. This, on account of his difference from others and of his celebrity, could not fail to grow round him in his village. In the cottage of his birth, in a Helpston enclosed and changed for ever, he went on writing.

The bulk of poetry from his long life of lyricism falls into two main categories. There are precise, 'sharp and exciting vignettes'. In these the telling detail from an abundance of plant, animal and rural lore is invested with strong emotional charge; but they must be sought in a repetitive profusion of descriptive verse, half of which is still unpublished. There are also his mature, semi-mystical poems amid over eight hundred quickly written sets of verse that he himself called Halfpenny Ballads. Such arbitrary divisions as these two naturally overlap and mingle.

From start to finish Clare had no one near enough, constant enough, discerning enough to help him discipline himself along that tightrope where spontaneity and craftsmanship strive for the poet's economy and balance. Thus there is a thin green line of Clare's readers who, despite the steady growth of an urban England, will always value him as our foremost country or 'nature' poet. These readers see him as the poet of—as Edmund Blunden put it—'that which grew from the incident and secrecy of wild life'. Not forgetting Andrew Marvell, Michael Drayton, or the naturalist verse-maker Erasmus Darwin; not excepting Edmund Blunden, Barnes or Edward Thomas—no other poet has Clare's wealth of accurate observation and naturalist's knowledge. Even more, this kind of reader sees him as spokesman for a unit of English society now lost for good. Equally there will always be readers who prize most the near-mystical, late poems of Clare's ultimate suffering.

By 1824 Clare was 'passing rich on forty pounds a year'. This income came from a fund raised by John Taylor, Lord Radstock, Eliza Louisa Emmerson and other literary friends. Making such a sum suffice for the needs of a growing family was not easy. The new system of enclosed farming needed fewer men. Casual work grew scarcer. According to working-family tradition, Clare took responsibility for his parents. You might think that under such practical burdens the lyric impulse would have withered, at least lessened. The problem—whether to abandon poetry or to eke out a precarious livelihood combining poetry and field-work—faced him. Round about 1824 he made the decision—to continue writing whatever it cost.

When he had made this decision his 'true voice' rang clearer in him. But two other books of country poetry, The Village Minstrel, 1821, and The Shepherd's Calendar, 1827, did not sell. The fashion that James Thomson had brought back passed. The Rural Muse, from the manuscript with Clare's own title 'The Midsummer Cushion', put out in 1835 and full of far better poetry than Clare's previous books had been, sold scarcely at all.

Failure and the determination to write on in spite of getting neither reputation nor a livelihood did not foster harmony between Clare and Patty. There is evidence of sexual restlessness on his part and some pointers toward, but no proof of, venereal disease. There is talk in a letter from Hessey about what sounds like an attempt on Clare's part at suicide. Interpreted less narrowly, and not necessarily less accurately, these references may indicate, rather, mental torment on Clare's part from the menace of a stern Bible and a God-fearing upbringing. Certainly by 1830 the pressures on a sensitive, if tough, constitution were beginning to tell.

In 1832 the Clares moved to a better cottage three miles from Helpston. Northborough, a village of Cromwellian memory, lies actually in the Fen. Clare is said to have refused to get into the cart, to have followed on foot behind it, in which the aged Parker, Patty and their six children sat among books, unpublished manuscripts, chairs, tables, pots and pans. The poet's head was bent. He was loath to move even three miles from his 'old home of homes' that faced the woodlands of rolling Northamptonshire.

Those lyrics written between 1832 and 1837 take on a new depth. They include a group of stark poems about cruelty, human and non-human. There is a series of sonnets and short poems, emotive descriptions so vivid and accurate as to light in the mind pictures of the actual bird and nest described. Dylan Thomas considered the very different poems in this group as among Clare's best work.

But by 1837 Clare's struggle to hold on to his personal identity had shown itself in two or three violent outbursts. He was developing an illusion that Mary Joyce was his first wife and Martha—Patty—his second. Stubborn and solitary, he would stay whole days in the fields and be found either angry or distracted; out of which states, and to home, only one or other of his two eldest sons could coax him.

On John Taylor's advice he was taken under the care of Matthew Allen, at Allen's private asylum of High Beech, in Epping Forest. What fees were paid were paid by old friends, Taylor, Mrs Emmerson. Clare was given kind and understanding treatment, relative freedom, and work to do in the gardens and fields. He stayed at High Beech four years. By July 1841 he was much stronger physically, but had grown too homesick. 'Weary of the place,' as he wrote to Matthew Allen a few weeks later, 'I heard the voice of freedom and started.'

He made his journey out of Essex on foot. In three and a half days he walked eighty miles. The first night

> I slept soundly but had a very uneasy dream I thought my first wife lay on my left arm & somebody took her away from my side which made me wake up rather unhappy I thought as I woke somebody said 'Mary' but nobody was near—I lay down with my head towards the north to show myself the steering point in the morning. . . .[1]

[1] *The Prose of John Clare*, pp. 245–6.

The third day

> I satisfied my hunger by eating the grass by the roadside which seemed to taste something like bread . . .

The Friday night that he reached Northborough, with characteristically wild energy he wrote two poems,[1] and next day he set about the account of his journey. It is one of the moving documents of English literature:

> Returned home out of Essex & found no Mary her & her family are nothing to me now though she herself was once the dearest of all—& how can I forget. . . .[2]

He was at home five months. However much his physical health had improved under High Beech treatment, he was obsessed—ambivalently as in most conflicts between emotion and reason—with the loss of Mary and at the same time with the deceit and faithlessness of all women:

> The worst is the road to ruin & the best is nothing like a good cow—man I never did like & woman has long sickened me. . . .[3]

Hallucination about phantoms and evil spirits tormented him: as the quaking thistle by the road from Maxey flour mill had, in the dark, made him almost swoon with fear when he was thirteen. His sense of everyday time and of people known and unknown grew shaky.

Yet the spring of 1841 at Epping and these five months at Northborough were when he wrote and finished the two long poems *Don Juan* and *Child Harold*. The one first finished, *Don Juan*, is, as Geoffrey Grigson says, 'an energetic mixture of madness and sanity'; more than it is a poem it is a fine quarry for the psycho-pathologist. In it a galaxy of associations denounces insincerity of many kinds. These mental associations that under a quick glance seem random are in reality brought from somewhere below to allow the poet to get away with speaking his mind. They betray what whipped him towards

---

[1] 'I've wandered many a weary mile' and 'Here's where Mary longed to be'. He intended both for the long poem *Child Harold*.

[2] *John Clare. A Life*, p. 405; also *The Prose of John Clare*, p. 44.

[3] Letter to Matthew Allen, August 1841. *The Letters of John Clare*, p. 295.

the invisible thorn-barriers that guard the grief-stricken
frontiers of madness. Besides using poetic ambiguity in *Don
Juan*, Clare was at the same time experiencing the acute pleasure, not confined to the psychotic, of mystifying his hearers:

> Put these two dishes into one and dress it
> And if there's a meaning—you may guess it.

Here are a couple of the less orthodox stanzas of *Don Juan*:

> . . . There's Doctor Bottle imp who deals in urine,
>   A keeper of state prisons for the Queen,
> As great a man as is the Doge of Turin
>   And save in London is but seldom seen—
> Yclep'd old A-ll-n—mad-brained ladies curing,
>   Some p-x-d like Flora and but seldom clean.
> The new road o'er the forest is the right one
> To see red hell, & further on the white one . . .
>
> O glorious Constitution what a picking
>   Ye've had from your tax harvest and your tythe.
> Old hens which cluck about that fair young chicken
>   —Cocks without spurs that yet can crow so blythe.
> Truth is shut up in prison while ye're licking
>   The gold from off the gingerbread—be lithe
> In winding that patched broken old state clock up.
> Playhouses open—but madhouses lock up . . .[1]

Don Juan is a poem of total disillusion. Clare had found the
world of words a fraud. Words and culture had given men
knowledge but had not made them more whole-hearted. The
poem is also a poem of sexual famine if ever there was one. It
lays bare Clare's extreme sense of lack or loss and at the same
time his sense of guilt, his resentments and his refusal to make
his feelings conform with accepted, 'normal', flexible stan-
dards. These were all part of the very complicated conflict
which drove him into the no man's land of madness.

The other poem that he was writing concurrently with
Don Juan during spring, summer, autumn and winter of 1841
was *Child Harold*. A much longer poem, *Child Harold* is more

---

[1] *Poems of John Clare's Madness*, ed. Geoffrey Grigson, 1949, pp. 70, 71;
also MS 6, Northampton.

tragic because its perspective of awareness is far deeper. In the following pages the poem is printed in the entirety Clare intended—of between seventy and eighty Spenserian, or nine-line, stanzas, with some twenty ballads and songs at intervals. These were to lighten and vary the rhythm. A poem about a life's failure, about, at the same time, hope, and about love as it pervades nature's and mankind's being, *Child Harold* approaches reconciliation of a rare kind. Like the whole of *Don Juan*, one or two stanzas of *Child Harold* are neither polite nor pretty. Bitter resentment and hate reveal themselves, necessary parts of the struggle to a reconciliation that must remain shadowy, never secure.

In December 1841 Clare was certified by two doctors. One of them, Fenwick Skrimshire, testified, without detail and as was customary in such documents [1] of that time, that Clare's disease was 'hereditary'. Up to now no evidence of any insanity or particular unbalance in the family has come to light. It is said that Clare resisted strongly when keepers came to take him away to the newly opened St Andrew's County Lunatic Asylum at Northampton. Eight shillings a week were kindly paid by Earl Fitzwilliam until Clare's death.

From the time he was forty-nine for almost twenty-three years until his death, 20th May 1864, Clare was confined at St Andrew's. As at Matthew Allen's, he met with the most enlightened treatment; and this at a time, the eighteen-thirties and forties, when Bedlam whip, chains and hunger on straw in solitude were by no means past remedies prescribed for the insane. In particular W. F. Knight, house-steward at St Andrew's from 1845 to 1850, encouraged Clare to write. For the first five years at least, medical superintendent Thomas S. Prichard allowed his patient freedom to walk into North-ampton town from the asylum more than a mile outside. Though later, when this freedom to roam was restricted, Clare wrote of his being in 'a prison that almost numbs common sense', at first he spent many hours sitting on the stone seat in the porch of the church that looks out over Northampton

[1] Peterborough MSS.

town square. The picture we have of him watching the children and the passers-by is from the pen of G. J. De Wilde.[1] The Northampton journalist's pen-sketch is not of him surrounded by acquaintances, but of him alone. A town square was not the kind of place Clare revelled in; and though—De Wilde wrote —he had 'a countenance beaming with sensitive intelligence', usually he was 'moody and taciturn and rather avoided society'.

A second phase of agony had set in. Clare's resolving of that agony resulted in those short, semi-mystical poems, important in any final assessment of his work. They include 'Love Lies Beyond the Tomb', 'I Hid my Love', 'Invite to Eternity', 'Love's Story', 'Born Upon an Angel's Breast', 'I Am', 'Enough of misery keeps my heart alive' and 'A Vision'. It is these, Geoffrey Grigson has truly said, that push this most intensely English of poets 'over the border between the pathetically interesting and exquisite into the great; however circumscribed his greatness'.[2]

Almost all the medical evidence upon which could be built any full analysis of the kind of madness from which Clare suffered was burnt by fire. Notes for his case-history exist for only the final two years at St Andrew's. These entries are without clinical detail. Best, therefore, to quote Dr Thomas Tennent, the late superintendent of St Andrew's Mental Hospital. Dr Tennent wrote on Clare's case in *The Journal of Mental Science*.[3] He described two or three epileptiform attacks at the age of seventeen, Clare's 'blue devils' of depression in the ensuing years, the 'inspiration' which drove him to write for days on end scarcely stopping to eat or sleep, his later delusions about being 'Boxer Byron', or a bruiser, or a wrestler, such as Jan Burns, Tom Spring or Ben Caunt. Dr Tennent then continued:

I have dealt in greater detail with this form of illness than might appear to have been necessary. This, however, was deliberate, as there are conflicting views regarding his type of illness. In my opinion this was a cyclothymic disorder, and not a

[1] Letter from De Wilde to Frederick Martin, Clare's first biographer, 25th February 1865. *Sketches in the Life of John Clare*, p. 39.
[2] Introduction to *Poems of John Clare's Madness*, p. 27.
[3] Vol. xcix, No. 414, January 1953.

schizophrenic one as suggested by one of his recent biographers. Apart from the actual symptomatology, the excellence of much of his poetry written in hospital and the slow development of deterioration support this diagnosis.

Confirmation of Dr Tennent's view that Clare's malady was cyclothymic rather than schizophrenic as was Hölderlin's, is given by Dr Russell Brain more recently in Some Reflections on Genius.[1] Clare endured this form of insanity, Dr Brain adds, in common with Smart, Cowper, Newton, Goethe and Samuel Johnson. It was a disorder to which men of broad general powers coupled with a sensitive imagination are naturally exposed.

But more valuable than the name which doctors of the mind have given to Clare's psychosis is our growing sense of him during those years when he wrote his best introspective lyrics, the eight hundred and more 'Halfpenny Ballads', and the last long poem A Rhapsody. This sense of him we owe chiefly to Geoffrey Grigson's lucid and beautiful Introduction to Poems of John Clare's Madness. In his later life as in his earlier, Clare wrote on, often making two or three drafts from memory of single verses or of whole poems. Each draft has slight variations. Variations later than the first draft are not necessarily meant as improvements.[2] He polished scarcely at all; and, after his first destroying when a boy, as far as is known he destroyed nothing. He wrote because for him to write was as natural and necessary an activity as speaking. The lastingness of his lyrical capacity and the extreme slowness of his mental and physical vitality to decline are characteristics of this St Andrew's period, as well as the rises, in 1844, 1847–8, 1860 and the intervening troughs of dissolution.

Our own unconscious fears are surely part of the complex reason why it is repugnant to think of any man as even momentarily sane—whatever sanity is?—during any part of a sojourn of more than twenty-two years in a nineteenth-century lunatic asylum. We would like to think of Clare's aberration as a little

[1] Pitman Medical Press, 1960, passim.
[2] As in 'No single hour can pass for nought' (Peterborough. MS. 57) and 'No single hour can stand for nought' (Northampton MS. 6).

less than madness if more than feigned. But his delusion about Mary Joyce, 'Mary Clare', 'my first wife and first love', with Patty, 'my second wife and second love'—each wife with a family that didn't grow up—saw no lessening. Whenever the long struggle to hold on to what he himself called 'self-identity' threatened to submerge him in the despair his spirit detested, as if he ducked mentally, he imagined himself one of several successful or well-known worldly figures:

> they're feeding me up for a fight but they can get nobody able to strip to me.[1]

His father had been a wrestling champion as well as ballad-singer at village May Day feasts, we recall. Another delusion, that he was Wellington, had won the battle of Waterloo, but had had his head shot off on that field, revealed the long bitterness of the fight for recognition on the field of poetry. These delusions he voiced, particularly in reply to unwelcome questions of the well-meaning. On other occasions he became Horatio Nelson. This Nelson could—and did, to his fellow 'prisoners'—recount happenings in the course of the battle of the Nile as vividly as if he had been an eye-witness. But this famous admiral

> Fell on the deck of the Belerophon
> Where his brains was knocked out
> With a Crowbar by the Crew [2]

These assertions that he was Nelson, Wellington or Byron variously voiced his unquenched longing for what, as far back as in 1824, he had called 'true fame' as opposed to 'common fame' or 'fashionable applause'. At times he maintained that he was Shakespeare:

> I'm the same man . . . but sometimes they called me Shakespeare and sometimes Byron and sometimes Clare.[3]

False because out of touch with accepted reality, such logic

[1] St. Andrew's notebook, Northampton MSS.
[2] Northampton MS. 10.
[3] De Wilde to Frederick Martin, 25th February 1865. *Sketches in the Life of John Clare*, pp. 39–40.

is, on a figurative plane, not entirely false. And after all these mental dives out of actuality, again and again Clare rose nearer the reconciliation of his vision, though never to achieve such reconcilement fully.

Frequently he knew he was in a 'Hell of a Madhouse', in, he wrote, this 'land of Sodom where all the people's brains are turned the wrong way'. Yet in such 'disordered company', during the scores of hours he spent writing, or as soon as subjects of his devotion were broached in conversation, he needed neither suspicion nor delusions. Words and thought, for a space, grew orderly.

Even in the hastily written 'Halfpenny Ballads' there are few touches of uncontrol. There are one or two. In 'Misfortune', for instance, it is not so much the straight thrusts, reminiscent of his *Don Juan*, against 'priest-craftcant', that betray, as a mental bafflement audible throughout the poem; in 'My Love in Disabille' the unknown girl in the street becomes without sufficient coherence 'my own true love in rags and disabille'. 'To Miss B——' is an inquiry into the complex old mental confusion between love and shame. And this inquiry echoes with madly painful directness.

The many St Andrew's ballads and songs are important chiefly because they follow out the themes of his best lyrics. He used the terms 'song' and 'ballad' interchangeably as they were used in earlier folk-verse. The 'Halfpenny Ballads' are like the songs and ballads of *Child Harold*. They have little or none of that intellectual content we associate with a literary tradition. Clare was still using writing as an anodyne, a form of 'emotional relief'. The ballads are the results of a few minutes' apparently effortless jotting on his instinctive 'singing note', as once George Darley called it. They are like the 'sentimental' ballads of the nineteenth century. They are in ancient rhythms—strong stresses with variable numbers of unaccented syllables, and often with successful innovations in rhyme-scheme and metre:

> O come to me i' the evening
> And let us walk together
> When talking is believing
> And beautiful the weather

> There's a siller bleb in the golden-eye
> A daisy's by the thorn
> On the wildling's blossoms diamonds eye
> The souls o' the summer morn
> But come to me i' the even Love
> When the lark drops i' the corn

or

> The night wind is born brief
> Ladybirds i' green corn sleep
> The dews on the thorn leaf
> Dearest meet for I'm lone
> I'm lone love and weary
> Where the hazels hang near thee
> O come love and cheer me
> And make me thy own

Their emphatic rhymes make them easily committed to memory. They could be sung. They are like the ballads of our twentieth-century ballad resurgence that continues strongly at the present day. And implicitly they convey those archetypal themes which Clare thought belonged to ballad and folk-verse: themes which continued to obsess him after the triumphant but temporary resolving of conflict in his greatest poems.

Frequently they are written to girls: as his Epping and St Andrew's notebooks contain lists of girls' and women's names, as he wrote to 'Eliza Phillips' whilst making his 'New Canto of Don Juan'. There are Jane Wilson, Helen Maria Gardiner, Lucy of Northampton, Caradora, Bonny Ann, Mary Featherstone, Mary o' the Plough and many other Marys.

It is not highly likely that a male patient of over fifty out for a couple of hours from his second asylum would achieve more than passing acquaintance with girls and women. That all these names were even contemporary is not altogether probable—remembering Clare's long lists of old friends (some dead) to whom he wished to be remembered in his St Andrew's letters home.

Jane Wilson and Miss B—— were undoubtedly real and contemporary, though. The tone of his terms with the second is revealed at the end of 'Song for Miss B——' in his note:

DEAR MISS

I beg your acceptance of the enclosed ballad as the best I could make. The spring may bring better days, and better opportunitys to write a better song,

Yours truly

JOHN CLARE.[1]

Still, one can't help wondering what the same, or another, girl made, if ever they were presented to her, of an earlier set of verses addressed to Miss B——:

> Odd rot it what a shame it is
>   That love should puzzles grow
> That we the one we seek should miss
>   And change from top to toe
>   The Gilafer's a Gilafer
>   And nature owns the plan
>   And strange a thing it is to me
>   A man can't be a man . . .
>
> The Bible says that God is Love
>   I like so wise a plan
> But was it ordered from above
>   That love was [not] wi' man?

Equally intriguing, however irrelevant, is what 'my lovely Miss Wilson thou beauteous creature', thus politely addressed at the beginning of an unpublished ballad, 'Come come in the Fields', thought about being invited to 'love before afternoon' at the end.

His loves had always been important to Clare. From Mary Joyce, who liked walking in the fields and by the brook with him when he was twelve and she eight, they range past dark-eyed Betty Sell, past serious Elizabeth Newbon (the Bessey of his last long poem, *A Rhapsody*, and of whom his 1845 pocket-book notes: 'they had been friends in youth'); his loves pass by kindly, sentimental, literary Mrs Eliza Louisa Emmerson; they pass buxom, bonny, practical, managing, unimaginative Patty, who retained her black hair to her death and against

---

[1] The note, in transcript, is punctuated, not necessarily by Clare.

whom Clare had periods of expletive-loaded fury, but whom he continued to recognize, if only as his 'second' wife.

He was reaching a time when

> love shall be nameless and I will be free. . .;

when, in wider context, 'my family'

> is not more dear than every girl and boy
> Which time matures and nothing can destroy. . . .

By then his love was 'one I cannot see'. She was 'a pleasant thought'; but she remained

> more living than a dream.

These ballads are poems of deprivation when the hungry personal vitality has lessened. Country girl after country girl emerges as a symbol of love. These symbols issue, not from Clare's rational use of immediate experience, but from below, after the responsibility and immediacy of experience have been lifted from him.

Over and over in the St Andrew's lesser poems he returned to this—for him—obsessional subject of love—gay, deep and of necessity innocent. He could not rid himself of hope, remote though his hope was, that this love was humanly realizable. About the earthly symbols of it he used threadbare phrases forced from their homes in poetry of past centuries and employed by hack and rhymster—'eyes like ony sloe', 'crow-black' hair, 'cheeks like the red rose tree', 'lips like cherries'. The phrases 'foggy dew' from 'I met a pleasant maiden' and 'grassy dew' from 'The daisy by the road side' both have the figurative meaning explained by James Reeves in *The Idiom of the People*.[1] They are part of the private speech used in folk poetry during the centuries when the Christian ethos was seeking to overcome pagan impulse.

This conflict about love has been fought in many guises and on many planes, as our moral code, century by century, has

[1] pp. 45-57.

grown more complicated. The battle is between 'innocent' primitiveness and human idealism; it is between romantic love and contractual marriage, between pleasurable, light, promiscuous sex, and a groping search for something more deeply pleasurable: this last is also thought to be more lasting.

'Innocence', in Blake's sense, in Clare's sense, may be 'out of poetry for good', as has been lately said. Twentieth-century poetry *may* need its 'built-in insurance against parody'. But Clare died in 1864. His is a bird's-eye view of life and poetry. That Nelson-Wellington-Spring-Caunt-Byron-Shakespeare-Clare theme was a viable, outward form of a desperate mental struggle to hold on to a few certainties which had become part of his stubbornest affirmation of life; and these he thought were being forgotten. Such wide affirmation included to the last 'the old cartwheel agen the hovel threw', the 'amber-trailed willow mouse-eared wi' leaves', and

> . . . a sweetness nothing could destroy
> The sunlight in the stream . . .

This rigid insistence on the innocence that is no part of ignorance but is beyond ignorance, and beyond the flexible, sophistication of much 'morality', was certainly within the complex of causes that kept Clare in the 'English Bastile a government Prison where harmless people are trapped and tortured till they die'.[1] Dr Nesbitt, succeeding Thomas Prichard, was medical superintendent at St Andrew's between 1844 and 1858. To Frederick Martin in 1865 Nesbitt wrote: 'I was always led to believe that [Clare's] mental affliction had its origin in dissipation.' After giving a new lease of life to an unproven assumption Nesbitt went on to describe Clare thus:

> He was generally docile and tranquil, but would brook no interference—anything approaching to this last would excite his ire in a torrent of ejaculation of no ordinary violence in which imprecations were conspicuous; but this was an exceptional state of things. . . . He was once asked how he had contrived to write his pretty poetry—his reply was that it came to him whilst walking

[1] Northampton MSS.

in the fields—that he kicked it out of the clods. On another occasion he presented me with the following scrap,

Where flowers are, God is, and I am free.[1]

Was Clare's refusal to recognize lust and lack of freedom as having anything to do with love a sentimental delusion? Or, in the particular form his insanity took, did some remnant of a candid and searching sanity remain in him to the last day in 'Prison'? What he was obstinately and obsessively convinced about was what far greater writers spend brilliant, reasonable lives to convey: it was the essential innocence of the physical basis of our time here.

Thus, from the time of writing *Child Harold* and *Don Juan*, through the writing of his best lyrics and his many ballads that look so simple but aren't so simple, Clare's preoccupations were with two perennial paradoxes: with that of joy linked, as joy must be, with grief, pain and disaster; and with that man-made antithesis between sexual shame and 'my everlasting love', between 'truth and friendship' in this life where lie and delusion must be lived out. May not his obsessive concern with love as not local or temporary but pervasive of all life be seen as a thread in the dream-haunted maze of humanity's journey since before medieval doctrinaire rationalism began to deflect the crude, more forthright impulse?

So often has he been written about as our greatest 'nature' poet that it might be of some little use to examine what this means traditionally, too. He has written at least half a dozen poems on the 'Eternity of Nature'. This sense of nature's 'eternity' can at last be seen not as 'romantic' or even as 'nineteenth-century'. Many scholars, like most people, then, believed in terms of a six-day Creation, a cataclysmic destruction by the Flood, a revelation to the white man only, a possible sudden call to judgment, and an eternity for some, but by no means all of us, in heaven. They were amazed when

[1] *Sketches in the Life of John Clare by Himself*, pp. 40–1; also Northampton MSS. Dr Nesbitt added: 'If there was one subject more than another that he [Clare] had an aversion to it was biography—he designated it a parcel of lies. . . .'

geographers such as Hutton and Lyell before Darwin began to reveal evidence of the astounding length and slowness of geological time. But now the 'unchanging laws of light in the eye of a four-hundred-million-year-old trilobite'[1] are known to geo-morphologists. Hints of 'nature's eternity', as Clare called it, intellectually emphasized, may be given to our children.

Worship of what both East and West have called 'Nature'— a Nature both bloody and kind—is recorded in the *Rig Vedas*. This attitude of the unity of all things may be said to have been with men well before 3000 B.C. In Greek intellectual thought the frenzied Dionysiac worship of Nature came into conflict with rational Apolline worship. Separation of human kindness into love and lust, typified under Agape and Eros, set in. Division intensified, with further cleavages between God and 'Nature', between Nature and Man, under Christian thought. Clare's 'nature' verse, or country verse, like his obsession with love, serves to illustrate his attempt to keep in touch at all costs with the simpler, unliterary poetry that belonged to men's earlier days: days when, he supposed, mind and heart were less divided.

Not always, however much one side of him might have longed to do so, could he endorse Wordsworth's 'looking through Nature up to Nature's God'. He was not, as the countryman often privately is not, religious in the dogmatic sense of the word. Throughout his poetry and prose there is evidence both for his trust in God and for scepticism. He was not consistent. But he could not always, in his feelings about natural eternity, agree even with Coleridge, whom he admired: 'Man . . . born an immortal soul that cannot die.' In one of the letters in the consonant code he sometimes used—where, if anywhere, we might expect private convictions alongside delusion—he wrote to a real or imaginary Mary Collingwood:

> . . . Foolish people tell me I have got no home in this world and as I don't believe in the other at any rate I make myself heaven. . . .

In this letter the word 'believe' is written in full.

Holding, as he does, the insight that love, including sexual

[1] Loren Eiseley, *The Firmament of Time*, Gollancz, 1961.

love, produces goodwill, whilst suppression, whether self-imposed or externally enforced, is likely to engender negation or even hatred, he reminds us of modern poets: of John Wain and his reason for not writing Orthodox Nature Poetry: simply that 'where you love you cannot break away'; of D. H. Lawrence's statement on that 'ponderous, primordial tenderness, such as made the world in the beginning'.

Since *The Waste Land* few poets confess to enthusiasm. There is instead a desolate acceptance of disintegration and disillusion; as in one of the most moving of modern ballads:

> Mercy, Pity, Peace, and Love,
> I saw him lift his gun.
> He lay like logic in the street
> And stared at the blind sun.[1]

This is a far cry from Clare who, surrounded by blank disaster, could yet write in *Child Harold*:

> At dusky eve or sober silent morn
> For such delights 'twere happy Man was born. . . .

Was Clare's clinging to positive aspects of human life, then, supremely heedless of most necessary sanctions? Or does such an outlook hold truths that he could say only in the way he did say them? His clarity in the midst of chaos resembles Blake's attitude, as Edmund Blunden pointed out in 1920.

This yes-saying is so much a part of Clare that it can hardly be minimized. His mature poetry, both introspective and when he was simply noting, at seventy years old, how 'the sprinkling rain blotches the thirsty dust', keeps these envisioned links with the past and the future. John Middleton Murry saw him as a non-intellectual, child-like poet who couldn't grow up. May it not rather be that he is a primitive poet in the sense that he insisted on writing almost from a fertility level?

> The wind of that eternal ditty sings
> Humming of future things, that burn the mind
> To leave some fragment of itself behind.[2]

[1] Robin Skelton, *Begging the Dialect*, 1960, p. 34, 'A Ballad of Despair'.
[2] Sonnet, 'The Shepherd's Tree'.

Perhaps all poetry of any merit keeps its lifeline with past and future. In Clare the links are so strong that on them rests the whole of what he rose above his mental agony to say. They shine through mischance to the last. The Clare whom Nesbitt remembered as 'essentially a kind-hearted, good-feeling man with an unusually large cerebral development' bought with madness the freedom to state again for us one or two elemental truths.

ANNE TIBBLE.

J. W. TIBBLE.

1964.

TEXT

THE text in this selection, except for that of *Child Harold* and of those lyrics from the Knight transcripts, is based on that of the two volumes, *The Poems of John Clare*, Dent, 1935. Poems not in the 1935 volumes are noted ( ) in Notes on the text at the end of this book; as also are certain corrections of the 1935 St Andrew's readings before Knight's transcripts came to light.

SELECT BIBLIOGRAPHY

Some of the more important books that may be of interest to the general reader.

CLARE'S WORKS

Poems Descriptive of Rural Life and Scenery. Printed for Taylor & Hessey, and E. Drury. London, 1820. Second and third editions, 1820. Fourth edition, 1821.

The Village Ministrel, and Other Poems. Printed for Taylor & Hessey, and E. Drury. Two volumes, London, 1821. Second issue, 1823.

The Shepherd's Calendar; with Village Stories, and Other Poems. Published for John Taylor by James Duncan, 1827.

The Rural Muse. Whittaker & Co., London, 1835.

SELECTIONS, BIOGRAPHIES AND IMPORTANT MISCELLANEA

The Life of John Clare. By Frederick Martin. Macmillan & Co., London and Cambridge, 1865.

Life and Remains of John Clare. By J. L. Cherry. Frederick Warne & Co., London; J. Taylor & Son, Northampton, 1873. Issued in Chandos Classics, 1873-7.

SELECT BIBLIOGRAPHY

Poems by John Clare. Selected and Introduced by Norman Gale. With a Bibliography by C. Ernest Smith. George E. Over, Rugby, 1901.

Poems by John Clare. Edited, with an Introduction, by Arthur Symons. Henry Frowde, London, 1908.

Northamptonshire Botanologia: John Clare. By G. Claridge Druce, 1912.

John Clare: Poems Chiefly from Manuscript. Edited by Edmund Blunden and Alan Porter; with an Introduction by Edmund Blunden. Cobden-Sanderson, London, 1920.

Madrigals and Chronicles: being newly found poems written by John Clare. Edited, with a Preface and Commentary, by Edmund Blunden. The Beaumont Press, London, 1924.

Sketches in the Life of John Clare by Himself; with an Introduction, Notes and Additions by Edmund Blunden. Cobden-Sanderson, London, 1931.

John Clare. A Life. By J. W. and Anne Tibble. Cobden-Sanderson, London, 1932.

The Poems of John Clare. Edited by J. W. Tibble. Dent, London, 1935.

Poems of John Clare's Madness. Edited by Geoffrey Grigson. Routledge & Kegan Paul, London, 1949.

The Letters of John Clare. Edited by J. W. and Anne Tibble. Routledge & Kegan Paul, London, 1950.

The Prose of John Clare. Edited by J. W. and Anne Tibble. Routledge & Kegan Paul, London, 1950.

Selected Poems of John Clare. Edited with an Introduction by Geoffrey Grigson. Routledge & Kegan Paul, London, 1950.

Selected Poems of John Clare. Edited with an Introduction by James Reeves. Heinemann, London, 1954.

John Clare. His Life and Poetry. By J. W. and Anne Tibble. Heinemann, London, 1956.

Later Poems of John Clare. Edited by Eric Robinson and Geoffrey Summerfield. Manchester University Press, 1964.

John Clare Letters. Edited by J. W. and Anne Tibble, 1970.

John Clare. A Life. By J. W. and Anne Tibble, 1972.

Clare. Edited by Mark Storey (Critical Heritage Series). Routledge & Kegan Paul, London, 1973.

Poetry of John Clare: A Critical Introduction. By Mark Storey. Macmillan, London, 1974.

A Right to Song: The Life of John Clare. By Edward Storey. Macmillan, 1982.

CONTENTS

Section II POEMS WRITTEN AT HELPSTONE, 1824–32

Poems Written in Northampton Asylum, 1842–64

ACKNOWLEDGMENTS

ACKNOWLEDGMENTS are due to the Northampton Public Libraries' Committee and to the Peterborough Museum Committee for permission to transcribe, over many years, Clare's poems in this book; to the Northampton Libraries' Committee for allowing us to have the cast of Clare's head photographed; and to the National Portrait Gallery for permission to reproduce the portrait of Clare by William Hilton, R.A.

We are indebted to Dr Alexander Bell of the Peterborough Museum Committee for the facilities he has given; and we thank Mr Halliday, the Chief of the Northampton Library, and the members of his staff, for the help they have so generously extended.

Certain hitherto unpublished lyrics are printed here by kind permission of the Clarendon Press.

SECTION I

HELPSTONE

(The dates given at the end of poems in this section were supplied by Clare in 1819)

HAIL, humble Helpstone! where thy valleys spread,
And thy mean village lifts its lowly head,
Unknown to grandeur, and unknown to fame,
No minstrel boasting to advance thy name:
Unletter'd spot! unheard in poets' song,
Where bustling labour drives the hours along,
Where dawning genius never met the day,
Where useless ignorance slumbers life away,
Unknown nor heeded, where low genius tries
Above the vulgar and the vain to rise.

Mysterious Fate! who can on thee depend?
Thou opes the hour, but hides its doubtful end:
In Fancy's view the joys have long appear'd,
Where the glad heart by laughing plenty's cheer'd,
And Fancy's eyes as oft, as vainly, fill,
At first but doubtful, and as doubtful still.
So little birds, in winter's frost and snow,
Doom'd, like to me, want's keener frost to know,
Searching for food and 'better life,' in vain
(Each hopeful track the yielding snows retain),
First on the ground each fairy dream pursue,
Though sought in vain; yet bent on higher view,
Still chirp, and hope, and wipe each glossy bill;
And undiscourag'd, undishearten'd still,
Hop on the snow-cloth'd bough, and chirp again,
Heedless of naked shade and frozen plain:
Till, like to me, these victims of the blast,
Each foolish, fruitless wish resign'd at last,
Are glad to seek the place from whence they went
And put up with distress, and be content.

Hail, scenes obscure! so near and dear to me,

3

The church, the brook, the cottage, and the tree:
Still shall obscurity rehearse the song,
And hum your beauties as I stroll along.
Dear, native spot! which length of time endears,
The sweet retreat of twenty lingering years;
And, oh! those years of infancy the scene,
Those dear delights, where once they all have been,
Those golden days, long vanish'd from the plain,
Those sports, those pastimes, now belov'd in vain;
When happy youth in pleasure's circle ran,
Nor thought what pains awaited future man,
No other thought employing, or employ'd,
But how to add to happiness enjoy'd:
Each morning wak'd with hopes before unknown,
And eve, possessing, made each wish their own;
The day gone by left no pursuit undone,
Nor one vain wish, save that it went too soon;
Each sport, each pastime, ready at their call,
As soon as wanted they possess'd them all:
These joys, all known in happy infancy,
And all I ever knew, were spent in thee.
And who but loves to view where these were past?
And who, that views, but loves them to the last?
Feels his heart warm to view his native place,
A fondness still those past delights to trace?
The vanish'd green to mourn, the spot to see
Where flourish'd many a bush and many a tree?
Where once the brook, for now the brook is gone,
O'er pebbles dimpling sweet went whimpering on;
Oft on whose oaken plank I've wondering stood
(That led a pathway o'er its gentle flood),
To see the beetles their wild mazes run,
With jetty jackets glittering in the sun:
So apt and ready at their reels they seem,
So true the dance is figur'd on the stream,
Such justness, such correctness they impart,
They seem as ready as if taught by art.
In those past days, for then I lov'd the shade,
How oft I've sigh'd at alterations made,

To see the woodman's cruel axe employ'd,
A tree beheaded, or a bush destroy'd:
Nay e'en a post, old standard, or a stone
Moss'd o'er by age, and branded as her own,
Would in my mind a strong attachment gain,
A fond desire that there they might remain;
And all old favourites, fond taste approves,
Griev'd me at heart to witness their removes.

Thou far fled pasture, long evanish'd scene!
Where nature's freedom spread the flow'ry green,
Where golden kingcups open'd into view,
Where silver daisies in profusion grew;
And, tottering, hid amidst those brighter gems,
Where silken grasses bent their tiny stems:
Where the pale lilac, mean and lowly, grew,
Courting in vain each gazer's heedless view;
While cowslips, sweetest flowers upon the plain,
Seemingly bow'd to shun the hand, in vain:
Where lowing oxen roam'd to feed at large,
And bleating there the shepherd's woolly charge,
Whose constant calls thy echoing valleys cheer'd,
Thy scenes adorn'd, and rural life endear'd;
No calls of hunger pity's feelings wound,
'Twas wanton plenty rais'd the joyful sound:
Thy grass in plenty gave the wish'd supply,
Ere sultry suns had wak'd the troubling fly;
Then blest retiring, by thy bounty fed,
They sought thy shades, and found an easy bed.

But now, alas! those scenes exist no more;
The pride of life with thee, like mine, is o'er,
Thy pleasing spots to which fond memory clings,
Sweet cooling shades, and soft refreshing springs.
And though Fate's pleas'd to lay their beauties by
In a dark corner of obscurity,
As fair and sweet they bloom'd thy plains among,
As bloom those Edens by the poets sung;
Now all's laid waste by desolation's hand,

Whose cursed weapons level half the land.
Oh! who could see my dear green willows fall,
What feeling heart, but dropt a tear for all?
Accursed Wealth! o'er-bounding human laws,
Of every evil thou remain'st the cause:
Victims of want, those wretches such as me,
Too truly lay their wretchedness to thee:
Thou art the bar that keeps from being fed,
And thine our loss of labour and of bread;
Thou art the cause that levels every tree,
And woods bow down to clear a way for thee.[1]

Sweet rest and peace! ye dear, departed charms,
Which industry once cherish'd in her arms;
When ease and plenty, known but now to few,
Were known to all, and labour had its due;
When mirth and toil, companions through the day,
Made labour light, and pass'd the hours away;
When nature made the fields so dear to me,
Thin scattering many a bush and many a tree;
Where the wood-minstrel sweetly join'd among,
And cheer'd my needy toilings with a song;
Ye perish'd spots, adieu! ye ruin'd scenes,
Ye well-known pastures, oft frequented greens!
Though now no more, fond Memory's pleasing pains,
Within her breast your every scene retains.
Scarce did a bush spread its romantic bower,
To shield the lazy shepherd from the shower;
Scarce did a tree befriend the chattering pie,
By lifting up its head so proud and high;
No, not a secret spot did then remain,
Throughout each spreading wood and winding plain,
But, in those days, my presence once possess'd,
The snail-horn searching, or the mossy nest.

Oh, happy Eden of those golden years
Which memory cherishes, and use endears,
Thou dear, beloved spot! may it be thine

[1] The preceding ten lines were omitted in the fourth edition of *Poems Descriptive*; Lord Radstock objected to them because they smacked of 'radical slang.'

To add a comfort to my life's decline,
When this vain world and I have nearly done,
And Time's drain'd glass has little left to run;
When all the hopes, that charm'd me once, are o'er,
To warm my soul in ecstasy no more,
By disappointments prov'd a foolish cheat,
Each ending bitter, and beginning sweet;
When weary age the grave, a rescue, seeks,
And prints its image on my wrinkled cheeks—
Those charms of youth, that I again may see,
May it be mine to meet my end in thee;
And, as reward for all my troubles past,
Find one hope true—to die at home at last!

1809.

IMPROMPTU ON WINTER

O WINTER, what a deadly foe
Art thou unto the mean and low!
What thousands now half pin'd and bare
Are forced to stand thy piercing air
All day, near numbed to death wi' cold
Some petty gentry to uphold,
Paltry proudlings hard as thee,
Dead to all humanity.
Oh, the weather's cold and snow,
Cutting winds that round me blow,
But much more the killing scorn!
Oh, the day that I was born
Friendless—poor as I can be,
Struck wi' death o' poverty!
But why need I the winter blame?
To me all seasons come the same:
Now winter bares each field and tree
She finds that trouble sav'd in me
Stript already, penniless,
Nothing boasting but distress;

And when spring chill'd nature cheers,
Still my old complaint she hears;
Summer too, in plenty blest,
Finds me poor and still distrest;
Kind autumn too, so liberal and so free,
Brings my old well-known present, Poverty.

1809–10.

THE ROBIN

Now the snow hides the ground, little birds leave the wood,
And fly to the cottage to beg for their food;
While the robin, domestic, more tame than the rest,
With its wings drooping down, and rough feathers undrest,
Comes close to our windows, as much as to say,
'I would venture in, if I could find a way:
I 'm starv'd, and I want to get out of the cold;
Oh! make me a passage, and think me not bold.'
Ah, poor little creature! thy visits reveal
Complaints such as these to the heart that can feel;
Nor shall such complainings be urged in vain;
I 'll make thee a hole, if I take out a pane.
Come in, and a welcome reception thou'lt find;
I keep no grimalkin to murder inclin'd.
But oh, little robin! be careful to shun
That house, where the peasant makes use of a gun;
For if thou but taste of the seed he has strew'd,
Thy life as a ransom must pay for the food:
His aim is unerring, his heart is as hard,
And thy race, though so harmless, he'll never regard.
Distinction with him, boy, is nothing at all;
Both the wren, and the robin, with sparrows must fall.
For his soul (though he outwardly looks like a man)
Is in nature a wolf of the Apennine clan;
Like them his whole study is bent on his prey:
Then be careful, and shun what is meant to betray.
Come, come to my cottage, and thou shalt be free

To perch on my finger and sit on my knee:
Thou shalt eat of the crumbles of bread to thy fill,
And have leisure to clean both thy feathers and bill.
Then come, little robin! and never believe
Such warm invitations are meant to deceive:
In duty I'm bound to show mercy on thee,
Since God don't deny it to sinners like me.

1809.

TO THE VIOLET

SWEET tiny flower of darkly hue,
   Lone dweller in the pathless shade;
How much I love thy pensive blue
   Of innocence so well display'd!

What time the watery skies are full
   Of streaming dappled clouds so pale,
And sideling rocks, more white than wool,
   Portending snowy sleet, or hail;

I 'gin to seek thy charming flower
   Along each hedgerow's mossy seat,
Where, dithering many a cold blea hour,
   I've hugg'd myself in thy retreat.

What makes me cherish such fond taste,
   What makes such raptures spring for thee,
Is that thou lov'st the dreary waste
   Which is so well belov'd by me.

For solitude should be my choice
   Could I this labouring life resign,
To see the little birds rejoice,
   And thy sweet flowers in clusters shine.

I'd choose a cave beside some rock,
　　Clos'd in all round with ash and thorn,
That near my door thy tribe might flock
　　To shed their sweets in early morn.

But, ah! that way would never prove
　　Means to sustain impending life;
I must forgo those scenes I love,
　　And still beat on with needy strife.

Sweet flower! we must reverse the plan,
　　Nor cherish such romantic views;
I'll strive to seek thee when I can,
　　Through noontide heat or evening dews.

To spring return, with all thy train
　　Of flow'rets cloth'd in varied hue,
I long to see that morn again
　　Which brings to light the violet blue.

SONG OF PRAISE

IMITATION OF THE 148TH PSALM

WARM into praises, kindling muse,
With grateful transport raise thy views
　　To Him, who moves this ball,
Who whirls, in silent harmony,
The earth, the ocean, air, and sky—
　　Oh, praise the Lord of all!

Ye angels—hymning round your King,
Praise Him who gives you power to sing,
　　Ye hosts—with raptures burn;
Who station'd you in bliss, proclaim!
Oh, bless your Benefactor's name,
　　Betokening kind return.

Ye spreading heavens, arching high,
Ye scenes unknown beyond the sky,
　　Creation's Maker own:
'Let there be light'—your Ruler said;
And instant your blue curtain spread
　　In triumph round His throne.

Thou moon, meek guardian of the night,
Ye planets of inferior light,
　　Ye lamps of rays divine,
Ye suns—dart forth your splendid rays
To Him who metes your nights and days,
　　And suffers you to shine.

Oh, praise His name, His mercy bless,
Ye poor, like me, in 'whelmed distress;
　　Oh, hail protection given:
When sin and sorrow die away,
Our hopes His promise still shall stay
　　Of recompensing heaven.

Thunders that fright the trembling ground,
Ye forked lightnings, flashing round,
　　Or quench'd in 'whelming shower;
While skies in vollied rolls are rent—
While nature pauses, silent bent—
　　Adore Almighty Power.

Ye minstrel birds, wild woodland's charms,
Whose song each child of nature warms
　　With your lov'd haunts in view;
From Him you borrow'd every note,
Then open wide your chanting throat
　　To give the tribute due.

Mis-shapen germs of parent earth,
Waiting, dependent for your birth,
　　The sun's enlivening rays;
Emerging from your silent tomb,
To join the hailing myriads, come,
　　And kindle into praise.

Bowing adorers of the gale,
Ye cowslips, delicately pale,
   Upraise your loaded stems;
Unfold your cups in splendour, speak!
Who deck'd you with that ruddy streak,
   And gilt your golden gems?

Violets, sweet tenants of the shade,
In purple's richest pride array'd,
   Your errand here fulfil;
Go bid the artist's simple stain
Your lustre imitate, in vain,
   And match your Maker's skill.

Daisies, ye flowers of lowly birth,
Embroiderers of the carpet earth,
   That stud the velvet sod;
Open to spring's refreshing air,
In sweetest smiling bloom declare
   Your Maker, and my God!

Thou humble clothing of the trees,
Moss, in whose meanness genius sees
   A world of wonders shine;
Put on your satin-smoothening green,
And let your Maker's power be seen,
   And workmanship divine.

Creation's universal round,
That beat the air, or press the ground,
   Or plough the seas, the same,
All join in chorusing accord,
Exalt your Maker and your Lord,
   And praise His holy name:

Till o'er this sin-consuming world
Destruction's fated doom is hurl'd,
   And ruin's self decays;
Then, freed from sin and Adam's fall,
All join, and hail Him Lord of all,
   In everlasting praise.

ADDRESS TO PLENTY

IN WINTER

OH, thou Bliss! to riches known,
Stranger to the poor alone,
Giving most where none's requir'd,
Leaving none where most's desir'd;
Who, sworn friend to miser, keeps
Adding to his useless heaps
Gifts on gifts, profusely stor'd,
Till thousands swell the mouldy hoard:
While poor, shatter'd Poverty,
To advantage seen in me,
With his rags, his wants, and pain,
Waking pity but in vain,
Bowing, cringing at thy side,
Begs his mite, and is denied,
Oh, thou Blessing! let not me
Tell, as vain, my wants to thee;
Thou, by name of Plenty styl'd,
Fortune's heir, her favourite child.
'Tis a maxim—hunger feed,
Give the needy when they need;
He whom all profess to serve
The same maxim did observe:
Their obedience here, how well,
Modern times will plainly tell.
Hear my wants, nor deem me bold,
Not without occasion told:
Hear one wish, nor fail to give;
Use me well, and bid me live.

'Tis not great, what I solicit;
Was it more, thou couldst not miss it:
Now the cutting winter's come,
'Tis but just to find a home,
In some shelter, dry and warm,
That will shield me from the storm.
Toiling in the naked fields,

Where no bush a shelter yields,
Needy Labour dithering stands,
Beats and blows his numbing hands;
And upon the crumping snows
Stamps, in vain, to warm his toes.
Leaves are fled, that once had power
To resist a summer shower;
And the wind so piercing blows,
Winnowing small the drifting snows,
The summer shade of loaded bough
Would vainly boast a shelter now;
Piercing snows so searching fall,
They sift a passage through them all.
Though all's vain to keep him warm,
Poverty must brave the storm.
Friendship none, its aid to lend;
Health alone his only friend,
Granting leave to live in pain,
Giving strength to toil in vain,
To be, while winter's horrors last,
The sport of every pelting blast.

Oh, sad sons of Poverty!
Victims doom'd to misery;
Who can paint what pain prevails
O'er that heart which want assails?
Modest shame the pain conceals;
No one knows, but he who feels.
Oh, thou charm which Plenty crowns,
Fortune! smile, now winter frowns:
Cast around a pitying eye;
Feed the hungry, ere they die.
Think, oh! think upon the poor,
Nor against them shut thy door;
Freely let thy bounty flow
On the sons of want and woe.

Hills and dales no more are seen
In their dress of pleasing green;
Summer's robes are all thrown by,

For the clothing of the sky;
Snows on snows in heaps combine,
Hillocks, rais'd as mountains, shine,
And at distance rising proud,
Each appears a fleecy cloud.
Plenty! now thy gifts bestow;
Exit bid to every woe;
Take me in, shut out the blast,
Make the doors and windows fast;
Place me in some corner, where,
Lolling in an elbow chair,
Happy, blest to my desire,
I may find a rousing fire;
While in chimney-corner nigh,
Coal, or wood, a fresh supply,
Ready stands for laying on,
Soon as t'other's burnt and gone.
Now and then, as taste decreed,
In a book a page I'd read;
And, inquiry to amuse,
Peep at something in the news;
See who's married, and who's dead,
And who, though bankrupt, beg their bread:
While on hob, or table nigh,
Just to drink before I'm dry,
A pitcher at my side should stand,
With the barrel nigh at hand,
Always ready as I will'd,
When 'twas empty, to be fill'd;
And, to be possess'd of all,
A corner cupboard in the wall,
With store of victuals lin'd complete,
That when hungry I might eat.
Then would I, in Plenty's lap,
For the first time take a nap;
Falling back in easy lair,
Sweetly slumb'ring in my chair,
With no reflective thoughts to wake
Pains that cause my heart to ache,

Of contracted debts, long made,
In no prospect to be paid,
And, to want, sad news severe,
Of provisions getting dear:
While the winter, shocking sight,
Constant freezes day and night,
Deep and deeper falls the snow,
Labour's slack, and wages low.
These, and more, the poor can tell,
Known, alas, by them too well,
Plenty! oh, if blest by thee,
Never more should trouble me.
Hours and weeks will sweetly glide,
Soft and smooth as flows the tide,
Where no stones or choking grass
Force a curve ere it can pass:
And as happy, and as blest,
As beasts drop them down to rest,
When in pastures, at their will,
They have roam'd and eat their fill,
Soft as nights in summer creep,
So should I then fall asleep;
While sweet visions of delight,
So enchanting to the sight,
Sweetly swimming o'er my eyes,
Would sink me into ecstasies,
Nor would pleasure's dreams once more,
As they oft have done before,
Cause be to create a pain,
When I woke, to find them vain:
Bitter past, the present sweet,
Would my happiness complete.
Oh! how easy should I lie,
With the fire up-blazing high
(Summer's artificial bloom),
That like an oven keeps the room,
Or lovely May, as mild and warm:
While, without, the raging storm
Is roaring in the chimney-top,

In no likelihood to drop;
And the witchen-branches nigh,
O'er my snug box towering high,
That sweet shelter'd stands beneath,
In convulsive eddies wreathe.
Then while, tyrant-like, the storm
Takes delight in doing harm,
Down before him crushing all,
Till his weapons useless fall;
And as in oppression proud
Peal his howlings long and loud,
While the clouds, with horrid sweep,
Give (as suits a tyrant's trade)
The sun a minute's leave to peep,
To smile upon the ruins made;
And to make complete the blast,
While the hail comes hard and fast,
Rattling loud against the glass;
And the snowy sleets, that pass,
Driving up in heaps remain
Close adhering to the pane,
Stop the light, and spread a gloom,
Suiting sleep, around the room:
Oh, how blest 'mid these alarms,
I should bask in Fortune's arms,
Who, defying every frown,
Hugs me on her downy breast,
Bids my head lie easy down,
And on winter's ruins rest.
So upon the troubled sea,
Emblematic simile,
Birds are known to sit secure,
While the billows roar and rave,
Slumbering in their safety sure,
Rock'd to sleep upon the wave,
So would I still slumber on,
Till hour-telling clocks had gone,
And, from the contracted day,
One or more had click'd away.

Then with sitting wearied out,
I for change's sake, no doubt,
Just might wish to leave my seat,
And, to exercise my feet,
Make a journey to the door,
Put my nose out, but no more;
There to village taste agree,
Mark how times are like to be,
How the weather's getting on,
Peep in ruts where carts have gone.
Or, by stones, a sturdy stroke,
View the hole the boys have broke,
Crizzling, still inclin'd to freeze;
And the rime upon the trees.
Then, to pause on ills to come,
Just look upward on the gloom;
See fresh storms approaching fast,
View them busy in the air,
Boiling up the brewing blast,
Still fresh horrors scheming there.
Black and dismal, rising high
From the north, they fright the eye:
Pregnant with a thousand storms
Huddled in their icy arms,
Heavy hovering as they come,
Some as mountains seem—and some
Jagg'd as craggy rocks appear
Dismally advancing near;
Earth unable seems to bear
The huge mass that's moving there.
Fancy, at the cumbrous sight,
Chills and shudders with affright,
Fearing lest the air in vain
Strives her station to maintain,
And wearied, yielding to the skies,
The world beneath in ruin lies.
So may Fancy think and feign;
Fancy oft imagines vain;
Nature's laws, by wisdom penn'd,

Mortals cannot comprehend;
Power Almighty Being gave,
Endless Mercy stoops to save;
Causes, hid from mortals' sight,
Prove 'whatever is, is right.'

Then to look again below,
Labour's former life I'd view,
Who, still beating through the snow,
Spite of storms their toils pursue,
Forc'd out by sad necessity,
That sad fiend that forces me.
Troubles, then no more my own,
Which I but too long had known,
Might create a care, a pain;
Then I'd seek my joys again,
Pile the fire up, fetch a drink,
Then sit down again and think;
Pause on all my sorrows past,
Think how many a bitter blast,
When it snow'd, and hail'd, and blew,
I have toil'd and batter'd through,
And how many a lengthen'd day,
Half the night as one may say,
Weary lowking in a barn,
Humble twenty pence to earn.
Then to ease reflective pain, ⎫
To my sports I'd fall again, ⎬
Till the clock had counted ten, ⎭
When I'd seek my downy bed,
Easy, happy, and well fed.

Then might peep the morn, in vain,
Through the rimy misted pane;
Then might bawl the restless cock,
And the loud-tongued village clock;
And the flail might lump away,
Waking soon the dreary day:
They should never waken me,

Independent, blest, and free;
Nor, as usual, make me start,
Yawning sigh with heavy heart,
Loath to ope my sleepy eyes,
Weary still, in pain to rise,
With aching bones and heavy head,
Worse than when I went to bed.
With nothing then to raise a sigh,
Oh, how happy should I lie
Till the clock was eight, or more,
Then proceed as heretofore.
Best of blessings! sweetest charm!
Boon these wishes while they're warm;
My fairy visions ne'er despise;
As reason thinks, thou realize:
Depress'd with want and poverty,
I sink, I fall, denied by thee.

1817.

DAWNINGS OF GENIUS

Genius! a pleasing rapture of the mind,
A kindling warmth to learning unconfin'd,
Glows in each breast, flutters in every vein,
From art's refinement to th'uncultur'd swain.
Hence is that warmth the lowly shepherd proves,
Pacing his native fields and willow groves;
Hence is that joy, when every scene unfolds,
Which taste endears and latest memory holds;
Hence is that sympathy his heart attends,
When bush and tree companions seem and friends;
Hence is that fondness from his soul sincere,
That makes his native place so doubly dear.
In those low paths which poverty surrounds,
The rough rude ploughman, off his fallow-grounds
(That necessary tool of wealth and pride),
While moil'd and sweating by some pasture's side,
Will often stoop inquisitive to trace
The opening beauties of a daisy's face;

Oft will he witness, with admiring eyes,
The brook's sweet dimples o'er the pebbles rise;
And often, bent as o'er some magic spell,
He'll pause, and pick his shaped stone and shell:
Raptures the while his inward powers inflame,
And joys delight him which he cannot name;
Ideas picture pleasing views to mind,
For which his language can no utterance find;
Increasing beauties, fresh'ning on his sight,
Unfold new charms, and witness more delight;
So while the present please, the past decay,
And in each other, losing, melt away.
Thus pausing wild on all he saunters by,
He feels enraptur'd though he knows not why,
And hums and mutters o'er his joys in vain,
And dwells on something which he can't explain.
The bursts of thought with which his soul's perplex'd,
Are bred one moment, and are gone the next;
Yet still the heart will kindling sparks retain,
And thoughts will rise, and fancy strive again.
So have I mark'd the dying ember's light,
When on the hearth it fainted from my sight,
With glimmering glow oft redden up again,
And sparks crack brightening into life, in vain;
Still lingering out its kindling hope to rise,
Till faint, and fainting, the last twinkle dies.
    Dim burns the soul, and throbs the fluttering heart,
Its painful pleasing feelings to impart;
Till by successless sallies wearied quite,
The memory fails, and fancy takes her flight.
The wick confin'd within its socket dies,
Borne down and smother'd in a thousand sighs.

EPIGRAM

FOR fools that would wish to seem learned and wise,
    This receipt a wise man did bequeath:
'Let 'em have the free use of their ears and their eyes;
    'But their tongue,' says he, 'tie to their teeth.'

AN EFFUSION TO POESY

ON RECEIVING A DAMP FROM A GENTEEL OPINIONIST IN POETRY, OF SOME SWAY, AS I AM TOLD, IN THE LITERARY WORLD

DESPIS'D, unskill'd, or how I will,
Sweet Poesy! I'll love thee still;
Vain (cheering comfort!) though I be,
I still must love thee, Poesy.
A poor, rude clown, and what of that?
I cannot help the will of fate,
A lowly clown although I be;
Nor can I help it loving thee.
Still must I love thee, sweetest charm!
Still must my soul in raptures warm;
Still must my rudeness pluck the flower,
That's plucked in an evil hour,
While Learning scowls her scornful brow,
And damps my soul—I know not how.
Labour! 'cause thou'rt mean and poor,
Learning spurns thee from her door;
But despise me as she will,
Poesy! I love thee still.
When on pillow'd thorns I weep,
And vainly stretch me down to sleep,
Then, thou charm from heav'n above,
Comfort's cordial dost thou prove:
Then, engaging Poesy!
Then how sweet to talk with thee.
And be despis'd, or how I will,
I cannot help but love thee still.
Endearing charm! vain though I be,
I still must love thee, Poesy.
Still must I! ay, I can't refrain:
Damp'd, despis'd, or scorn'd again,
With vain, unhallow'd liberty
Still must I sing thee, Poesy.
And poor, and vain, and press'd beneath
Oppression's scorn although I be,
Still will I bind my simple wreath,
Still will I love thee, Poesy.

BALLAD

Winter's gone, the summer breezes
  Breathe the shepherd's joys again,
Village scene no longer pleases,
  Pleasures meet upon the plain;
Snows are fled that hung the bowers,
  Buds to blossoms softly steal,
Winter's rudeness melts in flowers:
    Charmer, leave thy spinning wheel,
        And tend the sheep with me.

Careless here shall pleasures lull thee,
  From domestic troubles free;
Rushes for thy couch I'll pull thee,
  In the shade thy seat shall be;
All the flower-buds will I get
  Spring's first sunbeams do unseal,
Primrose, cowslip, violet:
    Charmer, leave thy spinning wheel,
        And tend the sheep with me.

Cast away thy 'twilly willy,'
  Winter's warm protecting gown,
Storms no longer blow to chill thee;
  Come with mantle loosely thrown,
Garments, light as gale's embraces,
  That thy lovely shape reveal;
Put thou on thy airy dresses:
    Charmer, leave thy spinning wheel,
        And tend the sheep with me.

Sweet to sit where brooks are flowing,
  Pleasant spreads the gentle heat,
On the green's lap thyme is growing,
  Every molehill forms a seat:
Fear not suns 'cause thou'rt so fair,
  In the thorn-bower we'll conceal;
Ne'er a sunbeam pierces there:
    Charmer, leave thy spinning wheel,
        And tend the sheep with me.

SONNETS

THE SETTING SUN

THIS scene, how beauteous to a musing mind,
 That now swift slides from my enchanted view;
The sun sweet setting yon far hills behind,
 In other worlds his visits to renew:
What spangled glories all around him shine;
 What nameless colours, cloudless and serene
(A heav'nly prospect, brightest in decline),
 Attend his exit from this lovely scene.
So sets the Christian's sun, in glories clear;
So shines his soul at his departure here:
 No clouding doubts, nor misty fears arise,
To dim hope's golden rays of being forgiven;
 His sun, sweet setting in the clearest skies,
In faith's assurance wings the soul to heaven.

1814.

THE PRIMROSE

WELCOME, pale Primrose! starting up between
 Dead matted leaves of ash and oak, that strew
 The every lawn, the wood, and spinney through,
Mid creeping moss and ivy's darker green;
 How much thy presence beautifies the ground:
How sweet thy modest, unaffected pride
Glows on the sunny bank, and wood's warm side.
 And where thy fairy flowers in groups are found,
The school-boy roams enchantedly along,
 Plucking the fairest with a rude delight:
While the meek shepherd stops his simple song,
 To gaze a moment on the pleasing sight,
O'erjoy'd to see the flowers that truly bring
The welcome news of sweet returning spring.

1811

24

POEMS WRITTEN AT HELPSTONE
1819–21

THE VILLAGE MINSTREL

While learned poets rush to bold extremes,
And sunbeams snatch to light the muse's fires,
An humble rustic hums his lowly dreams,
Far in the swale where poverty retires,
And sings what nature and what truth inspires:
The charms that rise from rural scenery,
Which he in pastures and in woods admires;
The sports, the feelings of his infancy,
And such-like artless things, how mean soe'er they be.

Though, far from what the learned's toils requite,
He unambitious looks at no renown,
Yet little hopes break his oblivious night,
To cheer the bosom of a luckless clown,
Where black neglect spreads one continual frown,
And threats her constant winter cold and chill,
Where toil and slavery bear each fancy down,
That fain would soar and sing 'albeit ill,'
And force him to submit to fate's controlling will.

Young Lubin was a peasant from his birth;
His sire a hind born to the flail and plough,
To thump the corn out and to till the earth,
The coarsest chance which nature's laws allow—
To earn his living by a sweating brow;
Thus Lubin's early days did rugged roll,
And mixt in timely [1] toil—but e'en as now,
Ambitious prospects fired his little soul,
And fancy soared and sung, 'bove poverty's control.

Small joy to him were childhood's tempting tricks,
Which schoolboys look for in their vacant hours;

[1] Clare uses the word in its older meaning, 'early.' Taylor emended to 'untimely.'

27

With other boys he little cared to mix;
Joy left him lonely in his hawthorn bowers,
As haply binding up his knots of flowers,
Or list'ning unseen birds to hear them sing;
Or gazing downward where the runnel pours
Through the moss'd bridge in many a whirling ring,
How would he muse o'er all on pleasure's fairy wing.

The 'I spy,' 'halloo,' and the marble-ring,
And many a game that infancy employs,
The spinning-top whirl'd from the twitching string,
The boastful jump of strong exulting boys,
Their sports, their pastimes, all their pleasing toys
We leave unsung—though much such rural play
Would suit the theme—yet they're not Lubin's joys:
Truth breathes the song in Lubin's steps to stray,
Through woods and fields and plains, his solitary way;

And tell how vales and shades did please his sight,
And how the wind breath'd music thro' each bough,
And how in rural charms he did delight—
To mark the shepherd's folds, and swains at plough,
And pasture speck'd with sheep, and horse, and cow,
With many a beauty that does intervene,
And steeple peeping o'er the wood's dark brow;
While young hope's fancy popt its smile between,
And wish'd man's days to spend in some such peaceful scene.

Each opening season, and each opening scene,
On his wild view still teem'd with fresh delight;
E'er winter's storms to him have welcome been,
That brought him comfort in its long dark night,
As joyful list'ning, while the fire burnt bright,
Some neighbouring labourer's superstitious tale,
How 'Jinny-burnt-arse,'[1] with her wisp alight,
To drown a 'nighted traveller once did fail,
He knowing well the brook that whimper'd down the vale.

[1] Taylor emended to 'Jack-a-lantern.'

And tales of fairy-land he lov'd to hear,
Those mites of human forms, like skimming bees,
That fly and flirt about but everywhere,
The fly-like tribes of night's un'scerning breeze,
That through a lock-hole even creep with ease:
The freaks and stories of this elfin crew,
Ah, Lubin gloried in such things as these;
How they rewarded industry he knew,
And how the restless slut was pinched black and blue.

How ancient dames a fairy's anger fear'd,
From gossips' stories Lubin often heard;
How they but every night the hearth-stone clear'd,
And 'gainst their visits all things neat prepar'd,
As fays naught more than cleanliness regard;
When in the morn they never fail'd to share
Or gold or silver as their meet reward,
Dropt in the water superstition's care
To make the charm succeed had cautious placed there.

And thousands such the village keeps alive:
Beings that people superstitious earth,
That e'er in rural manners will survive,
As long as wild rusticity has birth
To spread their wonders round the cottage-hearth.
On Lubin's mind these deeply were imprest;
Oft fear forbade to share his neighbour's mirth:
And long each tale, by fancy newly drest,
Brought fairies in his dreams, and broke his infant rest.

He had his dreads and fears, and scarce could pass
A churchyard's dreary mounds at silent night,
But footsteps trampled through the rustling grass,
And ghosts 'hind grave-stones peer'd in sheets of white,
Dread monsters fancy moulded on his sight:
Soft would he step lest they his tread should hear,
And creep and creep till past his wild affright;
Then on wind's wings would rally as it were,
So swift the wild retreat of childhood's fancied fear.

And when fear left him, on his corner-seat,
Much would he chatter o'er each dreadful tale:
Tell how he heard the sound of 'proaching feet,
And warriors jingling in their coats of mail,
And lumping knocks, as one would thump a flail,
Of spirits conjur'd in the charnel floor,
And many a mournful shriek and hapless wail,
Where maids self-murder'd their false loves deplore;
And from that time would vow to tramp on nights no more.

Oh, who can speak his joys when spring's young morn
From wood and pasture open'd on his view,
When tender green buds blush upon the thorn,
And the first primrose dips its leaves in dew:
Each varied charm how joy'd would he pursue,
Tempted to trace their beauties through the day;
Grey-girdled eve and morn of rosy hue
Have both beheld him on his lonely way,
Far, far remote from boys and their unpleasing play.

Sequester'd nature was his heart's delight;
Him would she lead thro' wood and lonely plain,
Searching the pooty from the rushy dyke;
And while the thrush sang her long-silenc'd strain,
He thought it sweet, and mock'd it o'er again;
And while he pluck'd the primrose in its pride,
He ponder'd o'er its bloom 'tween joy and pain,
And a rude sonnet in its praise he tried,
Where nature's simple way the aid of art supplied.

The freshen'd landscapes round his routes unfurl'd,
The fine-ting'd clouds above, the woods below,
Each met his eye a new-revealing world,
Delighting more as more he learn'd to know,
Each journey sweeter, musing to and fro.
Surrounded thus, not paradise more sweet,
Enthusiasm made his soul to glow;
His heart with wild sensations used to beat;
As nature seemly sang, his mutterings would repeat.

Upon a molehill oft he dropt him down,
To take a prospect of the circling scene,
Marking how much the cottage roof's-thatch brown
Did add its beauty to the budding green
Of sheltering trees it humbly peep'd between,
The stone-rock'd wagon with its rumbling sound,
The windmill's sweeping sails at distance seen,
And every form that crowds the circling round,
Where the sky stooping seems to kiss the meeting ground.

And dear to him the rural sports of May,
When each cot-threshold mounts its hailing bough,
And ruddy milkmaids weave their garlands gay,
Upon the green to crown the earliest cow,
When mirth and pleasure wear a joyful brow,
And join the tumult with unbounded glee
The humble tenants of the pale [1] and plough:
He lov'd 'old sports,' by them reviv'd, to see,
But never car'd to join in their rude revelry.

O'er brook-banks stretching, on the pasture-sward,
He gaz'd, far distant from the jocund crew;
'Twas but their feats that claim'd a slight regard;
'Twas his, his pastimes lonely to pursue—
Wild blossoms creeping in the grass to view,
Scarce peeping up the tiny bent as high,
Beting'd with glossy yellow, red, or blue,
Unnam'd, unnotic'd but by Lubin's eye,
That like low genius sprang to bloom their day and die.

Oh, who can tell the sweets of May-day's morn,
To waken rapture in a feeling mind,
When the gilt east unveils her dappled dawn,
And the gay woodlark has its nest resign'd,
As slow the sun creeps up the hill behind,
Morn redd'ning round, and daylight's spotless hue,
As seemly sweet with rose and lily lin'd;
While all the prospect round beams fair to view,
Like a sweet opening flower with its unsullied dew.

[1] Enclosed land. Taylor emended to 'pail.'

Ah, often brushing through the dripping grass
Has he been seen to catch this early charm,
List'ning the 'love song' of the healthy lass
Passing with milk-pail on her well-turn'd arm;
Or meeting objects from the rousing farm,
The jingling plough-teams driving down the steep,
Wagon and cart—and shepherd-dogs' alarm,
Raising the bleatings of unfolding sheep,
As o'er the mountain top the red sun 'gins to peep.

Nor could the day's decline escape his gaze;
He lov'd the closing as the rising day,
And oft would stand to catch the setting rays,
Whose last beams stole not unperceiv'd away;
When, hesitating like a stag at bay,
The bright unwearied sun seem'd loath to drop,
Till chaos' night-hounds hurried him away,
And drove him headlong from the mountain-top,
And shut the lovely scene, and bade all nature stop.

With contemplation's stores his mind to fill,
Oh, doubly happy would he roam as then,
When the blue eve crept deeper round the hill,
While the coy rabbit ventur'd from his den,
And weary labour sought his rest agen;
Lone wanderings led him haply by the stream
Where unperceiv'd he joy'd his hours at will,
Musing the cricket twittering o'er its dream,
Or watching o'er the brook the moonlight's dancing beam.

And here the rural muse might aptly say,
As sober evening sweetly siles along,
How she has chas'd black ignorance away
And warm'd his artless soul with feelings strong
To teach his reed to warble forth a song:
And how it echoed on the even-gale,
All by the brook the pasture-flowers among;
But, ah, such trifles are of no avail:
There's few to notice him, or hear his simple tale.

As most of nature's children prove to be,
His little soul was easy made to smart,
His tear was quickly born to sympathy,
And soon were rous'd the feelings of his heart
In others' woes and wants to bear a part.
Yon parish-huts, where want is shov'd to die,
He never view'd them but his tear would start;
He pass'd not by the doors without a sigh,
And felt for every woe of workhouse-misery.

O Poverty! thy frowns were early dealt
O'er him who mourn'd thee, not by fancy led
To whine and wail o'er woes he never felt,
Staining his rhymes with tears he never shed,
And heaving sighs a mock song only bred:
Alas! he knew too much of every pain
That shower'd full thick on his unshelter'd head;
And as his tears and sighs did erst complain,
His numbers took it up, and wept it o'er again.

Full well might he his early days recall,
When he a thresher with his sire has been,
When he a ploughboy in the fields did maul,
And drudg'd with toil through almost every scene;
How pinch'd with winter's frownings he has been;
And tell of all that modesty conceals,
Of what his friends and he have felt and seen:
But, useless naming what distress reveals,
As every child of want feels all that Lubin feels.

It might be curious here to hint the lad,
How in his earliest days he did appear;
Mean was the dress in which the boy was clad,
His friends so poor, and clothes excessive dear,
They oft were foil'd to rig him once a year;
And housewife's care in many a patch was seen;
Much industry 'gainst want did persevere;
His friends tried all to keep him neat and clean,
Though care has often fail'd, and shatter'd he has been.

Yet oft fair prospects cheer'd his parents' dreams,
Who had on Lubin founded many a joy;
But pinching want soon baffled all their schemes,
And dragg'd him from the school a hopeless boy,
To shrink unheeded under hard employ;
When struggling efforts warm'd him up the while,
To keep the little toil could not destroy;
And oft with books spare hours he would beguile,
And blunder oft with joy round Crusoe's lonely isle.

Folks much may wonder how the thing may be,
That Lubin's taste should seek refined joys,
And court th'enchanting smiles of poesy;
Bred in a village full of strife and noise,
Old senseless gossips, and blackguarding boys,
Ploughmen and threshers, whose discourses led
To nothing more than labour's rude employs,
'Bout work being slack, and rise and fall of bread,
And who were like to die, and who were like to wed:

Housewives discoursing 'bout their hens and cocks,
Spinning long stories, wearing half the day,
Sad deeds bewailing of the prowling fox,
How in the roost the thief had knav'd his way
And made their market-profits all a prey.
And other losses too the dames recite,
Of chick, and duck, and gosling gone astray,
All falling prizes to the swopping kite:
And so the story runs both morning, noon, and night.

Nor sabbath-days much better thoughts instil;
The true-going churchman hears the signal ring,
And takes his book his homage to fulfil,
And joins the clerk his amen-task to sing,
And rarely home forgets the text to bring:
But soon as service ends, he 'gins again
'Bout signs in weather, late or forward spring,
Of prospects good or bad in growing grain;
And if the sermon's long he waits the end with pain.

A more uncouthly lout was hardly seen
Beneath the shroud of ignorance than he;
The sport of all the village he has been,
Who with his simple looks oft jested free;
And gossips, gabbling o'er their cake and tea,
Time after time did prophecies repeat,
How half a ninny he was like to be,
To go so soodling up and down the street
And shun the playing boys whene'er they chanc'd to meet.

Nature look'd on him with a 'witching eye,
Her pleasing scenes were his delightful book,
Where [1] he, while other louts roam'd heedless by,
With wild enthusiasm us'd to look.
The kingcup vale, the gravel-paved brook,
Were paradise with him to muse among;
And haply sheltering in some lonely nook,
He often sat to see it purl along,
And, fir'd with what he saw, humm'd o'er his simple song.

When summer came, how eager has he sped
Where silence reign'd, and the old crowned tree
Bent with its sheltering ivy o'er his head;
And summer-breezes, breathing placidly,
Encroach'd upon the stockdove's privacy,
Parting the leaves that screen'd her russet breast:
'Peace!' would he whisper, 'dread no thief in me,'
And never rose to rob her careless nest;
Compassion's softness reign'd, and warm'd his gentle breast.

And he would trace the stagnant pond or lake,
Where flags sprang up or water-lilies smil'd,
And wipe the boughs aside of bush and brake,
And creep the woods with sweetest scenes beguil'd,
Tracking some channel on its journey wild,
Where dripping blue-bells on the bank did weep:
Oh, what a lovely scene to nature's child,
Through roots and o'er dead leaves to see it creep,
Watching on some moss'd stump in contemplation deep.

'Twas pleasing too, when meadows' browning swath
'Neath sultry sunbeams wither'd on the lea,
To mark the ploughboys at their Sunday bath,
When leisure left them at their wading free
In some clear pit hemm'd round wi' willow tree
And bush and brake to screen the dabbling crew,
Tho' bashful milkmaids couldn't help but see,
And doubtless, blushing by the naked crew,
Their bosoms might be warm'd to wish a nearer view.[1]

And he would mark in July's rosy prime,
Crossing the meadows, how a nameless fly
Of scarlet plumage, punctual to its time,
Perch'd on a flower would always meet his eye;
And plain-drest butterfly of russet dye,
As if awaken'd by the scythe's shrill sound,
Soon as the bent with ripeness 'gan to dye,
Was constant with him in each meadow-ground,
Flirting the withering swath and unmown blossom round.

No insect 'scap'd him, from the gaudy plume
Of dazzling butterflies so fine to view,
To the small midgen that at evening come
Like dust spots dancing o'er the water's blue,
Or, where the spreading oak above-head grew,
Tormenting maidens 'neath their kicking cow;
Who often murmur'd at the elfin crew,
And from th'endanger'd pail, with angry vow
Oft rose, their sport to spoil with switch of murdering bough.

And he has mark'd the curious stained rings,
Though seemly nothing in another's eye,
And bending o'er them thought them wondrous things,
Where nurses' night-fays circling dances hie
And set the cock to watch the morning's eye;
Light soon betrays 'em where their routes have been,
Their printing foot-marks leave a magic dye,
The grass grows gloomy in a darker green,
And look for years to come, and still the place is seen.

[1] Stanza added from MS.

And as declining day his stalking shade
A giant monster stretch'd, in fancy's view,
What bustle to his cottage has he made,
Ere sliving night around his journey threw
Her circling curtains of a grisly hue;
Then of the rings the fairy routs display'd
From gossips' wisdom much he glean'd, who knew
How they were haunts for ghosts as well as fays,
And told what things were seen in granny's younger days.

The verse might tremble with the 'haunted pond,'
And tell of terrors which his heart has found:
How he, to 'scape, shool'd many a pace beyond
Each dreaded, dangerous spot of haunted ground;
Here as he pass'd where Amy's woes were drown'd,
If late at night, his fears would turn him chill;
If naught was seen, he heard a squish-squash sound,
As when one's shoes the drenching waters fill,
And wet and dripping oft he saw her climb the hill.

And round his fields lay many a spot to dread;
'Twould note a history down to mark them all:
Oft monsters have been seen without a head;
And market-men oft got a dangerous fall,
When startled horses saw the sweeping pall
On the cross-roads where 'love-lorn Luce' was lain;
At other spots, like offspring of 'Old Ball,'
Or ploughman's senses often were mista'en,
A shagged foal would fright the early-rising swain.

In autumn-time he often stood to mark
What tumults 'tween the hogs and geese arose
Down the corn-litter'd street, and the rude bark
Of jealous watch-dog on his master's clothes,
E'en rous'd by quawking of the swopping crows,
And every tinkle in that busy toil,
In sultry field and dusty lane that flows:
He glean'd his corn, and lov'd to list the while,
For Lubin mingled there to share of autumn's spoil.

And when old women, overpower'd by heat,
Tuck'd up their clothes and sicken'd at the toil,
Seeking beneath the thorn the mole-hill seat,
To tell their tales and catch their breath awhile,
Their gabbling talk did Lubin's cares beguile;
And some would tell their tales, and some would sing,
And many a dame, to make the children smile,
Would tell of many a funny laughing thing,
While merrily the snuff went pinching round the ring.

Here Lubin listen'd with awe-struck surprise,
When 'Hickathrift's' great strength has met his ear,
How he kill'd giants as they were but flies,
And lifted trees as one would lift a spear,
Though not much bigger than his fellows were;
He knew no troubles wagoners have known,
Of getting stall'd, and such disasters drear;
Up he'd chuck sacks as one would hurl a stone,
And draw whole loads of grain unaided and alone.

And Goody's sympathy would fetch the tear
From each young list'ner seated by her side,
When 'Cruel Barbara Allen' they did hear,
The haughty stubbornness of female pride
To that fond youth who broke his heart and died:
And 'Jack the Giant-killer's' tales she'd say,
Which still the same enchanting power supplied;
The stagnant tear amazement wip'd away,
And Jack's exploits were felt for many an after-day.

These were such tales as Lubin did delight;
But should the muse narrate in Goody's strain,
And tell of all she told from morn till night,
Fays, ghosts, and giants would her songs detain
To be at day's return resumed again:
With 'Cinderella' she has charm'd awhile,
Then 'Thumb's' disasters gave a moment's pain;
Thus true-thought legends would each soul beguile,
As superstition will'd, to raise the tear or smile.

And as the load jogg'd homeward down the lane,
When welcome night shut out the toiling day,
Following he mark'd the simple-hearted swain;
Joying to listen, on his homeward way,
While rest's warm rapture rous'd the rustic's lay,
The threadbare ballad from each quavering tongue,
As 'Peggy Band,' or the 'Sweet Month of May';
Oh, how he joy'd to hear each 'good old song,'
That on night's pausing ear did echo loud and long.

The muse might sing too, for he well did know,
The freaks and plays that harvest-labour end,
How the last load is crown'd with boughs, and how
The swains and maids with fork and rake attend,
With floating ribbons 'dizen'd at the end;
And how the children on the load delight
With shouts of 'Harvest home!' their throats to rend;
And how the dames peep out to mark the sight:
And all the feats that crown the harvest-supper night.

He knew all well, a young familiar there,
And often look'd on all; for he himsen
Join'd with the sun-tann'd group the feast to share,
As years roll'd round him with the change agen,
And brought the masters level with their men,
Who push'd the beer about, and smok'd and drank
With freedom's plenty never shown till then;
Nor labourers dar'd, save now, so free and frank
To laugh, and joke, and play so many a harmless prank.

Much has he laugh'd each rude, rude act to see;
The long-neck'd sheet-clad 'crane' to poke about,
Spoiling each smoker's pipe, and cunningly,
Though blindfold, seen to pick each bald-head out,
And put each bashful maiden to the rout;
The 'fiery parrot' too, a laughing scene,
Where two maids on a sheet invite the lout,
Thrown o'er a water-tub, to sit between,
And as he drops they rise, and let him swearing in.

The 'dusty miller' playing many a rig;
And the 'Scotch pedlars,' with their jokes and fun;
The 'booted hogs drove over Lunnon brig,'
Boys, who had mischief in the harvest done,
As loads o'erturn'd, and foul on posts had run;
And brandy-burning ghosts most deadly blue,
That each old woman did with terror shun;
These with the rest did Lubin yearly view,
And join'd his mirth and fears with the low vulgar crew.

To close the ranting night, the master's health
Went round in bumping horns to every swain,
Who wish'd him best of crops t'increase his wealth,
And's merry sport when harvest came again;
And all in chorus rallied out amain:
The harvest-song (a tugging pull) begun,
Each ere its end the brimming horn must drain,
Or have it fill'd again—there lay the fun,
Till Hodge went drunk to bed, and morts of things were done.

Oh, dear to Lubin autumn's changing cloud,
Where shade and sunshine every minute sees;
And each rude-risen tempest, beetling loud,
Own'd every murmur his wild ear to please,
Sughing its vengeance through the yellow trees,
Pattering the acorns from their cups adown,
Fanning the sere leaf far upon the leas;
And picturesque to him each scrambling clown,
Tearing the woods among to search the nut-bunch brown.

How would he wander round the woods, the plains,
When every flower from nature's wreath had fled;
Tracing the shower-bedimpled sandy lanes,
And winding fountains to their infant bed,
With many a flag and rushy bunch bespread;
Marking each curdle boil and boil away,
And bubbles guggling born, that swell'd and fled
Like changing scenes in life's ephemeron-day:
Thus Lubin paus'd o'er all, and cheer'd his lonely way.

A solitaire through autumn's wan decay,
He heard the tootling robin sound her knell,
Observ'd the sun more coy to slink away,
And lingering oak-shade how it brown'd and fell;
And many a way of nature he could tell,
That secrets are to undiscerning eyes,
As how the bee most careful clos'd her cell,
The mouse with far-fetch'd ear his hole supplies,
And moles root deeper down, from winter's frowning skies,

And he could tell how the shy squirrel far'd,
Who often stood its busy toils to see;
How against winter it was well prepar'd
With many a store in hollow root or tree,
As if being told what winter's wants would be:
Its nuts and acorns he would often find,
And hips and haws too, heaped plenteously
In snug warm corner that broke off the wind,
With leafy nest made nigh, that warm green mosses lin'd.

'Twas thus his fond inquiry us'd to trace
Through nature's secrets with unwearied eye,
And watch the shifting seasons' changing grace:
Spring's first wild flower, and summer's painted sky,
The insect creeping, and the birds that fly,
The autumn's dying breeze, the winter-wind,
That bellow'd round his hut most mournfully:
And as his years increas'd his taste refin'd,
And fancy with new charms enlighten'd up his mind.

Beauty 'gan look too witching on his eye;
The sweetest image seen in nature's glass;
A swelling bosom 'neath its lily dye,
Without admiring, Lubin could not pass;
And downcast eye, and blush of shanny lass,
Had every power his heart to hold in thrall.
O beauteous woman! still thy charms surpass:
In spite of all thy failings and thy fall,
Thou art the comfort still that cheers this earthly ball.

Sure 'twas an oversight in nature's plan,
Such loveliness, that claims the tenderest care,
To leave defenceless with ungrateful man,
Such harden'd brutes as but too many are.
O pleasing flowers! as frail as ye are fair;
Sure some that live have souls to feel and sigh,
When, shrinking 'neath the storms ye cannot bear,
Your beauteous buds bow down to fade and die,
While not one pitying tear melts your seducer's eye.

Full oft, to see their witcheries divine,
He'd mix in circles which their charms did grace,
And merry routs he now began to join;
And though his heart denied to own its case,
It oft was smitten with a beauty's face,
And throbb'd with thrilling aggravating pain;
And many a long, long day has taken place,
Ere he forgot, and met his peace again,
While oft in beauty's praise he humm'd his amorous strain.

He knew the manners too of merry rout;
Statute and feast his village yearly knew;
And glorious revels too without a doubt
Such pastimes were to Hob, and Nell, and Sue,
Milkmaids and clowns that statute-joys pursue,
And rattle off, like hogs to Lunnon mart:
Weary of old, they seek for places new,
Where men hail maidens with a frothing quart,
And Hodge with sweetheart fix'd forgets his plough and
    cart:

Where cakes, and nuts, and gingerbread and all,
Tempt clowns to buy; and far more tempting still,
Where shining ribbons dizen out the stall,
And wenches drag poor sheepish Bob or Bill
Some long, long dallied promise to fulfil,
New wreath or bow for Sunday cap to buy—
'If yah set any store by one yah will!'
Each strings his purse, and makes them no reply,
But thinks returns at night will suit, for clowns are sly.

And there the ballad-singers rave and rant,
And Hodge, whose pockets won't stand treats more high,
Hears which his simpering lass may please to want,
And, brushing through the crowd most manfully,
Outs with his pence the pleasing song to buy,
And crams it in her hand with many a smile;
The trifling present makes the maid comply
To promise him her company the while,
And strutting on at night he hands her o'er the stile.

Here the poor sailor, with his hat in hand,
Hops through the crowd that wonderfully stares
To hear him talk of things in foreign land,
'Bout thundering cannons and most bloody wars;
And as he stops to show his seamy scars,
Pity soon meets the ploughman's penny then:
The sailor heartfelt thankfulness declares,
'God blesses' all, and styles them 'gentlemen,'
And fobs his money up, and 'gins his tale agen.

Here's 'Civil Will' too, with his 'pins and pegs,'
And he makes glorious fun among the chaps:
'Boys, miss my pegs,' he cries, 'and hit my legs,
'My timbers well can stand your gentle taps,'
Though sure enough he gets most ugly raps,
For here the rustic thinks the sports abound;
Whose aim at 'Civil's' legs his fellows caps
Meets most applause—still 'poor Will' stands his ground,
'Boys, throw your copper salve, and make another wound.'

But soldiers, they're the boys to make a rout,
With boasting bottle brimm'd with gin and rum,
The high-crown'd cap with ribbons hung about,
The tootling fife, and hoarse rap-tapping drum:
Lud, clowns are almost mad where'er they come;
They're like so many kings 'mong country folk,
They push their beer like water round the room,
Who will and welcome there may drink and smoke,
Though chaps have often found they dearly sell a joke.

The bumptious sergeant struts before his men,
And 'Clear the road, young whopstraws!' will he say;
And looks as big as if King George himsen,
And wields his sword around to make a way:
With lace and ribbons dizen'd out so gay,
So flashing smart—full oft, as well's the swain,
The tempted maid his finery does betray,
Who leaves poor slighted Hodge behind in pain,
And many a chiding dame to sorrow and complain.

And Lubin heard the echoing rabble-fight,
When men and maids were hir'd, and sports did close,
And wenches sought their sweethearts up at night,
And found 'em drunk, bedeck'd with soldier's clothes;
As they would pull and scold great tumults rose;
The sergeant's honour totter'd terribly,
From women's threat'nings hardly 'scap'd with blows;
—They 'd box his cap about his ears, if he
Gave not the contest up and set the prisoner free.

Some homeward-bound were coupled, maid and swain,
And Dick from Dolly now for gifts did sue,
He'd giv'n her ribbons, and he deem'd again
Some kind return as nothing but his due;
And he told things that ploughmen little knew,
Of bleeding hearts and pains—she seiz'd the spell,
And though at first she murmur'd 'bout the dew,
Spoiling her Sunday gown, he talk'd so well;
She gave consent at last to what no words dare tell.[1]

The statute nam'd, each servant's day of fun,
The village-feast next warns the muse's song;
'Tis Lubin's sphere, a thresher's lowly son;
Though little used to mix such routs among,
Such fitting subjects to the theme belong:
As pictur'd landscapes, destitute of trees,
Would doubtlessly be fancied painted wrong,
So lowly rural subjects, such as these,
Must have their simple ways discerning eyes to please.

[1] Preceding four lines restored from MS.

44

The lovely morn in July's blushes rose,
That brought the yearly feast and holiday,
When villagers put on their bran-new clothes,
And milk-maids, drest like any ladies gay,
Threw 'cotton drabs' and 'worsted hose' away,
And left their pails unscour'd, well pleas'd I ween
To join the dance where gipsy fiddlers play,
Accompanied with thumping tambourine,
From night till morning-light upon the rushy green,

Where the fond swain delighteth in the chance
To meet the sun-tann'd lass he dearly loves;
And, as he leads her down the giddy dance,
With many a token his fond passion proves,
Squeezing her hands, or snatching at her gloves,
And stealing kisses as chance prompts the while,
With eye fixt on her as she graceful moves,
To catch if such fond fancies her beguile,—
When happily her heart confesses in a smile.

O rural love! as spotless as the dove's;
No wealth gives fuel to a borrow'd flame,
To prompt the shepherd where to choose his loves,
And go a forger of that sacred name;
Both hearts in unison here beat the same;
Here nature makes the choice which love inspires;
Far from the wedded lord and haughty dame
This boon of heavenly happiness retires,
Not felon-like law-bound, but wedded in desires.

The woodman and the thresher now are found
Mixing and making merry with their friends;
Children and kin, from neighbouring towns around,
Each at the humble banquet pleas'd attends:
For though no costliness the feast pretends,
Yet something more than common they provide;
And the good dame her small plum-pudding sends
To sons and daughters fast in service tied,
With many a cordial gift of good advice beside.

'Tis pleasing then to view the cotter's cheer,
To mark his gentle and his generous mind;
How free he is to push about his beer;
And well's he knows, with ceremony kind,
Bids help themselves to such as they may find,
Tells them they're welcome as the flowers in May,
And, full of merrimental cheer inclin'd,
Drinks healths and sings when supper's clear'd away
And hopes they all may meet on next year's holiday;

And then for sake of's boys and wenches dear,
Gives leave a dancing in his hut shall be;
While he sits smoking in his elbow-chair,
And pleas'd as Punch his children round to see,
With each a sweetheart frisking merrily.
'God bless ye all!' quoth he, and drinks his beer,
'My boys and wenches, ye're a pride to me:
Lead but an honest life—no matter where,
And do as I have done, and ye'll have naught to fear.

'To bring ye up, from toil I never flinch'd,
Or fail'd to do the thing that's just and right;
Your mother knows ourselves were often pinch'd,
To fill your bellies and to keep ye tight:
May God look down and bless ye all this night!
May wives and husbands here, that are to be,
Instead of sorrows prove your heart's delight!—
I've brought ye up, expect no more from me,
So take your trundle now, and good luck may ye see!'

Thus talk'd the father to his pipe and beer,
For those whom he'd admonish were the while
Too occupied in dancing him to hear;
Yet still with talk and beer he does beguile
His short releasement from his cares and toil:
Then Sir John's spirit stops his merry glee
And lays him quiet down: his children smile,
Break up the dance, and pay the fiddler's fee,
And then the lass he loves each swain pulls on his knee.

And the long rural string of merry games,
That at such outings maketh much ado,
All were to Lubin's skill familiar names;
And he could tell each whole performance through,
As plann'd and practis'd by the jovial crew:
—Great sport to them was jumping in a sack,
For beaver hat bedeck'd with ribbons blue;
Soon one bumps down as though he'd broke his neck,
Another tries to rise, and wondrous sport they make.

And monstrous fun it makes to hunt the pig,
As soapt and larded through the crowd he flies:
Thus turn'd adrift he plays them many a rig;
A pig for catching is a wondrous prize,
And every lout to do his utmost tries;
Some snap the ear, and some the tunkey tail,
But still his slippery hide all hold denies,
While old men tumbled down sore hurts bewail,
And boys bedaub'd with muck run home with piteous tale.

And badger-baiting here, and fighting cocks—
But sports too barbarous these for Lubin's strains:
And red-fac'd wenches, for the holland smocks,
Oft puff and pant along the smooth green plains,
Where Hodge feels most uncomfortable pains
To see his love lag hindmost in the throng,
And of unfairness in her cause complains,
And swears and fights the jarring chaps among,
As in her part he'd die, 'fore they his lass should wrong.

And long-ear'd racers, fam'd for sport and fun,
Appear this day to have their swiftness tried;
Where some won't start, and 'Dick,' the race nigh won,
Enamour'd of some 'Jenny' by his side,
Forgets the winning-post to court a bride;
In vain the rout urge on the jockey-clown
To lump his cudgel on his harden'd hide,
Ass after ass still hee-haws through the town,
And in disgrace at last each jockey bumps adown.

And then the noisy rout, their sports to crown,
Form round the ring superior strength to show,
Where wrestlers join to tug each other down,
And thrust and kick with hard revengeful toe,
Till through their worsted hose the blood does flow:
For ploughmen would not wish for higher fame,
Than be the champion all the rest to throw;
And thus to add such honours to his name,
He kicks, and tugs, and bleeds to win the glorious game.

And when the night draws on, each mirthful lout
The ale-house seeks, and sets it in a roar;
And there, while fiddlers play, they rant about,
And call for brimming tankards frothing o'er:
For clouds of smoke ye'd hardly see the door;
No stint they make of 'bacco and of beer;
While money lasts they shout about for more,
Resolv'd to keep it merry when it's here—
As toils come every day, and feasts but once a year.

With village-merriments digress'd awhile,
We now resume poor Lubin's joys again,
And haply find him bending o'er a stile,
Or stretch'd in sabbath-musings on the plain,
Looking around and humming o'er a strain,
Painting the foliage of the woodland trees,
List'ning a bird that's lost its nest complain,
Noting the hummings of the passing bees,
And all the lovely things his musing hears and sees.

Where ling-clad heaths and pastures now may spread,
He oft has heard of castle and of hall;
And curiosity his steps hath led
To gaze on some old arch or fretting wall,
Where ivy scrambles up to stop the fall:
There would he sit him down, and look, and sigh,
And bygone days back to his mind would call,
The bloody-warring times of chivalry,
When Danes' invading routs made unarm'd Britons fly.

He lov'd to view the mossy-arched brigs,
Bending o'er wall or rail, the pits or springs
Below to mark, where willow's dripping twigs
To summer's silken zephyrs' feeblest wings
Bent in the flood, and curv'd its thousand rings;
And where the sunbeam twitter'd on the walls,
And nodding bulrush down its drowk head hings,
And down the rock the shallow water falls,
Wild fluttering through the stones in feeble whimpering
    brawls.

And oft, with shepherds leaning o'er their hooks,
He'd stand conjecturing on the ruins round:
Though little skill'd in antiquated books,
Their knowledge in such matters seem'd profound;
And they would preach of what did once abound,
Castles deep moated round, old haunted hall—
And something like to moats still 'camp the ground
Where beneath Cromwell's rage the towers did fall;
But ivy creeps the hill, and ruin hides it all.

And ancient songs he hung enraptur'd on,
Which herdsmen on a hill have sat to sing,
'Bout feats of Robin Hood and Little John,
Whose might was fear'd by country and by king,
Such strength had they to twitch the thrumming string;
Their darts oft suck'd the life-blood of the deer,
And Sherwood Forest with their horns did ring.
Ah, these were songs which he would joy to hear,
And these were such as warm'd when antique scenes appear.

But who can tell the anguish of his mind,
When reformation's formidable foes
With civil wars 'gainst nature's peace combin'd,
And desolation struck her deadly blows,
As curst improvement 'gan his fields inclose:
O greens, and fields, and trees, farewell, farewell!
His heart-wrung pains, his unavailing woes
No words can utter, and no tongue can tell,
When ploughs destroy'd the green, when groves of
    willows fell.

There once were springs when daisies' silver studs
Like sheets of snow on every pasture spread;
There once were summers when the crow-flower buds
Like golden sunbeams brightest lustre shed;
And trees grew once that shelter'd Lubin's head;
There once were brooks sweet whimpering down the vale:
The brook's no more—kingcup and daisy fled;
Their last fall'n tree the naked moors bewail,
And scarce a bush is left to tell the mournful tale.

Yon flaggy tufts, and many a rushy knot
Existing still in spite of spade and plough,
As seeming fond and loath to leave the spot,
Tell where was once the green—brown fallows now,
Where Lubin often turns a sadden'd brow,
Marks the stopt brook, and mourns oppression's power,
And thinks how once he waded in each slough
To crop the yellow 'horse-blob's' early flower
Or catch the 'miller's-thumb' in summer's sultry hour.

There once were days, the woodman knows it well,
When shades e'en echoed with the singing thrush;
There once were hours, the ploughman's tale can tell,
When morning's beauty wore its earliest blush,
How woodlarks caroll'd from each stumpy bush;
Lubin himself has mark'd them soar and sing:
The thorns are gone, the woodlark's song is hush,
Spring more resembles winter now than spring,
The shades are banish'd all—the birds have took to wing.

There once were lanes in nature's freedom dropt,
There once were paths that every valley wound—
Inclosure came, and every path was stopt;
Each tyrant fix'd his sign where paths were found,
To hint a trespass now who cross'd the ground:
Justice is made to speak as they command;
The high road now must be each stinted bound:
—Inclosure, thou'rt a curse upon the land,
And tasteless was the wretch who thy existence plann'd.

O England! boasted land of liberty,
With strangers still thou mayst thy title own,
But thy poor slaves the alteration see,
With many a loss to them the truth is known:
Like emigrating bird thy freedom's flown,
While mongrel clowns, low as their rooting plough,
Disdain thy laws to put in force their own;
And every village owns its tyrants now,
And parish-slaves must live as parish-kings allow.

Ye fields, ye scenes so dear to Lubin's eye,
Ye meadow-blooms, ye pasture-flowers, farewell!
Ye banish'd trees, ye make me deeply sigh—
Inclosure came, and all your glories fell:
E'en the old oak that crown'd yon rifled dell,
Whose age had made it sacred to the view,
Not long was left his children's fate to tell;
Where ignorance and wealth their course pursue,
Each tree must tumble down—old 'Lea-close Oak,' adieu!

Lubin beheld it all, and, deeply pain'd,
Along the paled road would muse and sigh,
The only path that freedom's rights maintain'd;
The naked scenes drew pity from his eye,
Tears dropt to memory of delights gone by;
The haunts of freedom, cowherd's wattled bower,
And shepherds' huts, and trees that tower'd high,
And spreading thorns that turn'd a summer shower,
All captives lost, and past to sad oppression's power.

And oft with shepherds he would sit, to sigh
O'er past delights of many a bygone day,
And look on scenes now naked to the eye,
And talk as how they once were clothed gay,
And how the runnel wound its weedy way,
And how the willows on its margin grew;
Talk o'er with them the rural feats of May—
Who got the blossoms 'neath the morning dew
That the last garland made, and where such blossoms grew:

And how he could remember well, when he,
Laden with blooming treasures from the plain,
Has mixt with them beneath a dotterel-tree,
Driv'n from his cowslips by a hasty rain,
And heard them there sing each delightful strain;
And how with tales what joys they us'd to wake;
Wishing with them such days would come again:
They lov'd the artless boy for talking's sake,
And said some future day a wondrous man he'd make.

And you, poor ragged outcasts of the land,
That lug your shifting camps from green to green,
He lov'd to see your humble dwellings stand,
And thought your groups did beautify the scene:
Though blam'd for many a petty theft you've been,
Poor wandering souls, to fate's hard want decreed,
Doubtless too oft such acts your ways bemean;
But oft in wrong your foes 'gainst you proceed,
And brand a gipsy's camp when others do the deed.

Lubin would love to list their gibberish talk,
And view the oddity their ways display;
And oft with boys pursued his Sunday walk,
Where warp'd the camp beneath the willows grey,
And its black tenants on the greensward lay;
While, on two forked sticks with cordage tied,
Their pot o'er pilfer'd fuel boils away,
With food of sheep that of red-water died,
Or any nauseous thing their frowning fates provide.

Yet oft they gather money by their trade,
And on their fortune-telling art subsist:
Where her long-hurded groat oft brings the maid,
And secret slives it in the sibyl's fist
To buy good luck and happiness—to list,
What occupies a wench's every thought,
Who is to be the man: while, as she wist,
The gipsy's tale with swains and wealth is fraught,
The lass returns well-pleas'd, and thinks all cheaply bought.

In summer, Lubin oft has mark'd and seen
How eagerly the village-maids pursue
Their Sunday rambles where the camps have been;
And how they give their money to the crew
For idle stories they believe as true;
Crossing their hands with coin or magic stick,
How quak'd the young to hear what things they knew;
While old experienc'd dames saw through the trick,
Who said that all their skill was borrow'd from Old Nick.

And thus the superstitious dread their harm,
And dare not fail relieving the distrest,
Lest they within their cot should leave a charm,
To let naught prosper and bring on some pest:
Of depth of cunning gipsies are possest,
And when such weakness in a dame they find,
Forsooth they prove a terrifying guest;
And though not one to charity inclin'd,
They mutter black revenge, and force her to be kind.

His native scenes! O sweet endearing sound!
Sure never beats a heart, howe'er forlorn,
But the warm'd breast has soft emotions found
To cherish the dear spot where he was born:
E'en the poor hedger, in the early morn
Chopping the pattering bushes hung with dew,
Scarce lays his mitten on a branching thorn,
But painful memory's banish'd thoughts in view
Remind him, when 'twas young, what happy days he knew.

When the old shepherd with his woolly locks
Crosses the green, past joys his eyes will fill,
Where when a boy he us'd to tend his flocks;
Each fringed rushy bed and swelling hill,
Where he has play'd, or stretch'd him at his will,
Freshening anew in life's declining years,
Will jog his memory with its pleasures still.
Oh, how the thought his native scenes endears!
No spot throughout the world so pleasingly appears.

The toil-worn thresher, in his little cot
Whose roof did shield his birth, and still remains
His dwelling-place, how rough soe'er his lot,
His toil though hard, and small the wage he gains
That many a child most piningly maintains;
Send him to distant scenes and better fare,
How would his bosom yearn with parting-pains;
How would he turn and look, and linger there,
And wish e'en now his cot and poverty to share.

How dear the soldier feels the relic prove
Took from his cot or giv'n by love's sweet hand—
A box that bears the motto of true love;
How will he take his quid, and musing stand,
Think on his native lass and native land,
And bring to mind all those past joys again
From which wild youth so foolish was trepann'd,
Kissing the pledge that doth these ways retain,
While fancy points the spot far o'er the barring main.

O dear delightful spots, his native place!
How Lubin look'd upon the days gone by;
How he, though young, would past delights retrace,
Bend o'er gull'd holes where stood his trees, and sigh,
With tears the while bemoist'ning in his eye;
How look'd he for the green, a green no more;
Mourning to scenes that made him no reply,
Save the strong accents they in memory bore,
'Our scenes that charm'd thy youth are dead, to bloom
    no more.'

O samely naked leas, so bleak, so strange!
How would he wander o'er ye to complain,
And sigh, and wish he ne'er had known the change,
To see the ploughshare bury all the plain,
And not a cowslip on its lap remain;
The rush-tuft gone that hid the skylark's nest:
Ah, when will May-morn hear such strains again?
The storms beat chilly on its naked breast,
No shelter grows to shield, no home invites to rest.

'Ah,' would he sigh, 'ye, 'neath the churchyard grass,
Ye sleeping shepherds, could ye rise again,
And see what since your time has come to pass,
See not a bush nor willow now remain,
Looking and list'ning for the brook in vain—
Ye'd little think such was your natal scene;
Ye'd little now distinguish field from plain,
Or·where to look for each departed green;
All plough'd and buried now, as though there naught had
    been.'

But still they beam'd with beauties on his eye;
No other scenes were half so sweet to view;
And other flowers but strove in vain to vie
With his few tufts that 'scap'd the wreck and grew;
And skylarks too their singing might pursue,
To claim his praise—he could but only say
Their songs were sweet but not like those he knew
That charm'd his native plains at early day,
Whose equals ne'er were found where'er his steps might
    stray.

When distant village feast or noisy fair
Short absence from his fields did him detain,
How would he feel when home he did repair,
And mix among his joys—the white-spire vane
Meeting his eye above the elms again:
Leaving his friends in the sweet summer-night,
No longer lost on unknown field or plain,
Far from the path with well-known haunts in sight,
He'd stray for scatter'd flowers with added new delight.

As travellers return'd from foreign ground
Feel more endearments for their native earth,
So Lubin cherish'd from each weary round
Still warmer fondness for those scenes of mirth,
Those plains, and that dear cot that gave him birth;
And oft this warmness for his fields he'd own,
Mix'd with his friends around the cottage-hearth,
Relating all the travels he had known,
And that he'd seen no spot so lovely as his own.

Nor has his taste with manhood e'er declin'd:
You still may see him on his lonely way,
O'er stile or gate in thoughtful mood reclin'd;
Or 'long the road with folded arms to stray,
Mixing with autumn's sighs or summer gay;
And curious, nature's secrets to explore,
Brushing the twigs of woods or copse away,
To roam the lonely shade so silent o'er,
Sweet muttering all his joys where clowns intrude no more.

Ah, who can tell the anxiousness of mind,
As now he doth to manhood's cares aspire:
The future blessings which he hopes to find,
The wisht-for prospects of his heart's desire,
And how chill fear oft damps the glowing fire,
And o'er hope's sunshine spreads a cloudy gloom:
Yet foil'd and foil'd, hopes still his songs inspire;
And, like the daisy on the cotter's tomb,
In melancholy scenes he 'joys his cheerless bloom.

He has his friends, compar'd to foes though few,
And like a cornflower in a field of grain
'Mong many a foe his wild weeds ope to view,
And malice mocks him with a rude disdain;
Proving pretensions to the muse as vain,
They deem her talents far beyond his skill,
And hiss his efforts as some forged strain:
But as hopes smile their tongues shall all be still,
E'en envy turns a friend when she's no power to kill.

Ah, as the traveller from the mountain-top
Looks down on misty kingdoms spread below,
And meditates beneath the steepy drop
What life and lands exist, and rivers flow;
How fain that hour the anxious soul would know
Of all his eye beholds—but 'tis in vain:
So Lubin eager views this world of woe,
And wishes time her secrets would explain,
If he may live for joys or sink in 'whelming pain.

Fate's close-kept thoughts within her bosom hide;
She is no gossip, secrets to betray:
Time's steady movements must her end decide,
And leave him painful still to hope the day,
And grope through ignorance his doubtful way,
By wisdom disregarded, fools annoy'd.
And if no worth anticipates the lay,
Then let his childish notions be destroy'd,
And he his time employ as erst it was employ'd.

THE GIPSY'S CAMP

How oft on Sundays, when I'd time to tramp,
My rambles led me to a gipsy's camp,
Where the real effigy of midnight hags,
With tawny smoked flesh and tatter'd rags,
Uncouth-brimm'd hat, and weather-beaten cloak,
'Neath the wild shelter of a knotty oak,
Along the greensward uniformly pricks
Her pliant bending hazel's arching sticks;
While round-topt bush, or brier-entangled hedge,
Where flag-leaves spring beneath, or ramping sedge,
Keep off the bothering bustle of the wind,
And give the best retreat she hopes to find.
How oft I've bent me o'er her fire and smoke,
To hear her gibberish tale so quaintly spoke,
While the old sibyl forc'd her boding clack,
Twin imps the meanwhile bawling at her back;
Oft on my hand her magic coin's been struck,
And hoping chink, she talk'd of morts of luck:
And still, as boyish hopes did first agree,
Mingled with fears to drop the fortune's fee,
I never fail'd to gain the honours sought,

And Squire and Lord were purchas'd with a groat.
But as man's unbelieving taste came round,
She furious stampt her shoeless foot aground,
Wip'd bye her soot-black hair with clenching fist,
While through her yellow teeth the spittle hist,

Swearing by all her lucky powers of fate,
Which like as footboys on her actions wait,
That fortune's scale should to my sorrow turn,
And I one day the rash neglect should mourn;
That good to bad should change, and I should be
Lost to this world and all eternity;
That poor as Job I should remain unblest;
   (Alas, for fourpence how my die is cast!)
Of not a hoarded farthing be possest,
   And when all's done, be shov'd to hell at last!

TO AN INFANT DAUGHTER

SWEET gem of infant fairy-flowers!
Thy smiles on life's unclosing hours,
Like sunbeams lost in summer showers,
     They wake my fears;
When reason knows its sweets and sours,
     They'll change to tears.

God help thee, little senseless thing!
Thou, daisy-like of early spring,
Of ambush'd winter's hornet sting
     Hast yet to tell;
Thou know'st not what to-morrows bring:
     I wish thee well.

But thou art come, and soon or late
'Tis thine to meet the frowns of fate,
The harpy grin of envy's hate,
     And mermaid-smiles
Of worldly folly's luring bait,
     That youth beguiles.

And much I wish, whate'er may be
The lot, my child, that falls to thee,
Nature may never let thee see
     Her glass betimes,
But keep thee from my failings free—
     Nor itch at rhymes.

Lord help thee in thy coming years
If thy mad father's picture 'pears
Predominant!—his feeling fears
        And jingling starts;
I'd freely now gi' vent to tears
        To ease my heart.

May thou, unknown to rhyming bother,
Be ignorant as is thy mother,
And in thy manners such another,
        Save sin's nigh quest;
And then with 'scaping this and t'other
        Thou mayst be blest.[1]

Lord knows my heart, it loves thee much;
And may my feelings, aches, and such,
The pains I meet in folly's clutch
        Be never thine:
Child, it's a tender string to touch,
        That sounds 'Thou'rt mine.'

PROPOSALS FOR BUILDING A COTTAGE

BESIDE a runnel build my shed,
    With stubbles cover'd o'er;
Let broad oaks o'er its chimney spread,
    And grass-plats grace the door.

The door may open with a string,
    So that it closes tight;
And locks would be a wanted thing,
    To keep out thieves at night.

A little garden, not too fine,
    Inclose with painted pales;
And woodbines, round the cot to twine,
    Pin to the wall with nails.

[1] Preceding two verses added from MS.

Let hazels grow, and spindling sedge,
  Bent bowering overhead;
Dig old man's beard from woodland hedge,
  To twine a summer shade.

Beside the threshold sods provide,
  And build a summer seat;
Plant sweetbrier bushes by its side,
  And flowers that blossom sweet.

I love the sparrows' ways to watch
  Upon the cotters' sheds,
So here and there pull out the thatch,
  That they may hide their heads.

And as the sweeping swallows stop
  Their flights along the green,
Leave holes within the chimney-top
  To paste their nest between.

Stick shelves and cupboards round the hut,
  In all the holes and nooks;
Nor in the corner fail to put
  A cupboard for the books.

Along the floor some sand I'll sift,
  To make it fit to live in;
And then I'll thank ye for the gift,
  As something worth the giving.

LANGLEY BUSH

O LANGLEY BUSH! the shepherd's sacred shade,
  Thy hollow trunk oft gain'd a look from me;
Full many a journey o'er the heath I've made,
  For such-like curious things I love to see.
What truth the story of the swain allows,
  That tells of honours which thy young days knew,

Of 'Langley Court' being kept beneath thy boughs,
  I cannot tell—thus much I know is true,
That thou art reverenc'd: even the rude clan
  Of lawless gipsies, driven from stage to stage,
Pilfering the hedges of the husbandman,
  Spare thee, as sacred, in thy withering age.
Both swains and gipsies seem to love thy name,
  Thy spot's a favourite with the sooty crew,
And soon thou must depend on gipsy-fame,
  Thy mouldering trunk is nearly rotten through.
My last doubts murmur on the zephyr's swell,
  My last look lingers on thy boughs with pain;
To thy declining age I bid farewell,
  Like old companions, ne'er to meet again.

SONGS AND BALLADS

COUNTRY SWEETHEARTS

'I'll ne'er walk at even grim
When the night is glimpt wi' grey;
When the light is waxing dim;
Deeds are done at closing day.
Ever sin' by blossom'd bean
While the gnats were dancing by,
Ye did on my bosom lean,
Aye the tear's bin in my eye.

'Ever sin' ye pass'd the morn
When ye little dreamt a spy,
Meeting Dolly 'hind the thorn,
Aye the tear's bin in my eye.
Ever sin' ye vow'd to wed,
And I prov'd wi' heavy sigh
Ye'd the vow to many made,
Aye the tear's bin in my eye.'

'Sweet the tear shines on thee, love,
Which I soon will wash away;
Tenderness has won me, love,
Fear thou not the even grey.
Sin' we sat by beans in bloom,
I have bin the ring to buy;
Think no harm from that shall come,
Wipe the tear from either eye.'

SONG

Swamps of wild rush-beds, and sloughs' squashy traces,
　　Grounds of rough fallows with thistle and weed,
Flats and low valleys of kingcups and daisies,
　　Sweetest of subjects are ye for my reed:
Ye commons left free in the rude rags of nature,
　　Ye brown heaths beclothed in furze as ye be,
My wild eye in rapture adores every feature,
　　Ye are dear as this heart in my bosom to me.

O native endearments! I would not forsake ye,
  I would not forsake ye for sweetest of scenes;
For sweetest of gardens that nature could make me,
  I would not forsake ye, dear valleys and greens:
Tho' nature ne'er dropt ye a cloud-resting mountain,
  Nor waterfalls tumble their music so free;
Had nature denied ye a bush, tree, or fountain,
  Ye still had been lov'd as an Eden by me.

And long, my dear valleys, long, long may ye flourish,
  Though rush-beds and thistles make most of your pride;
May showers never fail the green's daisies to nourish,
  Nor suns dry the fountain that rills by its side.
Your skies may be gloomy, and misty your mornings,
  Your flat swampy valleys unwholesome may be;
Still, refuse of nature, without her adornings
  Ye are dear as this heart in my bosom to me.

SONNET

TO THE MEMORY OF JOHN KEATS

THE world, its hopes, and fears, have pass'd away;
   No more its trifling thou shalt feel or see;
Thy hopes are ripening in a brighter day,
   While these left buds thy monument shall be.
When Rancour's aims have past in naught away,
   Enlarging specks discern'd in more than thee,
And beauties 'minishing which few display—
   When these are past, true child of Poesy,
Thou shalt survive.   Ah, while a being dwells,
   With soul, in nature's joys, to warm like thine,
With eye to view her fascinating spells,
   And dream entranced o'er each form divine,
Thy worth, Enthusiast, shall be cherish'd here,
Thy name with him shall linger, and be dear.

POEMS WRITTEN AT HELPSTONE
1821–4

THE SHEPHERD'S CALENDAR

JANUARY

I

WITHERING and keen the winter comes,
While Comfort flies to close-shut rooms,
And sees the snow in feathers pass
Winnowing by the window-glass;
Whilst unfelt tempests howl and beat
Above his head in chimney-seat.

Now, musing o'er the changing scene,
Farmers behind the tavern-screen
Collect; with elbow idly press'd
On hob, reclines the corner's guest,
Reading the news, to mark again
The bankrupt lists, or price of grain;
Or old Moore's annual prophecies
Of flooded fields and clouded skies;
Whose Almanac's thumb'd pages swarm
With frost and snow, and many a storm,
And wisdom, gossip'd from the stars,
Of politics and bloody wars.
He shakes his head, and still proceeds,
Nor doubts the truth of what he reads:
All wonders are with faith supplied—
Bible, at once, and weather-guide.
Puffing the while his red-tipt pipe,
He dreams o'er troubles nearly ripe;
Yet, not quite lost in profit's way,
He'll turn to next year's harvest-day,
And, winter's leisure to regale,
Hope better times, and sip his ale.

The schoolboy still, with dithering joys,
In pastime leisure hours employs,
And, be the weather as it may,
Is never at a loss for play:

Making rude forms of various names,
Snow-men, or aught his fancy frames;
Till, numb'd and shivering, he resorts
To brisker games and warmer sports—
Kicking, with many a flying bound,
The football o'er the frozen ground,
Or seeking bright glib ice, to play
And slide the wintry hours away,
As quick and smooth as shadows run,
When clouds in autumn pass the sun.
Some, hurrying rambles eager take
To skate upon the meadow lake,
Scaring the snipe from her retreat,
From shelving bank's unfrozen seat,
Or running brook, where icy spars,
Which the pale sunlight specks with stars,
Shoot crizzling o'er the restless tide,
To many a likeness petrified.
The moor-hen, too, with fear opprest,
Starts from her reedy shelter'd rest,
As skating by, with curving springs,
And arms outspread like heron's wings,
They race away, for pleasure's sake,
With hunter's speed along the lake.

Blackening through the evening sky,
In clouds the starnels daily fly
To Whittlesea's reed-wooded mere,
And osier holts by rivers near;
Whilst many a mingled swarthy crowd—
Rook, crow, and jackdaw—noising loud,
Fly to and fro to dreary fen,
Dull winter's weary flight again;
They flop on heavy wings away
As soon as morning wakens grey,
And, when the sun sets round and red,
Return to naked woods to bed.
Wood pigeons too in flocks appear,
By hunger tamed from timid fear;

They mid the sheep unstartled steal
And share with them a scanty meal,
Picking the green leaves want bestows
Of turnips sprouting thro' the snows.[1]

The sun is creeping out of sight
Behind the woods —whilst running night
Hastens to shut the day's dull eye,
And grizzle o'er the chilly sky,
Dark, deep and thick, by day forsook,
As cottage chimney's sooty nook.[2]
Now maidens, fresh as summer roses,
Journeying from the distant closes,
Haste home with yokes and swinging pail;
The thresher, too, sets by his flail,
And leaves the mice at peace again
To fill their holes with stolen grain;
Whilst owlets, glad his toils are o'er,
Swoop by him as he shuts the door.

Bearing his hook beneath his arm,
The shepherd seeks the cottage warm;
And, weary in the cold to roam,
Scenting the track that leads him home,
His dog goes swifter o'er the mead,
Barking to urge his master's speed;
Then turns, and looks him in the face,
And trots before with mending pace,
Till, out of whistle from the swain,
He sits him down and barks again,
Anxious to greet the open'd door,
And meet the cottage fire once more.

The robin, that with nimble eye
Glegs round a danger to espy,
Now pops from out the open door
From crumbs half left upon the floor,
Nor wipes his bill on perching chair,
Nor stays to clean a feather there,

[1] Six lines added from MS.   [2] Two lines added from MS.

Scared at the cat that slinketh in
A chance from evening's glooms to win,
To jump on chairs or tables nigh,
Seeking what plunder may supply,
The children's littered scraps to thieve
Or aught that negligence may leave,
Creeping, where housewives cease to watch
Or dairy doors are off the latch,
On cheese or butter to regale
Or new milk reeking in the pail.
The hedger now in leather coat,
From woodland wilds and fields remote,
After a journey far and slow,
Knocks from his shoes the caking snow
And opes the welcome creaking door,
Throwing his faggot on the floor;
And at his listening wife's desire
To eke afresh the blazing fire
With sharp bill cuts the hazel bands,
Then sits him down to warm his hands
And tell in labour's happy way
His story of the passing day;
While as the warm blaze cracks and gleams
The supper reeks in savoury steams
Or kettle murmurs merrily
And tinkling cups are set for tea;
Thus doth the winter's dreary day
From morn to evening wear away.[1]

II

The shutter closed, the lamp alight,
The faggot chopt and blazing bright—
The shepherd now, from labour free,
Dances his children on his knee;
While, underneath his master's seat,
The tired dog lies in slumbers sweet,

[1] Thirty-four lines added from MS. *January* appears in the MSS. as two
poems; the second begins here.

Starting and whimpering in his sleep,
Chasing still the straying sheep.
The cat's roll'd round in vacant chair,
Or leaping children's knees to lair,
Or purring on the warmer hearth,
Sweet chorus to the cricket's mirth.

The redcap, hanging overhead,
In cage of wire is perch'd abed;
Slumbering in his painted feathers,
Unconscious of the outdoor weathers;
Ev'n things without the cottage walls
Meet comfort as the evening falls,
As happy in the winter's dearth
As those around the blazing hearth.
The ass (frost-driven from the moor,
Where storms through naked bushes roar,
And not a leaf or sprig of green,
On ground or quaking bush, is seen,
Save grey-vein'd ivy's hardy pride,
Round old trees by the common side),
Litter'd with straw, now dozes warm,
Beneath his shed, from snow and storm:
The swine are fed and in the sty;
And fowls snug perch'd in hovel nigh,
With head in feathers safe asleep,
Where foxes cannot hope to creep,
And geese are gabbling in their dreams
Of litter'd corn and thawing streams.
The sparrow, too, a daily guest,
Is in the cottage eaves at rest;
And robin small, and smaller wren,
Are in their warm holes safe agen
From falling snows, that winnow by
The hovels where they nightly lie,
And ague winds, that shake the tree
Where other birds are forc'd to be.

The housewife, busy night and day,
Clears the supper-things away;

The jumping cat starts from her seat;
And stretching up on weary feet,
The dog wakes at the welcome tones
That call him up to pick the bones.

On corner walls, a glittering row,
Hang fire-irons—less for use than show,
With horse-shoe brighten'd, as a spell,
Witchcraft's evil powers to quell,
And warming-pan, reflecting bright
The crackling blaze's flickering light,
That hangs the corner wall to grace,
Nor oft is taken from its place:
There in its mirror, bright as gold,
The children peep, and straight behold
Their laughing faces, whilst they pass,
Gleam on the lid as plain as glass.

Supper removed, the mother sits,
And tells her tales by starts and fits.
Not willing to lose time or toil,
She knits or sews, and talks the while—
Something that may be warnings found
To the young listeners gaping round—
Of boys who in her early day
Stroll'd to the meadow-lake to play,
Where willows, o'er the bank inclined,
Shelter'd the water from the wind,
And left it scarcely crizzled o'er—
When one plopt in, to rise no more!
And how, upon a market-night,
When not a star bestow'd its light,
A farmer's shepherd, o'er his glass,
Forgot that he had woods to pass:
And having sold his master's sheep,
Was overta'en by darkness deep.
How, coming with his startled horse,
To where two roads a hollow cross,
Where, lone guide when a stranger strays,
A white post points four different ways,

Beside the woodride's lonely gate
A murdering robber lay in wait.
The frighten'd horse, with broken rein
Stood at the stable-door again;
But none came home to fill his rack,
Or take the saddle from his back:
The saddle—it was all he bore;
The man was seen alive no more!
In her young days, beside the wood,
The gibbet in his terror stood:
Though now decay'd, 'tis not forgot,
But dreaded as a haunted spot.

She from her memory oft repeats
Witches' dread powers and fairy feats:
How one has oft been known to prance
In cowcribs, like a coach, to France,
And ride on sheep-trays from the fold
A race-horse speed to Burton-hold,
To join the midnight mystery's rout,
Where witches meet the yews about:
And how, when met with unawares,
They turn at once to cats or hares,
And race along with hellish flight,
Now here, now there, now out of sight!
And how the other tiny things
Will leave their moonlight meadow-rings,
And, unperceiv'd, through key-holes creep,
When all around have sunk to sleep,
And crowd in cupboards as they please,
As thick as mites in rotten cheese,[1]
To feast on what the cotter leaves—
Mice are not reckon'd greater thieves.
They take away, as well as eat,
And still the housewife's eye they cheat,
In spite of all the folks that swarm
In cottage small and larger farm;
They through each key-hole pop and pop,

[1] Two lines added from MS.

Like wasps into a grocer's shop,
With all the things that they can win
From chance to put their plunder in;
As shells of walnuts, split in two
By crows, who with the kernels flew;
Or acorn-cups, by stock-doves pluck'd,
Or egg-shells by a cuckoo suck'd;
With broad leaves of the sycamore
They clothe their stolen dainties o'er,
And when in cellar they regale,
Bring hazel-nuts to hold their ale,
With bung-holes bor'd by squirrels well,
To get the kernel from the shell,
Or maggots a way out to win,
When all is gone that grew within;
And be the key-holes e'er so high,
Rush poles a ladder's help supply,
Where soft the climbers fearless tread
On spindles made of spiders' thread.
And foul, or fair, or dark the night,
Their wild-fire lamps are burning bright,
For which full many a daring crime
Is acted in the summer-time;
When glow-worm found in lanes remote
Is murder'd for its shining coat,
And put in flowers, that Nature weaves
With hollow shapes and silken leaves,
Such as the Canterbury bell,
Serving for lamp or lantern well;
Or, following with unwearied watch
The flight of one they cannot match,
As silence sliveth upon sleep,
Or thieves by dozing watch-dogs creep,
They steal from Jack-a-lantern's tails
A light, whose guidance never fails
To aid them in the darkest night
And guide their plundering steps aright,
Rattling away in printless tracks.
Some, housed on beetles' glossy backs,

Go whisking on —and others hie
As fast as loaded moths can fly:
Some urge, the morning cock to shun,
The hardest gallop mice can run,
In chariots, lolling at their ease,
Made of whate'er their fancies please;
Things that in childhood's memory dwell—
Scoop'd crow-pot-stone, or cockle-shell,
With wheels at hand of mallow seeds,
Where childish sport was stringing beads;
And thus equipp'd, they softly pass
Like shadows on the summer-grass,
And glide away in troops together
Just as the spring-wind drives a feather.
As light as happy dreams they creep,
Nor break the feeblest link of sleep:
A midgeon in their road abed,
Feels not the wheels run o'er his head,
But sleeps till sunrise calls him up,
Unconscious of the passing troop.

　　Thus dame the winter-night regales
With wonder's never-ceasing tales;
While in a corner, ill at ease,
Or crushing 'tween their father's knees,
The children—silent all the while—
And e'en repressed the laugh or smile—
Quake with the ague chills of fear,
And tremble though they love to hear,
Starting, while they the tales recall,
At their own shadows on the wall:
Till the old clock, that strikes unseen
Behind the picture-pasted screen
Where Eve and Adam still agree
To rob Life's fatal apple-tree,
Counts over bed-time's hour of rest,
And bids each be sleep's fearful guest.
She then her half-told tales will leave
To finish on to-morrow's eve.

The children steal away to bed,
And up the ladder softly tread,
Scarce daring—from their fearful joys—
To look behind or make a noise;
Nor speak a word, but still as sleep
They secret to their pillows creep,
And whisper o'er, in terror's way,
The prayers they dare no louder say,
Then hide their heads beneath the clothes,
And try in vain to seek repose;
While yet, to fancy's sleepless eye,
Witches on sheep-trays gallop by,
And fairies, like a rising spark,
Swarm twittering round them in the dark;
Till sleep creeps nigh to ease their cares,
And drops upon them unawares.

Oh, spirit of the days gone by—
Sweet childhood's fearful ecstasy!
The witching spells of winter nights,
Where are they fled with their delights?
When list'ning on the corner seat,
The winter evening's length to cheat,
I heard my mother's memory tell
Tales superstition loves so well:
Things said or sung a thousand times,
In simple prose or simpler rhymes.
Ah! where is page of poesy
So sweet as this was wont to be?
The magic wonders that deceived,
When fictions were as truths believed,
The fairy feats that once prevailed,
Told to delight, and never failed,
Where are they now, their fears and sighs,
And tears from founts of happy eyes?
I read in books, but find them not,
For poesy hath its youth forgot:
I hear them told to children still,
But fear numbs not my spirits chill:

I still see faces pale with dread,
While mine could laugh at what is said,
See tears imagined woes supply,
While mine with real cares are dry.
Where are they gone—the joys and fears,
The links, the life of other years?
I thought they twined around my heart
So close, that we could never part;
But Reason, like a winter's day,
Nipp'd childhood's visions all away,
Nor left behind one withering flower
To cherish in a lonely hour.
Memory may yet the themes repeat,
But childhood's heart hath ceased to beat
At tales, which Reason's sterner lore
Turns like weak gossips from her door:
The Magic Fountain, where the head
Rose up, just as the startled maid
Was stooping from the weedy brink
To dip her pitcher in to drink,
That did its half-hid mystery tell
To smooth its hair, and use it well;
Which, doing as it bade her do,
Turn'd to a king and lover too.
The tale of Cinderella, told
The winter through, and never old:
The pumpkin that, at her approach,
Was turn'd into a golden coach;
The rats that fairies' magic knew,
And instantly to horses grew;
The coachmen ready at her call,
To drive her to the Prince's ball,
With fur-changed jackets silver lined,
And tails hung 'neath their hats behind;
The golden glove, with fingers small,
She lost while dancing in the hall,
That was on every finger tried,
And fitted hers, and none beside,
When Cinderella, soon as seen,

Was woo'd and won, and made a Queen.
The Boy that did the Giant slay,
And gave his mother's cows away
For magic mask, that day or night,
When on, would keep him out of sight.
The running bean—not such as weaves
Round poles the height of cottage eaves,
But magic one—that travell'd high
Some steeple's journey up the sky,
And reach'd a giant's dwelling there,
A cloud-built castle in the air:
Where, venturing up the fearful height,
That serv'd him climbing half the night,
He search'd the giant's coffers o'er,
And never wanted riches more;
While, like a lion scenting food,
The giant roar'd, in hungry mood,
A storm of threats that might suffice
To freeze the hottest blood to ice.

I hear it now, nor dream of woes;
The storm is settled to repose.
Those fears are dead! What will not die
In fading Life's mortality?
Those truths have fled, and left behind
A real world and doubting mind.

APRIL

Now infant April joins the spring,
   And views the watery sky,
As youngling linnet tries its wing,
   And fears at first to fly;
With timid step she ventures on,
   And hardly dares to smile,
Till blossoms open one by one,
   And sunny hours beguile.

But finer days are coming yet,
  With scenes more sweet to charm,
And suns arrive that rise and set
  Bright strangers to a storm:
Then, as the birds with louder song
  Each morning's glory cheer,
With bolder step she speeds along,
  And loses all her fear.

In wanton gambols, like a child,
  She tends her early toils,
And seeks the buds along the wild,
  That blossoms while she smiles;
Or, laughing on, with naught to chide,
  She races with the Hours,
Or sports by Nature's lovely side,
  And fills her lap with flowers.

The shepherd on his pasture walks
  The first fair cowslip finds,
Whose tufted flowers, on slender stalks,
  Keep nodding to the winds.
And though the thorns withhold the may,
  Their shades the violets bring,
Which children stoop for in their play
  As tokens of the spring.

Those joys which childhood calls its own,
  Would they were kin to men!
Those treasures to the world unknown,
  When known, are wither'd then!
But hovering round our growing years,
  To gild Care's sable shroud,
Their spirit through the gloom appears
  As suns behind a cloud.

Since thou didst meet my infant eyes,
  As through the fields I flew,
Whose distance, where they meet the skies,
  Was all the world I knew;

That warmth of fancy's wildest hours,
  Which fill'd all things with life,
Which heard a voice in trees and flowers,
  Has swoon'd in reason's strife.

Sweet month! thy pleasures bid thee be
  The fairest child of spring;
And every hour, that comes with thee,
  Comes some new joy to bring:
The trees still deepen in their bloom,
  Grass greens the meadow-lands,
And flowers with every morning come,
  As dropt by fairy hands.

The field and garden's lovely hours
  Begin and end with thee;
For what's so sweet, as peeping flowers
  And bursting buds to see,
What time the dew's unsullied drops,
  In burnish'd gold, distil
On crocus flowers' unclosing tops,
  And drooping daffodil?

To see thee come, all hearts rejoice;
  And, warm with feelings strong,
With thee all Nature finds a voice,
  And hums a waking song.
The lover views thy welcome hours,
  And thinks of summer come,
And takes the maid the early flowers,
  To tempt her steps from home.

Along each hedge and sprouting bush
  The singing birds are blest,
And linnet green and speckled thrush
  Prepare their mossy nest;
On the warm bed thy plains supply,
  The young lambs find repose,
And mid thy green hills basking lie
  Like spots of ling'ring snows.

Thy open'd leaves and ripen'd buds
    The cuckoo makes his choice,
And shepherds in thy greening woods
    First hear his cheering voice:
And to thy ripen'd blooming bowers
    The nightingale belongs,
And, singing to thy parting hours,
    Keeps night awake with songs.

With thee the swallow dares to come,
    And primes his sooty wing;
And, urged to seek his yearly home,
    Thy suns the martin bring.
O lovely month! be leisure mine
    Thy yearly mate to be;
Though May-day scenes may brighter shine,
    Their birth belongs to thee.

I waked me with thy rising sun,
    And thy first glories viewed,
And, as thy welcome hours begun,
    Their sunny steps pursued.
And now thy sun is on thee set,
    Like to a lovely eve,
I view thy parting with regret,
    And linger loath to leave.

Though at her birth the northern gale
    Come with its withering sigh,
And hopeful blossoms, turning pale,
    Upon her bosom die,
Ere April seeks another place,
    And ends her reign in this,
She leaves us with as fair a face
    As e'er gave birth to bliss.

MAY

Come, Queen of Months! in company
With all thy merry minstrelsy:
The restless cuckoo, absent long,
And twittering swallows' chimney-song;
With hedgerow crickets' notes, that run
From every bank that fronts the sun;
And swarthy bees, about the grass,
That stop with every bloom they pass,
And every minute, every hour,
Keep teasing weeds that wear a flower;
And toil, and childhood's humming joys,
For there is music in the noise
When village children, wild for sport,
In school-time's leisure, ever short,
Alternate catch the bounding ball,
Or run along the churchyard wall,
Capp'd with rude figured slabs, whose claims
In time's bad memory have no names,
Or race around the nooky church,
Or raise loud echoes in the porch,
Throw pebbles o'er the weathercock,
Viewing with jealous eyes the clock,
Or leap o'er grave-stones' leaning heights,
Uncheck'd by melancholy sights,
Though green grass swells in many a heap
Where kin, and friends, and parents sleep.
They think not, in their jovial cry,
The time will come when they shall lie
As lowly and as still as they,
While other boys above them play,
Heedless, as they are now, to know
The unconscious dust that lies below.

The driving boy, beside his team,
Of May-month's beauty now will dream,
And cock his hat, and turn his eye
On flower, and tree, and deepening sky;

And oft burst loud in fits of song,
And whistle as he reels along,
Cracking his whip in starts of joy—
A happy, dirty, driving boy.
The youth, who leaves his corner stool
Betimes for neighbouring village-school,
Where, as a mark to guide him right,
The church spire's all the way in sight,
With cheerings from his parents given,
Beneath the joyous smiles of heaven
Saunters, with many an idle stand,
With satchel swinging in his hand,
And gazes, as he passes by,
On everything that meets his eye.
Young lambs seem tempting him to play,
Dancing and bleating in his way;
With trembling tails and pointed ears
They follow him, and lose their fears;
He smiles upon their sunny faces,
And fain would join their happy races.
The birds, that sing on bush and tree,
Seem chirping for his company;
And all—in fancy's idle whim—
Seem keeping holiday, but him.
He lolls upon each resting stile,
To see the fields so sweetly smile,
To see the wheat grow green and long;
And lists the weeder's toiling song,
Or short note of the changing thrush
Above him in the whitethorn bush,
That o'er the leaning stile bends low
Its blooming mockery of snow.

Each hedge is cover'd thick with green;
And where the hedger late hath been,
Young tender shoots begin to grow
From out the mossy stumps below.
But woodmen still on spring intrude,
And thin the shadow's solitude;

With sharpen'd axes felling down
The oak-trees budding into brown,
Which, as they crash upon the ground,
A crowd of labourers gather round.
These, mixing 'mong the shadows dark,
Rip off the crackling, staining bark,
Depriving yearly, when they come,
The green woodpecker of his home,
Who early in the spring began,
Far from the sight of troubling man,
To bore his round holes in each tree
In fancy's sweet security;
Now, startled by the woodman's noise,
He wakes from all his dreary joys.
The blue-bells too, that thickly bloom
Where man was never known to come;
And stooping lilies of the valley,
That love with shades and dews to dally,
And bending droop on slender threads,
With broad hood-leaves above their heads,
Like white-robed maids, in summer hours,
Beneath umbrellas shunning showers;
These, from the bark-men's crushing treads,
Oft perish in their blooming beds.
Stripp'd of its boughs and bark, in white
The trunk shines in the mellow light
Beneath the green surviving trees,
That wave above it in the breeze,
And, waking whispers, slowly bend,
As if they mourn'd their fallen friend.

Each morning, now, the weeders meet
To cut the thistle from the wheat,
And ruin, in the sunny hours,
Full many a wild weed with its flowers;
Corn-poppies, that in crimson dwell,
Call'd 'headaches,' from their sickly smell;
And charlocks, yellow as the sun,
That o'er the May-fields quickly run;

And 'iron-weed,' content to share
The meanest spot that spring can spare—
E'en roads, where danger hourly comes,
Are not without its purple blooms,
Whose leaves, with threat'ning thistles round
Thick set, that have no strength to wound,
Shrink into childhood's eager hold
Like hair; and, with its eye of gold
And scarlet-starry points of flowers,
Pimpernel, dreading nights and showers,
Oft call'd 'the shepherd's weather-glass,'
That sleeps till suns have dried the grass,
Then wakes, and spreads its creeping bloom
Till clouds with threatening shadows come—
Then close it shuts to sleep again:
Which weeders see, and talk of rain;
And boys, that mark them shut so soon,
Call them 'John-go-to-bed-at-noon.'
And fumitory too—a name
That superstition holds to fame—
Whose red and purple mottled flowers
Are cropp'd by maids in weeding hours,
To boil in water, milk, and whey,
For washes on a holiday,
To make their beauty fair and sleek,
And scare the tan from summer's cheek;
And simple small 'forget-me-not,'
Eyed with a pin's-head yellow spot
I' the middle of its tender blue,
That gains from poets notice due:
These flowers, that toil by crowds destroys,
Robbing them of their lowly joys,
Had met the May with hopes as sweet
As those her suns in gardens meet;
And oft the dame will feel inclined,
As childhood's memory comes to mind,
To turn her hook away, and spare
The blooms it loved to gather there.
—Now young girls whisper things of love,

And from the old dames' hearing move;
Oft making 'love-knots' in the shade,
Of blue-green oat or wheaten blade;
Or, trying simple charms and spells
Which rural superstition tells,
They pull the little blossom threads
From out the knotweed's button heads,
And put the husk, with many a smile,
In their white bosoms for a while—
Then, if they guess aright the swain
Their loves' sweet fancies try to gain,
'Tis said, that ere it lies an hour,
'Twill blossom with a second flower,
And from their bosom's handkerchief
Bloom as it ne'er had lost a leaf.
—But signs appear that token wet,
While they are 'neath the bushes met;
The girls are glad with hopes of play,
And harp upon the holiday:
A high blue bird is seen to swim
Along the wheat, when skies grow dim
With clouds; slow as the gales of spring
In motion, with dark-shadow'd wing
Beneath the coming storm he sails:
And lonely chirp the wheat-hid quails,
That come to live with spring again,
But leave when summer browns the grain;
They start the young girls' joys afloat,
With 'wet my foot'—their yearly note:
So fancy doth the sound explain,
And oft it proves a sign of rain!

The thresher, dull as winter days,
And lost to all that spring displays,
Still mid his barn-dust forced to stand,
Swings round his flail with weary hand;
While o'er his head shades thickly creep,
That hide the blinking owl asleep,
And bats, in cobweb-corners bred,

Sharing till night their murky bed.
The sunshine trickles on the floor
Through ev'ry crevice of the door:
This makes his barn, where shadows dwell,
As irksome as a prisoner's cell;
And, whilst he seeks his daily meal,
As schoolboys from their task will steal,
So will he stand with fond delay
To see the daisy in his way,
Or wild weeds flowering on the wall;
For these to memory still recall
The joys, the sports that come with spring—
The twirling top, the marble ring,
The jingling halfpence hustled up
At pitch-and-toss, the eager stoop
To pick up *heads*, the smuggled plays
'Neath hovels upon sabbath-days,
The sitting down, when school was o'er,
Upon the threshold of the door,
Picking from mallows, sport to please,
Each crumpled seed he call'd a cheese,
And hunting from the stack-yard sod
The stinking henbane's belted pod,
By youth's warm fancies sweetly led
To christen them his loaves of bread.
He sees, while rocking down the street
With weary hands and crimpling feet,
Young children at the self-same games,
And hears the self-same boyish names
Still floating on each happy tongue:
Touch'd with the simple scene so strong,
Tears almost start, and many a sigh
Regrets the happiness gone by;
Thus, in sweet Nature's holiday,
His heart is sad while all is gay.

How lovely now are lanes and balks,
For lovers in their Sunday walks!
The daisy and the buttercup—

For which the laughing children stoop
A hundred times throughout the day,
In their rude romping summer play—
So thickly now the pasture crowd,
In a gold and silver sheeted cloud,
As if the drops of April showers
Had woo'd the sun, and changed to flowers.
The brook resumes her summer dresses,
Purling 'neath grass and water-cresses,
And mint and flagleaf, swording high
Their blooms to the unheeding eye,
And taper, bow-bent, hanging rushes,
And horsetail, children's bottle-brushes; [1]
The summer tracks about its brink
Are fresh again where cattle drink;
And on its sunny bank the swain
Stretches his idle length again;
While all that lives enjoys the birth
Of frolic summer's laughing mirth.

JUNE

Now summer is in flower, and Nature's hum
Is never silent round her bounteous bloom;
Insects, as small as dust, have never done
With glitt'ring dance, and reeling in the sun;
And green wood-fly, and blossom-haunting bee,
Are never weary of their melody.
Round field and hedge, flowers in full glory twine,
Large bindweed bells, wild hop, and streak'd woodbine,
That lift athirst their slender-throated flowers,
Agape for dew-falls, and for honey showers;
These o'er each bush in sweet disorder run,
And spread their wild hues to the sultry sun.
The mottled spider, at eve's leisure, weaves
His webs of silken lace on twigs and leaves,

[1] Two lines added from MS.

Which every morning meet the poet's eye,
Like fairies' dew-wet dresses hung to dry.
The wheat swells into ear, and hides below
The May-month wild flowers and their gaudy show,
Leaving a schoolboy's height, in snugger rest,
The leveret's seat, and lark and partridge nest.

The mowers now bend o'er the beaded grass,
Where oft the gipsy's hungry journeying ass
Will turn his wishes from the meadow paths,
List'ning the rustle of the falling swaths.
The ploughman sweats along the fallow vales,
And down the sun-crack'd furrow slowly trails,
Oft seeking, when athirst, the brook's supply,
Where, brushing eagerly the bushes by
For coolest water, he disturbs the rest
Of ring-dove, brooding o'er its idle nest.
The shepherd's leisure hours are over now;
No more he loiters 'neath the hedgerow bough,
On shadow-pillowed banks and lolling stile;
The wilds must lose their summer friend awhile.
With whistle, barking dogs, and chiding scold,
He drives the bleating sheep from fallow fold
To wash-pits, where the willow shadows lean,
Dashing them in, their stained coats to clean;
Then, on the sunny sward, when dry agen,
He brings them homeward to the clipping pen,
In hurdles pent, where elm or sycamore
Shut out the sun—or to some threshing-floor.
There with the scraps of songs, and laugh, and tale,
He lightens annual toil, while merry ale
Goes round, and glads some old man's heart to praise
The threadbare customs of his early days:
How the high bowl was in the middle set
At breakfast time, when clippers yearly met,
Fill'd full of furmety, where dainty swum
The streaking sugar and the spotting plum.
The maids could never to the table bring
The bowl, without one rising from the ring

To lend a hand; who, if 'twere ta'en amiss,
Would sell his kindness for a stolen kiss.
The large stone pitcher in its homely trim,
And clouded pint-horn with its copper rim,
Were there; from which were drunk, with spirits high,
Healths of the best the cellar could supply;
While sung the ancient swains, in uncouth rhymes,
Songs that were pictures of the good old times.
Thus will the old man ancient ways bewail,
Till toiling shears gain ground upon the tale,
And break it off—then from the timid sheep
The fleece is shorn, and with a fearful leap
He starts, while with a pressing hand
His sides are printed by the tarry band,[1]
Shaking his naked skin with wond'ring joys,
And others are tugged in by sturdy boys.

  Though fashion's haughty frown hath thrown aside
Half the old forms simplicity supplied,
Yet there are some pride's winter deigns to spare,
Left like green ivy when the trees are bare.
And now, when shearing of the flocks is done,
Some ancient customs, mix'd with harmless fun,
Crown the swain's merry toils.   The timid maid,
Pleased to be praised, and yet of praise afraid,
Seeks the best flowers; not those of woods and fields,
But such as every farmer's garden yields—
Fine cabbage-roses, painted like her face,
The shining pansy, trimm'd with golden lace,
The tall-topp'd larkheels, feather'd thick with flowers,
The woodbine, climbing o'er the door in bowers,
The London tufts, of many a mottled hue,
The pale pink pea, and monkshood darkly blue,
The white and purple gilliflowers, that stay
Ling'ring, in blossom, summer half away,
The single blood-walls, of a luscious smell,
Old-fashion'd flowers which housewives love so well,
The columbines, stone-blue, or deep night-brown,

[1] Three lines added from MS.

Their honeycomb-like blossoms hanging down,
Each cottage-garden's fond adopted child,
Though heaths still claim them, where they yet grow wild
'Mong their old wild companion summer blooms—
Furze brake and mozzling ling and golden broom;
Snapdragons gaping like to sleepy clowns
And 'clipping pinks' (which maidens' Sunday gowns
Full often wear, catched at by teasing chaps),
Pink as the ribbons round their snowy caps;
'Bess in her bravery' too, of glowing dyes
As deep as sunset's crimson pillowed skies,[1]
With marjoram knots, sweetbrier, and ribbon-grass,
And lavender, the choice of ev'ry lass,
And sprigs of lad's-love—all familiar names,
Which every garden through the village claims.
These the maid gathers with a coy delight,
And ties them up, in readiness for night;
Then gives to every swain, 'tween love and shame,
Her 'clipping posies' as his yearly claim.
He rises, to obtain the custom'd kiss:
With stifled smiles, half hankering after bliss,
She shrinks away, and blushing, calls it rude;
Yet turns to smile, and hopes to be pursued;
While one, to whom the hint may be applied,
Follows to claim it, and is not denied.
The rest the loud laugh raise, to make it known—
She blushes silent, and will not disown.
Thus ale, and song, and healths, and merry ways,
Keep up a shadow still of former days;
But the old beechen bowl, that once supplied
The feast of furmety, is thrown aside,
And the old freedom that was living then,
When masters made them merry with their men,
When all their coats alike were russet brown,
And his rude speech was vulgar as their own—
All this is past, and soon will pass away
The time-torn remnant of the holiday.

[1] Eight lines added from MS.

JULY

JULY, the month of summer's prime,
Again resumes his busy time;
Scythes tinkle in each grassy dell,
Where solitude was wont to dwell;
And meadows, they are mad with noise
Of laughing maids and shouting boys,
Making up the withering hay
With merry hearts as light as play.
The very insects on the ground
So nimbly bustle all around,
Among the grass, or dusty soil,
They seem partakers in the toil.
The landscape even reels with life,
While mid the busy stir and strife
Of industry, the shepherd still
Enjoys his summer dreams at will,
Bent o'er his hook, or listless laid
Beneath the pasture's willow shade,
Whose foliage shines so cool and grey
Amid the sultry hues of day,
As if the morning's misty veil
Yet linger'd in its shadows pale;
Or lolling in a musing mood
On mounds where Saxon castles stood,
Upon whose deeply-buried walls
The ivied oak's dark shadow falls,
He oft picks up with wond'ring gaze
Some little thing of other days,
Saved from the wrecks of time—as beads,
Or broken pots among the weeds,
Of curious shapes—and many a stone
From Roman pavements thickly strown,
Oft hoping, as he searches round,
That buried riches may be found,
Though, search as often as he will,
His hopes are disappointed still;
Or watching, on his mossy seat,

The insect world beneath his feet,
In busy motion here and there
Like visitors to feast or fair,
Some climbing up the rush's stem,
A steeple's height or more to them,
With speed, that sees no fear to stop,
Till perch'd upon its spiry top,
Where they awhile the view survey,
Then prune their wings, and flit away;
And others journeying to and fro
Among the grassy woods below,
Musing, as if they felt and knew
The pleasant scenes they wander'd through,
Where each bent round them seems to be
Huge as a giant timber-tree.
Shaping the while their dark employs
To his own visionary joys,
He pictures such a life as theirs,
As free from summer's sweating cares,
And only wishes that his own
Could meet with joys so thickly sown:
Sport seems the all that they pursue,
And play the only work they do.

The cow-boy still cuts short the day,
By mingling mischief with his play;
Oft in the pond, with weeds o'ergrown,
Hurling quick the plashing stone
To cheat his dog, who watching lies,
And instant plunges for the prize;
And though each effort proves in vain,
He shakes his coat, and dives again,
Till, wearied with the fruitless play,
He drops his tail, and sneaks away,
Nor longer heeds the bawling boy,
Who seeks new sports with added joy:
Now on some bank's o'erhanging brow
Beating the wasp's nest with a bough,
Till armies from the hole appear,

And threaten vengeance in his ear
With such determined hue-and-cry
As makes the bold besieger fly;
Then, pelting with excessive glee
The squirrel on the woodland-tree,
Who nimbles round from grain to grain,
And cocks his tail, and peeps again,
Half-pleased, as if he thought the fray
Which mischief made was meant for play,
Till scared and startled into flight,
He instant tumbles out of sight.
Thus he his leisure hour employs,
And feeds on busy meddling joys,
While in the willow-shaded pool
His cattle stand, their hides to cool.

Loud is the summer's busy song;
The smallest breeze can find a tongue;
While insects of each tiny size
Grow teasing with their melodies,
Till noon burns with its blistering breath
Around, and day dies still as death.
The busy noise of man and brute
Is on a sudden lost and mute;
Even the brook that leaps along
Seems weary of its bubbling song,
And, so soft its waters creep,
Tired silence sinks in sounder sleep.
The cricket on its banks is dumb,
The very flies forget to hum;
And, save the wagon rocking round,
The landscape sleeps without a sound.
The breeze is stopt, the lazy bough
Hath not a leaf that dances now;
The totter-grass upon the hill,
And spiders' threads, are standing still;
The feathers dropt from moor-hen's wing,
Which to the water's surface cling,
Are steadfast, and as heavy seem

As stones beneath them in the stream;
Hawkweed and groundsel's fanning downs
Unruffled keep their seedy crowns;
And in the oven-heated air,
Not one light thing is floating there,
Save that to the earnest eye,
The restless heat seems twittering by.
Noon swoons beneath the heat it made,
And flowers e'en wither in the shade,
Until the sun slopes in the west,
Like weary traveller, glad to rest
On pillowed clouds of many hues;
Then nature's voice its joy renews,
And chequer'd field and grassy plain
Hum, with their summer songs again,
A requiem to the day's decline,
Whose setting sunbeams coolly shine,
As welcome to day's feeble powers
As falling dews to thirsty flowers.

Now to the pleasant pasture dells,
Where hay from closes sweetly smells,
Adown the pathway's narrow lane
The milking maiden hies again,
With scraps of ballads never dumb,
And rosy cheeks of happy bloom,
Tann'd brown by summer's rude embrace,
Which adds new beauties to her face,
And red lips never pale with sighs,
And flowing hair, and laughing eyes
That o'er full many a heart prevailed,
And swelling bosom loosely veiled,
White as the love it harbours there,
Unsullied with the taunts of care.

The mower now gives labour o'er,
And on his bench beside the door
Sits down to see his children play,
Smoking a leisure hour away:

While from her cage the blackbird sings,
That on the woodbine arbour hings;
And all with soothing joys receive
The quiet of a summer's eve.

SEPTEMBER

HARVEST awakes the morning still,
And toil's rude groups the valleys fill;
Deserted is each cottage hearth
To all life, save the cricket's mirth;
Each burring wheel its sabbath meets,
Nor walks a gossip in the streets;
The bench beneath the eldern bough,
Lined o'er with grass, is empty now,
Where blackbirds, caged from out the sun,
Would whistle while their mistress spun:
All haunt the thronged fields, to share
The harvest's lingering bounty there.

As yet, no meddling boys resort
About the streets in idle sport;
The butterfly enjoys its hour,
And flirts, unchased, from flower to flower;
The humming bees, which morning calls
From out the low hut's mortar walls,
And passing boy no more controls,
Fly undisturb'd about their holes;
The sparrows in glad chirpings meet,
Unpelted in the quiet street.
None but imprison'd children now
Are seen, where dames with angry brow
Threaten each younker to his seat,
Who, through the window, eyes the street,
Or from his hornbook turns away,
To mourn for liberty and play.

Yet loud are morning's early sounds;
The farm or cottage yard abounds
With creaking noise of opening gate,
And clanking pumps, where boys await
With idle motion, to supply
The thirst of cattle crowding nigh.
Upon the dovecote's mossy slates,
The pigeons coo around their mates;
And close beside the stable wall,
Where morning sunbeams earliest fall,
The basking hen, in playful rout,
Flaps the powdery dust about.
Within the barn-hole sits the cat
Watching to seize the thirsty rat,
Who oft at morn its dwelling leaves
To drink the moisture from the eaves;
The redbreast, with his nimble eye,
Dares scarcely stop to catch the fly,
That, tangled in the spider's snare,
Mourns in vain for freedom there.
The dog beside the threshold lies,
Mocking sleep, with half-shut eyes—
With head crouch'd down upon his feet,
Till strangers pass his sunny seat—
Then quick he pricks his ears to hark,
And bustles up to growl and bark;
While boys in fear stop short their song,
And sneak in startled speed along;
And beggar, creeping like a snail,
To make his hungry hopes prevail
O'er the warm heart of charity,
Leaves his lame halt and hastens by.

The maid afield now leaves the farm,
With dinner-basket on her arm,
Loitering unseen in narrow lane,
To be o'ertook by following swain,
Who, happy thus her truth to prove,
Carries the load and talks of love.

Soon as the dew is off the ground,
Rumbling like distant thunder round,
The wagons haste the corn to load,
And hurry down the dusty road;
While driving boy with eager eye
Watches the church clock passing by—
Whose gilt hands glitter in the sun—
To see how far the hours have run;
Right happy, in the breathless day,
To see time wearing fast away.
But now and then a sudden shower
Will bring to toil a resting hour;
Then, under sheltering shocks, a crowd
Of merry voices mingle loud,
Draining, with leisure's laughing eye,
Each welcome, bubbling bottle dry;
Till peeping suns dry up the rain,
Then off they start to toil again.

Anon the fields are getting clear,
And glad sounds hum in labour's ear;
When children halloo, 'Here they come!'
And run to meet the Harvest Home,
Covered with boughs, and thronged with boys,
Who mingle loud a merry noise,
And, when they meet the stack-thronged yard
Cross-buns and pence their shouts reward.
Then comes the harvest-supper night,
Which rustics welcome with delight;
When merry game and tiresome tale,
And songs, increasing with the ale,
Their mingled uproar interpose,
To crown the harvest's happy close;
While Mirth, that at the scene abides,
Laughs, till she almost cracks her sides.

Now harvest's busy hum declines,
And labour half its help resigns.
Boys, glad at heart, to play return;
The shepherds to their peace sojourn,

Rush-bosom'd solitudes among,
Which busy toil disturb'd so long.
The gossip, happy all is o'er,
Visits again her neighbour's door,
On scandal's idle tales to dwell,
Which harvest had no time to tell;
And free from all its sultry strife,
Enjoys once more her idle life.
A few, whom waning toil reprieves,
Thread the forest's sea of leaves,
Where the pheasant loves to hide,
And the darkest glooms abide,
Beneath the old oaks moss'd and grey,
Whose shadows seem as old as they;
Where time hath many seasons won,
Since aught beneath them saw the sun;
Within these brambly solitudes,
The ragged, noisy boy intrudes,
To gather nuts, that, ripe and brown,
As soon as shook will patter down.

Thus harvest ends its busy reign,
And leaves the fields their peace again,
Where autumn's shadows idly muse
And tinge the trees in many hues:
Amid whose scenes I'm fain to dwell,
And sing of what I love so well.
But hollow winds, and tumbling floods,
And humming showers, and moaning woods,
All startle into sadden strife,
And wake a mighty lay to life,
Making, amid their strains divine,
Unheard a song so mean as mine.

OCTOBER

NATURE now spreads around, in dreary hue,
A pall to cover all that summer knew;
Yet, in the poet's solitary way,
Some pleasing objects for his praise delay,

Something that makes him pause and turn again,
As every trifle will his eye detain:
The free horse rustling through the stubble field,
And cows at lair in rushes, half conceal'd,
With groups of restless sheep who feed their fill,
O'er clear'd fields rambling wheresoe'er they will;
The hedger stopping gaps, amid the leaves,
Which time, o'erhead, in every colour weaves;
The milkmaid stepping with a timid look,
From stone to stone, across the brimming brook;
The cotter journeying with his noisy swine,
Along the wood-side where the brambles twine,
Shaking from mossy oaks the acorns brown,
Or from the hedges red haws dashing down;
The nutters, rustling in the yellow woods,
Who tease the wild things in their solitudes;
The hunters, from the thicket's avenue,
In scarlet jackets, startling on the view,
Skimming a moment o'er the russet plain,
Then hiding in the motley woods again;
The plopping guns' sharp, momentary shock,
Which Echo bustles from her cave to mock;
The bawling song of solitary boys,
Journeying in rapture o'er their dreaming joys.
Haunting the hedges in their reveries,
For wilding fruit that shines upon the trees;
The wild wood music from the lonely dell,
Where merry gipsies o'er their raptures dwell,
Haunting each common's wild and lonely nook,
Where hedges run as crooked as the brook,
Shielding their camps beneath some spreading oak,
And but discovered by the circling smoke
Puffing, and peeping up, as wills the breeze,
Between the branches of the coloured trees:
Such are the pictures that October yields,
To please the poet as he walks the fields;
While Nature—like fair woman in decay,
Whom pale consumption hourly wastes away—
Upon her waning features, winter chill,

Wears dreams of beauty that seem lovely still.
Among the heath-furze still delights to dwell,
Quaking, as if with cold, the harvest bell;
And mushroom-buttons each moist morning brings,
Like spots of snow-shine in dark fairy rings.
Wild shines each hedge in autumn's gay parade;
And, where the eldern trees to autumn fade,
The glossy berry picturesquely cleaves
Its swarthy bunches mid the yellow leaves,
On which the tootling robin feeds at will
And coy hedge-sparrow stains its little bill.
The village dames, as they get ripe and fine,
Gather the bunches for their 'eldern wine,'
Which, bottled up, becomes a rousing charm,
To kindle winter's icy bosom warm,
And, with its merry partner, nut-brown beer,
Makes up the peasant's Christmas-keeping cheer.

Like to a painted map the landscape lies;
And wild above, shine the cloud-thronged skies,
That chase each other on with hurried pace,
Like living things, as if they ran a race.
The winds, that o'er each sudden tempest brood,
Waken like spirits in a startled mood,
Flirting the sear leaves on the bleaching lea,
That litter under every fading tree,
And pausing oft, as falls the patting rain,
Then gathering strength, and twirling them again,
Till drops the sudden calm: the hurried mill
Is stopt at once, and every noise is still;
Save crows, that from the oak-trees quawking spring,
Dashing the acorns down with beating wing,
Waking the wood's short sleep in noises low,
Patting the crimpt brakes withering brown below;
And whirr of starling crowds, that dim the light
With mimic darkness, in their numerous flight;
Or shrilly noise of puddocks' feeble wail,
As in slow circles round the woods they sail;
While huge black beetles, revelling alone,

In the dull evening hum their heavy drone.
These trifles linger through the shortening day,
To cheer the lone bard's solitary way;
Till surly winter comes with biting breath,
And strips the woods, and numbs the scene with death;
Then all is still o'er wood and field and plain,
As naught had been, and naught would be again.

NOVEMBER

THE landscape sleeps in mist from morn till noon;
And, if the sun looks through, 'tis with a face
Beamless and pale and round, as if the moon,
When done the journey of her nightly race,
Had found him sleeping, and supplied his place.
For days the shepherds in the fields may be,
Nor mark a patch of sky—blindfold they trace
The plains, that seem without a bush or tree,
Whistling aloud by guess to flocks they cannot see.

The timid hare seems half its fears to lose,
Crouching and sleeping 'neath its grassy lair,
And scarcely startles, tho' the shepherd goes
Close by its home, and dogs are barking there;
The wild colt only turns around to stare
At passer by, then knaps his hide again;
And moody crows beside the road, forbear
To fly, tho' pelted by the passing swain;
Thus day seems turn'd to night, and tries to wake in vain.

The owlet leaves her hiding-place at noon,
And flaps her grey wings in the doubting light;
The hoarse jay screams to see her out so soon,
And small birds chirp and startle with affright;
Much doth it scare the superstitious wight,
Who dreams of sorry luck, and sore dismay;
While cow-boys think the day a dream of night,
And oft grow fearful on their lonely way,
Fancying that ghosts may wake, and leave their graves by day.

Yet but awhile the slumbering weather flings
Its murky prison round—then winds wake loud;
With sudden stir the startled forest sings
Winter's returning song—cloud races cloud,
And the horizon throws away its shroud,
Sweeping a stretching circle from the eye;
Storms upon storms in quick succession crowd,
And o'er the sameness of the purple sky
Heaven paints, with hurried hand, wild hues of every dye.

At length it comes among the forest oaks,
With sobbing ebbs, and uproar gathering high;
The scared, hoarse raven on its cradle croaks,
And stockdove-flocks in hurried terrors fly,
While the blue hawk hangs o'er them in the sky.
The hedger hastens from the storm begun,
To seek a shelter that may keep him dry;
And foresters, low bent the wind to shun,
Scarce hear amid the strife the poacher's muttering gun.

The ploughman hears its humming rage begin,
And hies for shelter from his naked toil;
Buttoning his doublet closer to his chin,
He bends and scampers o'er the elting soil,
While clouds above him in wild fury boil,
And winds drive heavily the beating rain;
He turns his back to catch his breath awhile,
Then ekes his speed and faces it again,
To seek the shepherd's hut beside the rushy plain.

The boy, that scareth from the spiry wheat
The melancholy crow, in hurry weaves,
Beneath an ivied tree, his sheltering seat
Of rushy flags and sedges tied in sheaves,
Or from the field a shock of stubble thieves.
There he doth dithering sit, and entertain
His eyes with marking the storm-driven leaves;
Oft spying nests where he spring eggs had ta'en,
And wishing in his heart 'twas summer-time again.

Thus wears the month along, in chequer'd moods,
Sunshine and shadows, tempests loud and calms;
One hour dies silent o'er the sleepy woods,
The next wakes loud with unexpected storms;
A dreary nakedness the field deforms—
Yet many a rural sound and rural sight
Lives in the village still about the farms,
Where toil's rude uproar hums from morn till night,
Noises in which the ears of Industry delight.

At length the stir of rural labour's still,
And Industry her care awhile forgoes;
When Winter comes in earnest to fulfil
His yearly task, at bleak November's close,
And stops the plough, and hides the field in snows;
When frost locks up the stream in chill delay,
And mellows on the hedge the jetty sloes
For little birds—then Toil hath time for play,
And naught but threshers' flails awake the dreary day.

DECEMBER

GLAD Christmas comes, and every hearth
    Makes room to give him welcome now,
E'en want will dry its tears in mirth,
    And crown him with a holly bough;
Though tramping 'neath a winter sky,
    O'er snowy paths and rimy stiles,
The housewife sets her spinning by
    To bid him welcome with her smiles.

Each house is swept the day before,
    And windows stuck with evergreens,
The snow is besom'd from the door,
    And comfort crowns the cottage scenes.
Gilt holly, with its thorny pricks,
    And yew and box, with berries small,
These deck the unused candlesticks,
    And pictures hanging by the wall.

Neighbours resume their annual cheer,
    Wishing, with smiles and spirits high,

Glad Christmas and a happy year
  To every morning passer-by;
Milkmaids their Christmas journeys go,
  Accompanied with favour'd swain;
And children pace the crumping snow,
  To taste their granny's cake again.

The shepherd, now no more afraid,
  Since custom doth the chance bestow,
Starts up to kiss the giggling maid
  Beneath the branch of misletoe
That 'neath each cottage beam is seen,
  With pearl-like berries shining gay;
The shadow still of what hath been,
  Which fashion yearly fades away.

The singing waits, a merry throng,
  At early morn, with simple skill,
Yet imitate the angels' song,
  And chant their Christmas ditty still;
And, mid the storm that dies and swells
  By fits, in hummings softly steals
The music of the village bells,
  Ringing round their merry peals.

When this is past, a merry crew,
  Bedeck'd in masks and ribbons gay,
The 'Morris-dance,' their sports renew,
  And act their winter evening play.
The clown turn'd king, for penny-praise,
  Storms with the actor's strut and swell;
And Harlequin, a laugh to raise,
  Wears his hunchback and tinkling bell.

And oft for pence and spicy ale,
  With winter nosegays pinn'd before,
The wassail-singer tells her tale,
  And drawls her Christmas carols o'er.
While prentice boy, with ruddy face,
  And rime-bepowder'd, dancing locks,
From door to door with happy pace,
  Runs round to claim his 'Christmas box.'

The block upon the fire is put,
    To sanction custom's old desires;
And many a faggot's bands are cut,
    For the old farmers' Christmas fires;
Where loud-tongued Gladness joins the throng,
    And Winter meets the warmth of May,
Till feeling soon the heat too strong,
    He rubs his shins, and draws away.

While snows the window-panes bedim,
    The fire curls up a sunny charm,
Where, creaming o'er the pitcher's rim,
    The flowering ale is set to warm;
Mirth, full of joy as summer bees,
    Sits there, its pleasures to impart,
And children, 'tween their parents' knees,
    Sing scraps of carols o'er by heart.

And some, to view the winter weathers,
    Climb up the window-seat with glee,
Likening the snow to falling feathers,
    In fancy's infant ecstasy;
Laughing, with superstitious love,
    O'er visions wild that youth supplies,
Of people pulling geese above,
    And keeping Christmas in the skies.

As tho' the homestead trees were drest,
    In lieu of snow, with dancing leaves,
As tho' the sun-dried martin's nest,
    Instead of ickles, hung the eaves,
The children hail the happy day—
    As if the snow were April's grass,
And pleas'd, as 'neath the warmth of May,
    Sport o'er the water froze to glass.

Thou day of happy sound and mirth,
    That long with childish memory stays,
How blest around the cottage hearth
    I met thee in my younger days!

Harping, with rapture's dreaming joys,
  On presents which thy coming found,
The welcome sight of little toys,
  The Christmas gift of cousins round:

The wooden horse with arching head,
  Drawn upon wheels around the room,
The gilded coach of gingerbread,
  And many-colour'd sugar-plum,
Gilt-cover'd books for pictures sought,
  Or stories childhood loves to tell,
With many an urgent promise bought,
  To get to-morrow's lesson well;

And many a thing, a minute's sport,
  Left broken on the sanded floor,
When we would leave our play, and court
  Our parents' promises for more.
Tho' manhood bids such raptures die,
  And throws such toys aside as vain,
Yet memory loves to turn her eye,
  And count past pleasures o'er again.

Around the glowing hearth at night,
  The harmless laugh and winter tale
Go round, while parting friends delight
  To toast each other o'er their ale;
The cotter oft with quiet zeal
  Will musing o'er his Bible lean;
While in the dark the lovers steal
  To kiss and toy behind the screen.

Old customs! Oh! I love the sound,
  However simple they may be:
Whate'er with time hath sanction found,
  Is welcome and is dear to me.
Pride grows above simplicity,
  And spurns them from her haughty mind,
And soon the poet's song will be
  The only refuge they can find.

TO THE SNIPE

LOVER of swamps
And quagmire overgrown
With hassock-tufts of sedge, where fear encamps
Around thy home alone,

The trembling grass
Quakes from the human foot,
Nor bears the weight of man to let him pass
Where thou, alone and mute,

Sittest at rest
In safety, near the clump
Of huge flag-forest that thy haunts invest
Or some old sallow stump,

Thriving on seams
That tiny islands swell,
Just hilling from the mud and rancid streams,
Suiting thy nature well;

For here thy bill,
Suited by wisdom good,
Of rude unseemly length, doth delve and drill
The jellied mass for food;

And here, mayhap,
When summer suns have drest
The moor's rude, desolate and spongy lap,
May hide thy mystic nest—

Mystic indeed;
For isles that oceans make
Are scarcely more secure for birds to build
Than this flag-hidden lake.

Boys thread the woods
To their remotest shades;
But in these marshy flats, these stagnant floods,
Security pervades.

From year to year
Places untrodden lie,
Where man nor boy nor stock hath ventured near,
Naught gazed on but the sky

And fowl that dread
The very breath of man,
Hiding in spots that never knew his tread,
A wild and timid clan,

Widgeon and teal
And wild duck—restless lot,
That from man's dreaded sight will ever steal
To the most dreary spot.

Here tempests howl
Around each flaggy plot,
Where they who dread man's sight, the water fowl,
Hide and are frightened not.

'Tis power divine
That heartens them to brave
The roughest tempest and at ease recline
On marshes or the wave.

Yet instinct knows
Not safety's bounds:—to shun
The firmer ground where skulking fowler goes
With searching dogs and gun,

By tepid springs
Scarcely one stride across
(Though bramble from its edge a shelter flings
Thy safety is at loss)

—And never choose
The little sinky foss,
Streaking the moors whence spa-red water spews
From pudges fringed with moss;

Freebooters there,
Intent to kill or slay,
Startle with cracking guns the trepid air,
And dogs thy haunts betray.

From danger's reach
Here thou art safe to roam,
Far as these washy flag-sown marshes stretch
A still and quiet home.

In these thy haunts
I've gleaned habitual love;
From the vague world where pride and folly taunts
I muse and look above.

Thy solitudes
The unbounded heaven esteems,
And here my heart warms into higher moods
And dignifying dreams.

I see the sky
Smile on the meanest spot,
Giving to all that creep or walk or fly
A calm and cordial lot.

Thine teaches me
Right feelings to employ—
That in the dreariest places peace will be
A dweller and a joy.

SUMMER IMAGES [1]

Now swarthy summer, which rude health embrowns,
Takes precedence of rosy-fingered spring
    And litters from her lap
    A world of varied hues.

Joy, never silent with her laugh and song,
And health robust with bosom soft as down,
    And patient industry
    Still plying busy toils—

[1] This is the first rough draft of the *Summer Images* in Volume II.

These in her merry path run jovial on,
Or hang upon her arm in smiling guise,
    And from her happy face
    Steal smiles that grace their own.

Thee with thy sultry locks all loose and rude,
And mantle laced with gems of tawdry hues,
    I love thee, and as wont
    Win pleasure from thy smiles.

And thus delighted, on I thread with thee
Rude wood, wild heath, and cornfield laced with
        streams,
    And feel life's stirring pulse
    Throb into genial song.

Me not the noise of brawling pleasure cheers,
In mighty revels or in city streets,
    But joys which soothe
    And not distract mine ear,

That one at musing leisure ever meets
In the green woods and meadows summer-shorn,
    Or fields where gadfly sounds
    Its small and tiresome horn.

Jet-black and shining, from the dripping hedge
Slow peeps the fearful snail,
    And from each tiny bent
    Withdraws his timid horn.

The yellow frog from underneath the swath
Leaps startling as the dog with heavy feet
    Brushes across the path
    And runs the timid hare.

And mark the bird-boy peep from out the corn,
Bawling aloud to know the passing hour,
    And at the lessening day
    To list his louder song.

The aspen leaves, enamoured of the wind,
Turn up their silver lining to the sun,
    And rustle on the ear
    Like fast-approaching showers.

The south-west wind—I love the sudden sound,
And then to feel it gush upon my cheek,
    And then with weary pause
    Await the creeping storm.

To me right luscious sing the stirring leaves,
Just bade to dance attendance on the storm,
    That blackens in the south
    And threatens hasty showers.

I love the wizard noise, and rave in turn,
Half-vacant thoughts in self-imagined rhymes,
    Then hide me from the shower,
    And mutter to the winds.

Now sound the village bells; how musical,
Across the valley of that winding flood,
    Upon the listening ear
    Comes the soft pealing chime;

As glad and healthful as the morning sun,
The shepherd boy leans o'er the meadow bridge
    To list their mellow sounds
    And muse in vacant joy.

Woods, meadows, cornfields, all around
Glow in their harmony of varied greens,
    While o'er them, lost in light,
    Far spreads the laughing sky.

THE TOPER'S RANT

Give me an old crone of a fellow
  Who loves to drink ale in a horn,
And sing racy songs when he's mellow,
  Which topers sung ere he was born.
For such a friend fate shall be thankèd,
  And, line but our pockets with brass,
We'd sooner suck ale through a blanket
  Than thimbles of wine from a glass.

Away with your proud thimble-glasses
  Of wine foreign nations supply,
A toper ne'er drinks to the lasses
  O'er a draught scarce enough for a fly.
Club me with the hedger and ditcher
  Or beggar that makes his own horn,
To join o'er an old gallon pitcher
  Foaming o'er with the essence of corn.

I care not with whom I get tipsy
  Or where with brown stout I regale,
I'll weather the storm with a gipsy
  If he be a lover of ale.
I'll weather the toughest storm weary
  Altho' I get wet to the skin,
For my outside I never need fear me
  While warm with real stingo within.

We'll sit till the bushes are dropping
  Like the spout of a watering pan,
And till the cag's drained there's no stopping,
  We'll keep up the ring to a man.
We'll sit till Dame Nature is feeling
  The breath of our stingo so warm,
And bushes and trees begin reeling
  In our eyes like to ships in a storm.

We'll start it three hours before seven,
  When larks wake the morning to dance,

And we'll stand it till night's black eleven,
   When witches ride over to France;
And we'll sit it in spite of the weather
   Till we tumble dead drunk on the plain,
When the morning shall find us together,
   All willing to stand it again.

ENCLOSURE

FAR spread the moory ground, a level scene
Bespread with rush and one eternal green,
That never felt the rage of blundering plough,
Though centuries wreathed spring blossoms on its brow.
Autumn met plains that stretched them far away
In unchecked shadows of green, brown, and grey.
Unbounded freedom ruled the wandering scene;
No fence of ownership crept in between
To hide the prospect from the gazing eye;
Its only bondage was the circling sky.
A mighty flat, undwarfed by bush and tree,
Spread its faint shadow of immensity,
And lost itself, which seemed to eke its bounds,
In the blue mist the horizon's edge surrounds.

Now this sweet vision of my boyish hours,
Free as spring clouds and wild as forest flowers,
Is faded all—a hope that blossomed free,
And hath been once as it no more shall be.
Enclosure came, and trampled on the grave
Of labour's rights, and left the poor a slave;
And memory's pride, ere want to wealth did bow,
Is both the shadow and the substance now.
The sheep and cows were free to range as then
Where change might prompt, nor felt the bonds of men.
Cows went and came with every morn and night
To the wild pasture as their common right;
And sheep, unfolded with the rising sun,
Heard the swains shout and felt their freedom won,

Tracked the red fallow field and heath and plain,
Or sought the brook to drink, and roamed again;
While the glad shepherd traced their tracks along,
Free as the lark and happy as her song.
But now all's fled, and flats of many a dye
That seemed to lengthen with the following eye,
Moors losing from the sight, far, smooth, and blea,
Where swopt the plover in its pleasure free,
Are banished now with heaths once wild and gay
As poet's visions of life's early day.
Like mighty giants of their limbs bereft,
The skybound wastes in mangled garbs are left,
Fence meeting fence in owner's little bounds
Of field and meadow, large as garden-grounds,
In little parcels little minds to please,
With men and flocks imprisoned, ill at ease.
For with the poor scared freedom bade farewell,
And fortune-hunters totter where they fell;
They dreamed of riches in the rebel scheme
And find too truly that they did but dream.

THE ENTHUSIAST.   A DAYDREAM IN SUMMER [2]

WEARIED with his lonely walk,
Hermit-like with none to talk,
And cloyed with often-seen delight,
His spirits sickened at the sight
Of life's realities and things
That spread around his wanderings,
Of wood and heath in brambles clad,
That seemed like him in silence sad,
The lone enthusiast, weary worn,
Sought shelter from the heats of morn,
And in a cool nook by the stream,
Beside a bridge-wall, dreamed a dream;
And instant from his half-closed eye
Reality seemed fading by;

Dull fields and woods that round him lay
Like curtains to his dreaming play
All slided by, and on his sight
New scenes appeared in fairy light;
The skies lit up a brighter sun,
The birds a cheery song begun,
And flowers bloomed fair and wildly round
As ever grow on dreaming ground;
And mid the sweet enchanting view,
Created every minute new,
He swooned at once from care and strife
Into the poesy of life.
A stranger to the thoughts of men,
He felt his boyish limbs agen
Revelling in all the glee
Of life's first fairy infancy;
Chasing by the rippling spring
Dragon-flies of purple wing,
Or setting mushroom tops afloat,
Mimicking the sailing boat;
Or vainly trying by surprise
To catch the settling butterflies;
And oft with rapture driving on
Where many partner boys had gone,
Wading through the rustling wheat,
Red and purple flowers to meet,
To weave and trim a wild cockade
And play the soldiers' gay parade;
Now tearing through the clinging thorns,
Seeking kecks for bugle horns.
Thus with a schoolboy's heart again
He chased and hallo'd o'er the plain,
Till the church clock counted one
And told them freedom's hour was gone;
In its dull, humming, drowsy way,
It called them from their sports and play.
How different did the sound appear
To that which brought the evening near,
That lovely, humming, happy strain,

That brought them liberty again.
The desk, the books, were all the same,
Marked with each well-known little name,
And many a cover blotched and blurred
With shapeless forms of beast and bird;
And the old master, white with years,
Sat there to waken boyish fears,
While the tough sceptre of his sway,
That awed to silence all the day,
The peeled wand, acting at his will,
Hung o'er the smoke-stained chimney still.
The churchyard still its trees possessed,
And jackdaws sought their boughs to rest,
In whose old trunks they did acquire
Homes safe as in the mossy spire.
The school they shadowed as before,
With its white dial o'er the door,
And bees hummed round in summer's pride,
In its time-creviced walls to hide.
The gravestones childhood eager reads
Peeped o'er the rudely clambering weeds,
Where cherubs gilt, that represent
The slumbers of the innocent,
Smiled glittering to the slanting sun,
As if death's peace with heaven was won.
All, all was blest, and peace and plays
Brought back the enthusiast's fairy days;
And leaving childhood unperceived,
Scenes sweeter still his dream relived,
Life's calmest spot that lingers green
Manhood and infancy between,
When youth's warm feelings have their birth,
Creating angels upon earth,
And fancying woman born for joy,
With naught 'to wither and destroy.'
That picture of past youth's delight
Was swimming now before his sight,
And love's soft thrill of pleasant pain
Was whispering its deceits again,

And Mary, pride of pleasures gone,
Was at his side to lead him on.
And on they went through field and lane,
Haunts of their loves to trace again;
Clung to his arm, she skipt along
With the same music on her tongue,
The selfsame voice as soft and dear
As that which met his youthful ear;
The sunny look, the witching grace
Still blushed upon her angel face,
As though one moment's harmless stay
Had never stole a charm away,
The selfsame bloom—and in her eye
That blue of thirteen summers by.
The pleasant spots where they had met
All shone as naught had faded yet;
The sun was setting o'er the hill,
The thorn-bush it was blooming still,
As it was blooming on the day
When last he reached her boughs of may,
And pleased he clomb the thorny grain
To crop its firstling buds again,
And claimed in eager ecstasies
Love's favours as he reached the prize.
Objects of summer all the same
Were nigh, her gentle praise to claim.
The lark was rising from his nest
To sing the setting sun to rest,
And her fair hand was o'er her eyes
To see her favourite to the skies;
And oft his look was turned to see
If love still felt that melody;
And blooming flowers were at her feet,
Her bending lovely looks to meet,
The blooms of spring and summer days,
Lingering as to wait her praise;
And though she showed him weeds the while,
He praised and loved them for a smile.
The cuckoo sang in soft delight

Its ditty to departing light,
And murmuring children far away
Mocked the music in their play;
And in the ivied tree the dove
Breathed its soothing song to love.
He loved to watch her wistful look
Following white moths down the brook,
And thrilled to mark her beaming eyes
Brightening in pleasure and surprise
To meet the wild mysterious things
That evening's soothing presence brings;
And stepping on with gentle feet
She strove to shun the lark's retreat;
And as he near the bushes prest,
And scared the linnet from its nest,
Fond chidings from her bosom fell,
Then blest the bird and wished it well.
His heart was into rapture stirred,
His very soul was with the bird;
He felt that blessing by her side
As only to himself applied,
And in his rapture's gushing whim
He told her it was meant for him.
She ne'er denied, but looked the will
To own as though she blessed him still.
Yet he had fearful thoughts in view,
Joy seemed too happy to be true;
He doubted if 'twas Mary by,
Yet could not feel the reason why;
He loitered by her as in pain,
And longed to hear her voice again;
He called her by her witching name,
She answered—'twas the very same,
And looked as if she knew his fears,
Smiling to cheer him through her tears,
And whispering in a tender sigh,
''Tis youth and Mary standing by.'
His heart revived, yet in its mirth
Felt fears that they were not of earth,

That both were shadows of the mind,
Picturing the joys it wished to find.
Yet he did feel as like a child,
And sighed in fondness till she smiled,
Vowing that they would part no more,
Nor act so foolish as before.
She nestled closer by his side,
And vowed, 'We never will,' and sighed.
He grasped her hand; it seemed to thrill;
He whispered, 'No, we never will,'
And thought in rapture's mad extreme
To hold her though it proved a dream.
And instant as that thought begun
Her presence seemed his love to shun,
And deaf to all he had to say
Quick turned her tender face away;
When her small waist he strove to clasp,
She shrunk like water from his grasp.

THE PROGRESS OF RHYME

O SOUL-ENCHANTING poesy,
Thou'st long been all the world with me;
When poor, thy presence grows my wealth,
When sick, thy visions give me health,
When sad, thy sunny smile is joy
And was from e'en a tiny boy.
When trouble came, and toiling care
Seemed almost more than I could bear,
While threshing in the dusty barn
Or squashing in the ditch to earn
A pittance that would scarce allow
One joy to smooth my sweating brow
Where drop by drop would chase and fall,
Thy presence triumphed over all:
The vulgar they might frown and sneer,
Insult was mean but never near.
'Twas poesy's self that stopt the sigh

And malice met with no reply.
So was it in my earlier day
When sheep to corn had strayed away
Or horses closen gaps had broke,
Ere sunrise peeped or I awoke;
My master's frowns might force the tear,
But poesy came to check and cheer.
It glistened in my shamèd eye
But ere it fell the swoof was by.
I thought of luck in future days
When even he might find a praise.
I looked on poesy like a friend
To cheer me till my life should end.
'Twas like a parent's first regard
And love when beauty's voice was heard,
'Twas joy, 'twas hope, and maybe fear,
But still 'twas rapture everywhere.
My heart were ice unmoved to dwell,
Nor care for one I loved so well
Through rough and smooth, through good and ill,
That led me and attends me still.
Thou wert an early joy to me:
That joy was love and poesy;
And but for thee my idle lay
Had ne'er been urged in early day;
The harp imagination strung
Had ne'er been dreamed of; but among
The flowers in summer's fields of joy
I'd lain an idle rustic boy,
No hope to think of, fear or care,
And even love a stranger there.
But poesy that vision flung
Around me as I hummed and sung;
I glowered on beauty passing by,
Yet hardly turned my sheepish eye;
I worshipped, yet could hardly dare
To show I knew the goddess there,
Lest my presumptuous stare should gain
But frowns, ill humour, and disdain.

My first ambition was its praise,
My struggles aye in early days.
Had I by vulgar boldness torn
That hope when it was newly born,
By rudeness, gibes, and vulgar tongue,
The curse of the unfeeling throng,
Their scorn had frowned upon the lay
And hope and song had died away.
And I with nothing to atone
Had felt myself indeed alone.
But promises of days to come
The very fields would seem to hum,
Those burning days when I should dar
To sing aloud my worship there,
When beauty's self might turn its eye
Of praise: what could I do but try?
'Twas winter then, but summer shone
From heaven when I was all alone;
And summer came, and every weed
Of great or little had its meed;
Without its leaves there wa'n't a bower
Nor one poor weed without its flower.
'Twas love and pleasure all along;
I felt that I'd a right to song
And sung—but in a timid strain—
Of fondness for my native plain;
For everything I felt a love,
The weeds below, the birds above;
And weeds that bloomed in summer's hours,
I thought they should be reckoned flowers;
They made a garden free for all,
And so I loved them great and small,
And sung of some that pleased my eye,
Nor could I pass the thistle by,
But paused and thought it could not be
A weed in nature's poesy.
No matter for protecting wall,
No matter though they chance to fall
Where sheep and cows and oxen lie,

The kindly rain when they're adry
Falls on them with as plenteous showers
As when it waters garden flowers;
They look up with a blushing eye
Upon a tender watching sky,
And still enjoy the kindling smile
Of sunshine though they live with toil,
As garden flowers with all their care,
For nature's love is ever there.
And so it cheered me while I lay
Among their beautiful array,
To think that I in humble dress
Might have a right to happiness
And sing as well as greater men;
And then I strung the lyre agen
And heartened up o'er toil and fear
And lived with rapture everywhere,
Till dayshine to my themes did come.
Just as a blossom bursts to bloom
And finds itself in thorny ways,
So did my musings meet with praise,
And though no garden care had I
My heart had love for poesy,
A simple love, a wild esteem,
As heartfelt as the linnet's dream
That mutters in its sleep at night
Some notes from ecstasy's delight.
Thus did I dream o'er joys and lie
Muttering dream-songs of poesy.
The night dislimned and waking day
Shook from wood leaves the drops away;
Hope came, storms calmed, and hue and cry
With her false pictures herded by,
With tales of help when help was not,
Of friends who urged to write or blot,
Whose taste were such that mine were shame
Had they not helped it into fame.
Poh! let the idle rumour ill,
Their vanity is never still;

My harp, though simple, was my own.
When I was in the fields alone
With none to help and none to hear
To bid me either hope or fear,
The bird or bee its chords would sound,
The air hummed melodies around;
I caught with eager ear the strain
And sung the music o'er again;
Or love or instinct flowing strong,
Fields were the essence of the song.
And fields and woods are still as mine,
Real teachers that are all divine;
So if my song be weak or tame
'Tis I, not they, who bear the blame;
But hope and cheer through good and ill,
They are my aids to worship still,
Still growing on a gentle tide
Nor foes could mar nor friends could guide;
Like pasture brooks through sun and shade,
Crooked as channels chance hath made,
It rambles as it loves to stray
And hope and feeling lead the way.
—Ay, birds, no matter what the tune,
Or 'croak' or 'tweet,' 'twas nature's boon
That brought them joy, and music flung
Its spell o'er every matin sung,
And e'en the sparrow's chirp to me
Was song in its felicity.
When grief hung o'er me like a cloud
Till hope seemed even in her shroud,
I whispered poesy's spell till they
Gleamed round me like a summer's day;
When tempests o'er my labours sung,
My soul to its responses rung,
And joined the chorus till the storm
Fell all unheeded, void of harm;
And each old leaning shielding tree
Were princely palaces to me,
Where I would sit me down and chime

My unheard rhapsodies to rhyme.
All I beheld of grand, with time
Grew up to beautiful's sublime:
The arching grove of ancient limes
That into roofs like churches climbs,
Grain intertwisting into grain,
That stops the sun and stops the rain
And spreads a gloom that never smiles,
Like ancient halls and minster aisles,
While all without a beauteous screen
Of summer's luscious leaves is seen,
While heard that everlasting hum
Of insects haunting where they bloom,
As though 'twas nature's very place
Of worship, where her mighty race
Of insect life and spirits too
In summer-time were wont to go,
Both insects and the breath of flowers,
To sing their maker's mighty powers.
I've thought so as I used to rove
Through Burghley Park, that darksome grove
Of limes where twilight lingered grey
Like evening in the midst of day.
I felt without a single skill
That instinct that would not be still,
To think of song sublime beneath
That heaved my bosom like my breath,
That burned and chilled and went and came
Without or uttering or a name,
Until the vision waked with time
And left me itching after rhyme,
Where little pictures idly tell
Of nature's powers and nature's spell.
I felt and shunned the idle vein,
Laid down the pen and toiled again;
But, spite of all, through good and ill,
It was and is my worship still.
No matter how the world approved,
'Twas nature listened, I that loved;

No matter how the lyre was strung,
From my own heart the music sprung.
The cowboy with his oaten straw,
Although he hardly heard or saw
No more of music than he made,
'Twas sweet; and when I pluckt the blade
Of grass upon the woodland hill
To mock the birds with artless skill,
No music in the world beside
Seemed half so sweet, till mine was tried.
So my boy-worship poesy
Made e'en the muses pleased with me,
Until I even danced for joy,
A happy and a lonely boy,
Each object to my ear and eye
Made paradise of poesy.
I heard the blackbird in the dell
Sing sweet; could I but sing as well,
I thought, until the bird in glee
Seemed pleased and paused to answer me.
And nightingales—Oh, I have stood
Beside the pingle and the wood,
And o'er the old oak railing hung
To listen every note they sung,
And left boys making taws of clay
To muse and listen half the day.
The more I listened and the more
Each note seemed sweeter than before,
And aye so different was the strain
She'd scarce repeat the note again:
'Chew-chew chew-chew,' and higher still:
'Cheer-cheer cheer-cheer,' more loud and shrill:
'Cheer-up cheer-up cheer-up,' and dropt
Low: 'tweet tweet jug jug jug,' and stopt
One moment just to drink the sound
Her music made, and then a round
Of stranger witching notes was heard,
As if it was a stranger bird:
'Wew-wew wew-wew, chur-chur chur-chur,

Woo-it woo-it': could this be her?
'Tee-rew tee-rew tee-rew tee-rew,
Chew-rit chew-rit,' and ever new:
'Will-will will-will, grig-grig grig-grig.'
The boy stopt sudden on the brig
To hear the 'tweet tweet tweet' so shrill,
Then 'jug jug jug,' and all was still
A minute, when a wilder strain
Made boys and woods to pause again;
Words were not left to hum the spell.
Could they be birds that sung so well?
I thought, and maybe more than I,
That music's self had left the sky
To cheer me with its magic strain;
And then I hummed the words again,
Till fancy pictured, standing by,
My heart's companion, poesy.
No friends had I to guide or aid
The struggles young ambition made.
In silent shame the harp was tried
And rapture's griefs the tune applied,
Yet o'er the songs my parents sung
My ear in silent musings hung.
Their kindness wishes did regard,
They sung, and joy was my reward.
All else was but a proud decree,
The right of bards and naught to me,
A title that I dared not claim
And hid it like a private shame.
I whispered aye and felt a fear
To speak aloud though none was near;
I dreaded laughter more than blame,
I dared not sing aloud for shame;
So all unheeded, lone and free,
I felt it happiness to be
Unknown, obscure, and like a tree
In woodland peace and privacy.
No, not a friend on earth had I
But my own kin and poesy,

Nor wealth, and yet I felt indeed
As rich as anybody need
To be, for health and hope and joy
Was mine, although a lonely boy,
And what I felt, as now I sing,
Made friends of all and everything
Save man the vulgar and the low;
The polished 'twas not mine to know
Who paid me in my after days
And gave me even more than praise:
'Twas then I found that friends indeed
Were needed when I'd less to need.
The pea, that independent springs,
When in its blossom, trails and clings
To every help that lingers by,
And I, when classed with poesy,
Who stood unbrunt the heaviest shower,
Felt feeble as that very flower
And helpless all; but beauty's smile
Is harvest for the hardest toil,
Whose smiles I little thought to win
With ragged coat and downy chin,
A clownish, silent, aguish boy
Who even felt ashamed of joy,
So dirty, ragged, and so low,
With naught to recommend or show
That I was worthy e'en a smile.
Had I but felt amid my toil
That I in days to come should be
A little light in minstrelsy,
And in the blush of after days
Win beauty's smile and beauty's praise,
My heart with lonely fancy warm
Had even bursted with the charm;
And Mary, thou whose very name
I loved, whose look was even fame,
From those delicious eyes of blue
In smiles and rapture ever new,
Thy timid step, thy fairy form,

Thy face with blushes ever warm,
When praise my schoolboy heart did move,
I saw thy blush and thought it love.
And all ambitious thee to please
My heart was ever ill at ease;
I saw thy beauty grow with days,
And tried song-pictures in thy praise,
And all of fair or beautiful
Were thine akin, nor could I pull
The blossoms that I thought divine
Lest I should injure aught of thine.
So where they grew I let them be,
And though I dare not talk to thee
Of love, to them I talked aloud,
And grew ambitious from the crowd
With hopes that I one day should be
Beloved, Mary, e'en by thee.
But I mistook in early day
The world, and so our hopes decay.
Yet that same cheer in after toils
Was poesy, and still she smiles
As sweet as blossoms to the tree,
And hope, love, joy, are poesy.

TO THE RURAL MUSE

MUSE of the fields, oft have I said farewell
To thee, my boon companion, loved so long,
And hung thy sweet harp in the bushy dell,
For abler hands to wake an abler song.
Much did I fear my homage did thee wrong:
Yet, loath to leave, as oft I turned again;
And to its wires mine idle hands would cling,
Torturing it into song.   It may be vain;
Yet still I try, ere fancy droops her wing,
And hopeless silence comes to numb its every string.

Muse of the pasture brooks, on thy calm sea
Of poesy I've sailed; and though the will
To speed were greater than my prowess be,
I've ventured with much fear of usage ill,
Yet more of joy.   Though timid be my skill,
As not to dare the depths of mightier streams,
Yet rocks abide in shallow ways, and I
Have much of fear to mingle with my dreams.
Yet, lovely muse, I still believe thee by,
And think I see thee smile, and so forget I sigh.

Muse of the cottage hearth, oft did I tell
My hopes to thee, nor feared to plead in vain;
But felt around my heart thy witching spell,
That bade me as thy worshipper remain:
I did so, and still worship.   Oh! again
Smile on my offerings, and so keep them green;
Bedeck my fancies like the clouds of even,
Mingling all hues which thou from heaven dost glean.
To me a portion of thy power be given,
If theme so mean as mine may merit aught of heaven.

For thee in youth I culled the simple flower,
That on thy bosom gained a sweeter hue,
And took thy hand along life's sunny hour,
Meeting the sweetest joys that ever grew;
More friends were needless, and my foes were few.
Though freedom then be deemed as rudeness now,
And what once won thy praise now meet disdain,
Yet the last wreath I braided for thy brow
Thy smiles did so commend, it made me vain
To weave another one and hope for praise again.

With thee the spirit of departed years
Wakes that sweet voice which time hath rendered dumb
And freshens—like to spring—loves, hopes and fears
That in my bosom found an early home,
Wooing the heart to ecstasy.   I come
To thee, when sick of care, of joy bereft,

Seeking the pleasures that are found in bloom.
O happy hopes, that time hath only left
Around the haunts where thou didst erst sojourn!
Then smile, sweet cherubim, and welcome my return.

With thee the raptures of life's early day
Appear, and all that pleased me when a boy.
Though pains and cares have torn the best away,
And winters creep between us to destroy,
Do thou commend, the recompense is joy:
The tempest of the heart shall soon be calm.
Though sterner truth against my dreams rebel,
Hope feels success; and all my spirits warm
To strike with happier mood thy simple shell
And seize thy mantle's hem—Oh! say not fare-thee-well.

Still, sweet enchantress, youth's strong feelings move,
That from thy presence their existence took:
The innocent idolatry and love,
Paying thee worship in each secret nook,
That fancied friends in tree, and flower, and brook,
Shaped clouds to angels and beheld them smile,
And heard commending tongues in every wind.
Life's grosser fancies did these dreams defile,
Yet not entirely root them from the mind;
I think I hear them still, and often look behind.

Ay, I have heard thee in the summer wind,
As if commending what I sung to thee;
Ay, I have seen thee on a cloud reclined,
Kindling my fancies into poesy;
I saw thee smile, and took the praise to me.
In beauties, past all beauty, thou wert drest;
I thought the very clouds around thee knelt:
I saw the sun to linger in the west,
Paying thee worship; and as eve did melt
In dews, they seemed thy tears for sorrows I had felt.

Sweeter than flowers on beauty's bosom hung,
Sweeter than dreams of happiness above,
Sweeter than themes by lips of beauty sung,
Are the young fancies of a poet's love,
When round his thoughts thy trancing visions move.
In floating melody no notes may sound,
The world is all forgot and past his care,
While on thy harp thy fingers lightly bound,
As winning him its melody to share;
And heaven itself, with him, where is it then but there?

E'en now my heart leaps out from grief, and all
The gloom thrown round by care's o'ershading wing;
E'en now those sunny visions to recall,
Like to a bird I quit dull earth and sing:
Life's tempests swoon to calms on every string.
Ah! sweet enchantress, if I do but dream,
If earthly visions have been only mine,
My weakness in thy service woos esteem,
And proves my truth as almost worthy thine:
Surely true worship makes the meanest theme divine.

And still, warm courage, calming many a fear,
Heartens my hand once more thy harp to try,
To join the anthem of the minstrel year:
For summer's music in thy praise is high;
The very winds about thy mantle sigh
Love-melodies; thy minstrel bards to be,
Insects and birds, exerting all their skill,
Float in continued song for mastery;
While in thy haunts loud leaps the little rill,
To kiss thy mantle's hem; and how can I be still?

There still I see thee fold thy mantle grey,
To trace the dewy lawn at morn and night;
And there I see thee, in the sunny day,
Withdraw thy veil and shine confest in light;
Burning my fancies with a wild delight,

To win a portion of thy blushing fame.
Though haughty fancy treat thy power as small,
And fashion thy simplicity disclaim,
Should but a corner of thy mantle fall
O'er him who woos thy love, 'tis recompense for all.[1]

Not with the mighty to thy shrine I come,
In anxious sighs or self-applauding mirth,
On Mount Parnassus as thine heir to roam:
I dare not credit that immortal birth;
But mingling with the lesser ones on earth,
Like as the little lark from off its nest
Beside the mossy hill awakes in glee
To seek the morning's throne, a merry guest,
So do I seek thy shrine, if that may be,
To win by new attempts another smile from thee.

If without thee 'neath storms and clouds and wind,
I've roamed the wood and field and meadow lea,
And found no flowers but what the vulgar find,
Nor met one breath of living poesy,
Among such charms where inspirations be,
The fault is mine—and I must bear the lot
Of missing praise to merit thy disdain.
To feel each idle plea, though urged, forgot,
I can but sigh—though foolish to complain—
O'er hopes so fair begun, to find them end so vain.

Then will it prove presumption thus to dare
To add fresh failings to each faulty song,
Urging thy blessings on an idle prayer,
To sanction silly themes: it will be wrong
For one so lowly to be heard so long.

[1] In another MS. the preceding five lines read:

> That wasteth life away to win a name,
> Of aught else reckless, tho' the chance be small;
> And if so be that death's the price of fame,
> Should but a portion of thy prize befall
> To him who dies to live, 'tis recompense for all.

Yet, sweet enchantress, yet a little while
Forgo impatience and from frowns refrain;
The strong are ne'er debarred thy cheering smile,
Why should the weak, who need them most, complain
Alone, in solitude, soliciting in vain?

But if my efforts on thy harp prove true,
Which bashful youth at first so feared to try;
If aught of nature be in sounds I drew
—From hope's young dreams and doubt's uncertainty,
To these late offerings, not without their sigh—
Then on thine altar shall these themes be laid,
And past the deeds of graven brass remain,
Filling a space in time that shall not fade;
And if it be not so—avert disdain,
Till dust shall feel no sting, nor know it toiled in vain.

The following four stanzas are taken from rough drafts not used in the final version.

Is poesy dwelling in a nice-culled sound,
Or soft smooth words that trifle on the ear
Unmeaning music? Is it to be found
In rhymes run mad, that paint to startled fear
Monsters that are not and that never were?
Is it in declamations frothing high,
Worked like machinery to its mad career?
No, poetry lives in its simplicity,
And speaks from its own heart, to which all hearts reply.

Fame's hopes with me are faint to look upon;
The cloud of doubt with gloom her skies defiles;
Though fluttering pulse and burning thrills urge on,
And hope at intervals the way beguiles,
The flowers she plucks me wear precarious smiles.
Yet do I follow with unwearied eyes
The shadowy recompense for real toils:
Ah, would the heart cease aching and be wise,
And think life vainly spent, staked for a doubtful prize.

Thy smiles are dear to him that needs thy smiles;
He feels their raptures in no less degree
Than bolder votaries, whose ambition toils
Up the steep road of immortality;
And while their souls expand and rise with thee,
On humbler wing, with unpresuming powers,
He shares a portion of thy ecstasy,
Hiding among thy valleys, brooks, and bowers,
Cheered by thy sunny smiles with other lowly flowers.

I've heard of Parnass Hill, Castalia's stream,
And in my dreams have worshipped beauty long;
I've heard, alas, but never could I dream
That aught of birthright did to me belong
In that rich paradise of sacred song.
Yet have I loved and worshipped, and the spring
Of hope—though not an eagle in the sun—
Did like a young bird to thy kindness cling;
Friend of my visions, though my race be run,
I'll feel the triumph still to know thy praises won.

SONNETS

EVENING PASTIME

Musing beside the crackling fire at night,
　　While singing kettle merrily prepares
Woman's solacing beverage, I delight
　　To read a pleasant volume, where the cares
Of life are sweetened by the muse's voice—
　　Thomson, or Cowper, or the bard that bears
Life's humblest name, though nature's favoured choice,
　　Her pastoral Bloomfield;—and as evening wears,
Weary with reading, list the little tales
　　Of laughing children, who edge up their chairs
To tell the past day's sport, which never fails
　　To cheer the spirits.　While my fancy shares
Their artless talk, man's sturdy reason quails,
　　And memory's joy grows young again with theirs.

TO CHARLES LAMB ON HIS ESSAYS

Elia, thy reveries and visioned themes
　　To care's lorn heart a luscious pleasure proves,
Wild as the mystery of delightful dreams,
　　Soft as the anguish of remembered loves;
Like records of past days their memory dances
　　Mid the cool feelings manhood's reason brings,
As the unearthly visions of romances
　　Peopled with sweet and uncreated things;
And yet thy themes thy gentle worth enhances;
　　Then wake again thy wild harp's tenderest strings,
Sing on, sweet bard, let fairy loves again
　　Smile in thy dreams with angel ecstasies;
Bright o'er our minds will break the witching strain
　　Through the dull gloom of earth's realities.

TO DE WINT

De Wint! I would not flatter; nor would I
  Pretend to critic-skill in this thy art;
Yet in thy landscape I can well descry
  The breathing hues as nature's counterpart.
No painted peaks, no wild romantic sky,
  No rocks, nor mountains, as the rich sublime,
Hath made thee famous; but the sunny truth
  Of nature, that doth mark thee for all time,
Found on our level pastures—spots, forsooth,
  Where common skill sees nothing deemed divine.
Yet here a worshipper was found in thee;
  And thy young pencil worked such rich surprise
That rushy flats, befringed with willow tree,
  Rivalled the beauties of Italian skies.

TO THE MEMORY OF BLOOMFIELD

Sweet unassuming minstrel! not to thee
  The dazzling fashions of the day belong;
Nature's wild pictures, field, and cloud, and tree,
  And quiet brooks, far distant from the throng,
In murmurs tender as the toiling bee,
  Make the sweet music of thy gentle song.
Well, Nature owns thee: let the crowd pass by;
  The tide of fashion is a stream too strong
For pastoral brooks, that gently flow and sing:
  But Nature is their source, and earth and sky
Their annual offering to her current bring.
  Thy gentle muse and memory need no sigh;
For thine shall murmur on to many a spring,
  When prouder streams are summer-burnt and dry.

IZAAK WALTON

Some blame thee, honest Izaak! ay, and deem
Thy pastime cruel, by the silent stream
Of the unwooded Lea: but he that warms

In eloquence of grief o'er suffering worms
Throws by his mourning quill, and hunts the hare
Whole hours to death, yet feels no sorrow there.
Yet this mock-sentimental man of moods
On every pastime but his own intrudes:
Not so with thee, thou man of angel-mind!
That, like thy Master, gentle was, and kind;
Fit emblem of the prime apostles' days,
And worthy even of the scripture praise;
For men of God's own heart must surely be
Those honest souls that most resemble thee.

TO MARY (I)

I MET thee like the morning, though more fair,
And hopes 'gan travel for a glorious day;
And though night met them ere they were aware,
Leading the joyous pilgrims all astray,
Yet know I not, though they did miss their way,
That joyed so much to meet thee, if they are
To blame or bless the fate that bade such be.
Thou seem'dst an angel when I met thee first,
Nor has aught made thee otherwise to me:
Possession had not cloyed my love, nor curst
Fancy's wild visions with reality.
Thou art an angel still; and Hope, awoke
From the fond spell that early raptures nurst,
Still feels a joy to think that spell ne'er broke.

CROWLAND ABBEY

In sooth, it seems right awful and sublime
    To gaze by moonlight on the shattered pile
Of this old abbey, struggling still with time—
    The grey owl hooting from its rents the while,
And tottering stones, as wakened by the sound,

Crumbling from arch and battlement around,
  Urging dread echoes from the gloomy aisle,
To sink more silent still.—The very ground
  In desolation's garment doth appear,
The lapse of age and mystery profound.
We gaze on wrecks of ornamented stones,
  On tombs whose sculptures half erased appear,
On rank weeds, battening over human bones,
  Till even one's very shadow seems to fear.

THE PARISH: A SATIRE [1]

THE parish hind, oppression's humble slave,
Whose only hope of freedom is the grave,
The cant miscalled religion in the saint,
And justice mocked while listening want's complaint,
The parish laws and parish queens and kings,
Pride's lowest classes of pretending things,
The meanest dregs of tyranny and crime,
I fearless sing: let truth attend my rhyme.
That good old fame the farmers earned of yore,
That made as equals, not as slaves, the poor,
That good old fame did in two sparks expire—
A shooting coxcomb and a hunting squire;
And their old mansions that were dignified
With things far better than the pomp of pride,
At whose oak table, that was plainly spread,
Each guest was welcomed and the poor were fed,
Where master, son, and serving-man and clown
Without distinction daily sat them down,
Where the bright rows of pewter by the wall
Served all the pomp of kitchen or of hall—
These all have vanished like a dream of good;
And the slim things that rise where they once stood
Are built by those whose clownish taste aspires
To hate their farms and ape the country squires.
And where's that lovely maid, in days gone by

---

[1] Clare wrote most of this poem between 1820 and 1824, though he added several passages at a later date. Both its length and its subject prevented its inclusion in *The Shepherd's Calendar* or *The Rural Muse*; his plan to have it published by a local printer fell through, so that he did not prepare a final draft. Hence the text given here excludes a number of passages which were not sufficiently worked in. Clare left the following notes on the poem: 'This poem was begun and finished under the pressure of heavy distress, with embittered feelings under a state of anxiety and oppression almost amounting to slavery, when the prosperity of one class was founded on the adversity and distress of the other. The haughty demand by the master to his labourer was "Work for the little I choose to allow you and go to the parish for the rest—or starve." To decline working under such "advantages" was next to offending a magistrate, and no opportunity was lost in marking the insult by some unqualified oppression. . . .

'Each character is a true one and as little coloured as possible.'

The farmer's daughter, unreserved though shy,
That milked her cows and old songs used to sing,
As red and rosy as the lovely spring?
Ah, these have dwindled to a formal shade
As pale and bedrid as my lady's maid,
Who cannot dare to venture in the street,
Sometimes thro' cold, at other times for heat,
And vulgar eyes to shun and vulgar winds,
Shrouded in veils green as their window-blinds;
These, taught at school their stations to despise
And view old customs with disdainful eyes,
Deem all as rude their kindred did of yore,
And scorn to toil or foul their fingers more;
They sit before their glasses hour by hour,
Or paint unnatural daubs of fruit or flower;
E'en poetry in these high-polished days
Is oft profaned by their dislike or praise;
Thus housed mid cocks and hens in idle state,
Aping at fashions which their betters hate,
Affecting high life's airs to scorn the past,
Trying to be something makes them naught at last;
These are the shadows that supply the place
Of famous daughters of the vanished race.
And what are these? Rude names will do them harm.
Oh, rather call them 'Ladies of the Farm.'
Miss Peevish Scornful, once the village toast,
Deemed fair by some and prettyish by most;
Brought up a lady, tho' her father's gain
Depended still on cattle and on grain,
She followed shifting fashions and aspired
To the high notions baffled pride desired;
And all the profits pigs and poultry made
Were given to Miss for dressing and parade,
To visit balls and plays, fresh hopes to chase,
And try her fortune with a simpering face;
She now and then in London's crowds was shown,
To know the world and to the world be known;
All leisure hours while Miss at home sojourned
Passed in preparing till new routs returned,

Or tittle-tattling o'er her shrewd remarks
Of ladies' dresses or attentive sparks:
How Mr. So-and-so at such a rout
Fixed his eyes on her all the night about;
And young Squire Dandy, just returned from France,
How he first chose her from the rest to dance;
How this squire bowed polite at her approach,
And lords e'en nodded as she passed their coach.
Thus she went on, and visited and drest,
And deemed things earnest that were spoke in jest,
And dreamed at night o'er pride's unchecked desires
Of nodding gentlemen and smiling squires;
To Gretna Green her visions often fled,
And rattling coaches lumbered in her head;
Till hopes, grown weary with too long delay,
Caught the green sickness and declined away,
And beauty, like a garment worse for wear,
Fled her pale cheek and left it much too fair.
Then she gave up sick-visits, balls, and plays,
Where whispers turned to anything but praise;
All were thrown by like an old-fashioned song
Where she had played show-woman much too long;
She condescended to be kind and plain,
And 'mong her equals hoped to find a swain;
Past follies now were hateful to review,
And they were hated by her equals too;
Notice from equals vain she tried to court,
Or if they noticed 'twas but just in sport;
At last, grown husband-mad, away she ran,
Not with young Squire Dandy, but the servant man.

Young Farmer Bigg, of this same flimsy class,
Wise among fools and with the wise an ass,
A farming sprout with more than farmer's pride,
Struts like a lord and dresses dignified;
They call him squire, at which his weakness aimed;
But others view him as a fool misnamed.
Yet dress and tattle ladies' hearts can charm,
And he's the choice with madams of the farm,

Now with that lady strutting, now with this,
Braced up in stays as slim as sickly miss,
Shining at Christmas rout and vulgar ball,
The favourite spark and rival of them all.
And oft he'll venture to bemean his pride,
—Tho' bribes and mysteries do their best to hide—
Teasing weak maidens with his pert deceit,
Whose lives are humble and whose looks are sweet,
Whose beauty happens to outrival those
With whom the dandy as an equal goes.
Thus maids are ruined oft and mothers made,
As if bewitched, without a father's aid;
Tho' nods and winks and whispers urge a guess,
Weakness is bribed and hides its heart's distress,
To live dishonoured and to die unwed;
For clowns grow jealous when they're once misled.
Thus pointed fingers brand the passing spark,
And whispers often guess his deeds are dark;
But friends deny and urge that doubts mislead,
And prove the youth above so mean a deed.
The town agrees and leaves his ways at will,
A proud, conceited, meddling fellow still.

Nature in various moods pursues her plan,
And moulds by turns the monkey or the man;
With one she deals out wisdom as a curse,
To follow fortune with an empty purse;
The next in opposite extremes is bred—
O'erflowing pockets and an empty head;
Beggars in merit share a squire's estate,
And squires untitled meet a beggar's fate.
Fortune's great lottery owns nor rules nor laws;
Fate holds the wealth, and reason rarely draws;
Blanks are her lot, and merit vainly tries,
While heedless folly blunders on the prize.

Young Headlong Racket's to the last akin,
Who only deals more openly in sin,
And apes forged love with less mysterious guile,

A high-flown dandy in its lowest style;
By fashion hated, with the vulgar gay,
He deems it wit to tempt their steps astray.
No maid can pass him but his leering eye
Attempts to prove her forward or too shy.
He brags o'er wine of loves his wits have won,
And loves betrayed—and deems it precious fun.
Horses and dogs and women o'er his wine
Is all his talk, and he believes it fine;
And fools may join him, but to common sense
His head pleads empty and has no pretence.
He courts his maids and shuns the better sort,
And hunts and courses as a change of sport,
And hates all poachers, game-destroying brutes,
Altho' with both the name as aptly suits,
With this one difference—darkness brings their prey,
And he more brazen murders his by day.
And thus he lives a hated sort of life,
Loves wedded wantons while he scorns a wife,
Prepares by turns to hunt and whore and shoot,
Less than a man and little more than brute.

Next on the parish list in paltry fame
Shines Dandy Flint, Esquire, whose dirty name
Has grown into a proverb for bad deeds;
And he who reads it all that's filthy reads.
Ne'er did a single sentence more express
Of downright evil or of goodness less
Than Dandy Flint, grown old in youthful shame
By loathed diseases which no words can name,
And worn so spare that wit, as passing by,
Swears Nick will thread him through a bodkin's eye;
A sot who spouts short morals o'er his gin,
And when most drunk rails most against the sin;
A dirty hog that on the puddle's brink
Stirs up the mud and quarrels with the stink.

These are the things that o'er inferiors flirt,
That spring from pride like summer flies from dirt,

And tease and buzz their summer season by,
Bantering the poor and struggling to be high.

Some of the old school yet my verse could tell;
And one from boyhood I remember well,
Who ne'er aspired on folly's wings to soar,
A plain, mean man, scarce noticed from the poor,
Who ne'er expected, as he walked the street,
Bows from inferiors whom he chanced to meet;
Inferiors, bred from fashion's idle whim,
Equals and neighbours all appeared to him;
And tho' wealth scorned in such low walks to go,
And pride disdained and called his manners low,
He sought nor paid pride's homage unto man,
But lived unshining in his humble plan;
And when his rights tyrannic power assailed,
His courage triumphed tho' his pocket failed;
For he was doomed to feel that worldly curse,
An upright spirit and an empty purse;
Nor did he try the shameless fault to cure,
Still keeping honest and remaining poor.
But he has left, and one of different race
Spoilt his old mansion and supplied his place.

Proud Farmer Cheetum turned a rogue by stealth,
Whom prosperous times had ripened into health;
Hunting and shooting had its ceaseless charm
When his full purse cared little for a farm;
A trusty hand was left to plough and plan
The double trade of master and of man;
He kept his stud for hunts and races then,
And dogs fed even better than his men,
Bought loves and changed them when the freak was old,
And drank his wine without a wife to scold,
And gained a dashing name and lived in style,
And wore a mask to profit by't the while,
And made large credit while his name was good,
For all would trust him, draw on whom he would;
A man so stylish none could dream to doubt,

Till changing times the secret brought about;
The grain's sunk price o'er knavery's tricks was thrown,
And others' failings well excused his own;
The times, he said, and frowned, disturbed and sad,
Needed no comment to explain them bad.
So ere he broke he honestly confest
His wealth all gone and credit had the rest,
And proved to all a smuggling rogue too late:
Cheat creditors—turn bankrupt—and still great,
Hunts, shoots, and rackets as he did before,
And still finds wealth for horses, dogs, and whore.
And dogs and whore and horses in his train
Are all that have no reason to complain;
These show his kindness in their varied ways
And gild his rotting name with dirty praise;
Like as when brooks are dry, the village sinks
Boast their full dingy tide that flows and stinks.

Old Saveall next, whose dirty deeds and fame
Might put a young bard's silken lines to shame;
But my plain homespun verse lets none escape,
Nor passes folly in its rudest shape;
When satire's muse puts on a russet gown,
Tho' vermin start as game, she runs them down.
So Saveall shall have place—tho' fortune's smiles,
Unmixed with frowns, have made him known for miles;
Who tries to buy a good name and deceive
With fair pretensions that but few believe;
Who seldom swears, and that but now and then
A smuggled oath when vext by better men,
That beard hypocrisy with honest grace
And tear the mask from cant's deceiving face;
Yet in religion he is made elect
And buys with wine the favours of the sect,
Making each spouter welcome when he comes
And turning beggars from their fallen crumbs,
Pleading up charity in whining tones
And driving dogs at dinner from the bones;
The scraps which beggars plead for serve his swine,

So their lorn hopes seek other doors to dine;
The broken bones enrich his land for grain,
So dogs beneath his table wait in vain;
On neighbourly goodwill he often dwells,
And in dry times locks up his very wells,
And if 'twas but of worth we might suppose
He'd even save the droppings of his nose.
Such is this Saveall, first of fortune's fellows,
Famous for wealth, great farms, and small-beer cellars,
With the elect most saintish or most civil,
And with the rest a cunning knave or devil.

Religion now is little more than cant,
A cloak to hide what godliness may want;
Men love mild sermons with few threats perplexed,
And deem it sinful to forget the text;
Then turn to business ere they leave the church,
And linger oft to comment in the porch
Of fresh rates wanted from the needy poor
And list of taxes nailed upon the door;
Little religion in each bosom dwells,
And that sleeps sound till Sunday's chiming bells.
Some with reform religion's shade pursue,
And vote the old church wrong to join the new;
Casting away their former cold neglects—
Paying religion once a week respects,
They turn from regular old forms as bad
To pious maniacs regularly mad,
A chosen race, so their conceit would teach,
Whom cant inspired to rave and not to preach,
A set of upstarts late from darkness sprung
With this new light, like mushrooms out of dung;
Tho' blind as owls i'the sun they lived before,
Conceit inspired and they are blind no more.
The drunken cobbler leaves his wicked life,
Hastes to save others, and neglects his wife;
To mend men's souls he thinks himself designed,
And leaves his shoes to the uncalled and blind;
He then like old songs runs the scriptures o'er

And makes discoveries never known before,
Makes darkest points as plain as A B C,
And wonders why his hearers will not see,
Shouts facts on facts to prove that dark is light
And all are blind till he restore their sight,
And swears the old church which he cast away
As full of errors and as blind as they.
Then learning's looked on as an idle jest,
And the old cobbler preaches far the best,
Who soothes with honeyed hopes the deep-dyed sinner,
And earns reward—a lodging and a dinner.
Their former teachers as blind guides they mock,
Nor think them chosen for the crazy flock;
The crazy flock believe and are depraved,
And just in time turn idiots to be saved.

The Ranter priests, that take the street to teach,
Swear God builds churches wheresoe'er they preach;
While on the other hand Protestant people
Will have no church but such as wears a steeple.
Thus creeds all differ; yet each different sect,
From the free agents to the grand elect,
Who cull a remnant of the promised land,
And wear heaven's mark as sheep their owner's brand,
Each thinks his own as right and others wrong,
And thus keeps up confusion's babel-song;
While half the tribes at bottom are no more
Than saints skin-deep and devils at the core.
Old Ralph, the veriest rake the town possessed,
Felt sins prick deep and all his crimes confessed,
Groaned o'er confessions to his ranting priest,
And prayed and sang and felt his soul released;
The new-birth's struggle made him wondrous wan,
And feebly prayed at first the baby man
'Twixt doubts and fears, yet viewed the cured complaint
And scarce perceived the devil from the saint;
But soon the 'outward man,' grown godly mad,
Felt the good spirit triumph o'er the bad;
He then whined lectures in a happier strain

And coaxed poor sinner to be born again,
Shunned old companions once beloved so well,
As condemned transports on the way to hell,
And prayed and sang from sin and pain released,
And smoothed his hair and strove to act the priest.
And then as priest he exercised his wits,
Forced men to prayers and women into fits,
And heard and cured each difficult complaint,
And midst his flock seemed little less than saint.
But hell, untired with everlasting watch
(The fox grows cunning when prey's hard to catch),
Crept into Ralph's new-planted paradise,
And met success in tempting him to vice.
A simpering Eve did in his garden dwell,
And she was fair, and he grew fond—and fell.
'Twas love at first, but e'en when that began
The sinking saint grew more and more the man,
And with his Eve, so treacherously fair,
Could feel more joy than kneeling down to prayer;
Yet still he prayed nor deemed his case so bad
As stone-blind sinners, tho' his heart was sad;
Tho' sinful love had overpowered his skill,
From other sins he kept unspotted still;
When brethren met he would his joys express,
Groaned when they prayed and said amen by guess;
Till the completion of his serpent sin,
Urged by the devil, sunk him to the chin.
Eve, tho' beguiled forbidden fruit to taste,
Had loved an Adam ere she loved the priest;
And ere disgrace had ripened into light,
Ralph had no power to wed her and be right;
His fate was evident; it came at last;
His sheep were judge and shepherd Ralph was cast;
Then drink and racket joined their former friends,
And new-born saint in the old sinner ends.

   In politics and politicians' lies
The modern farmer waxes wondrous wise,
Opinionates with wisdom all compact,

And e'en could tell a nation how to act,
Throws light on darkness with excessive skill,
Knows who acts well and whose designs are ill,
Proves half the members naught but bribery's tools,
And calls the past a dull dark age of fools.
As wise as Solomons they read the news,
Not with their blind forefathers' simple views,
Who read of wars, and wished that wars would cease,
And blessed the king and wished his country peace;
Who marked the weight of each fat sheep or ox,
The price of grain and rise and fall of stocks;
Who thought it learning how to buy and sell,
And him a wise man who could manage well.
No, not with such old-fashioned idle views
Do these newsmongers traffic with the news;
They read of politics and not of grain,
And speechify and comment and explain,
And know so much of parliament and state
You'd think them members when you heard them prate;
And know so little of their farms the while
That can but urge a wiser man to smile.
Young Bragg, a Jack of all trades save his own,
From home is little as the farmer known;
Opinions gratis gives in men's affairs,
Fool in his own but wondrous wise in theirs,
Scrats paragraphs and sends them to the *News*,
Signed 'Constant Reader,' lest they should refuse
The ill-spelt trash on patriotic cavils,
Leaving corrections to the printer's devils:
Skits upon those by whom they're never read
(He might as well write letters to the dead)
Or puffs upon himself in various ways,
Which none but self will either read or praise;
And poems, too, the polished patriot chimes,
Stanzas to Cobbett's truth and comic rhymes,
To which he fits a hackneyed tune that draws
From patriot dinners echoes of applause.
But when election mobs for battle meet,
And dirty flags and ribbons throng the street,

Hunting for votes some dirty borough town,
'Tis then his genius meets the most renown;
When on the hustings bawling spouters throng,
Who fight and war like women with the tongue,
All speakers and no hearers, where the cries
Pile up.confusion's babel to the skies,
And croaking at the top in proud renown
Each party sits till t'other pulls them down;
Here shines our orator in all his plumes,
Nor prouder bantam to a dunghill comes
Than he to crow and peck and peck and crow,
And hurl bad English at retorting foe.
He games and drinks and rackets up and down,
A low-lived mocker of high life in town;
And sips his wine in fashionable pride,
And thrusts in scorn the homely ale aside.
His father's riches bought such foolish airs,
But wasting fortunes e'en must need repairs;
As parching summer checks the runnel's haste,
The greatest wealth will lessen, spent in waste;
Tho' credit proves him poor, his stubborn pride
O'eracts his purse and struggles dignified;
Yet, stung with tidings that his conscience vents,
He rails at tithes and hopes for falling rents,
Curses all taxes as tyrannic things,
And hates the pride of government and kings.
Turned radical in spirit and in purse,
He prays reform and deems the laws a curse,
Speaks treasonous things before his friends and cousins
And toasts reforming patriots by dozens,
And aping wit with ignorant delight
A village politician turns outright.
He hails his country's foes his only friends,
Damns peace and prays for war that never ends;
Its ruin's looked on as the way to wealth,
And grace for all meals is reform's good health.
And why is all this hubbub for reforms,
This anxious looking for expected storms,
That turns each fireside into parliaments,

In strong debates of taxes, tithes, and rents?
Is aught of general good or general view
Sketched in the pathway which reform pursues?
Or is the rich man's lands or miser's pelf
But grudged in other to be claimed by self?
With other nations, mid tyrannic strife,
This miscalled mania struggles oft to life;
Fair is the mask that hides its visage first,
But soon the infant to a fiend is nursed,
That like a wolf howls hungrily and high
A cry for blood—and freedom apes that cry;
For freedom, unrestrained, forsakes her cause,
And lawless pleasures are her only laws.

Thus village politics and hopes for pelf
Live in one word and centre all in self;
Thus village politicians urge repairs,
And deem all governments as wrong but theirs,
Versed in low cunning, which, to handle brief,
Is but a genteel title for a thief;
Nay, start not, reader, such harsh words to hear,
Nor think the pen of satire too severe.
What is that shuffling shadow of a man
Where self-deceptions shine in every plan,
Who spouts of wisdom as the thing he craves
And treats the poor o'er whom he rules as slaves,
Who votes equality that all men share
And stints the pauper of his parish fare,
Who damns all taxes both of church and state
And on the parish lays a double rate?
Such is our hero in his tyrant pride,
Then is his honour's title misapplied;
Such with one breath scoff at the poor's distress
And bawl out freedom for their own redress.
These soft politic saints may freedom preach,
And vacant minds believe the lies they teach;
Who think them walking Canaans, flowing o'er
With milk and honey for the starving poor.
And sure enough, their wants may richly fare

If like chameleons they can feed on air;
Their promises, sown thick, degenerate run
And mildew into broken ones when done;
And though a plenteous seed-time dreams of gain,
A blighted harvest falsifies the pain;
Such promises to-day to-morrow straight,
Like an old almanack, are out of date,
And they who break them no more credit break
Than Moore's new year does for the old's mistake;
Thus freedom-preaching is but knavery's game
And old self-interest by another name.

Churchwardens, constables, and overseers
Make up the round of commons and of peers;
With learning just enough to sign a name,
And skill sufficient parish rates to frame,
And cunning deep enough the poor to cheat,
This learned body for debatings meet;
Their secretary is the parish clerk,
Whom like a shepherd's dog they keep to bark,
And gather rates, and, when the next are due,
To cry them o'er at church-time from his pew.
He as their Jack of all trades steady shines
Thro' thick and thin to sanction their designs,
Who apes the part of king and magistrate
And acts Grand Signior of this Turkish state,
Who votes new laws to those already made
And acts by force when one is disobeyed;
Having no credit which he fears to lose,
He does whatever dirty jobs they choose,
Tasking the pauper labourer to stand,
Or clapping on his goods the parish brand,
Lest he should sell them for the want of bread,
On parish bounty rather pined than fed;
Or carrying the parish book from door to door,
Claiming fresh taxes from the needy poor.
And if one's hunger overcomes his hate
And buys a loaf with what should pay the rate,
He instant sets his tyrant laws to work,

In heart and deed the essence of a Turk,
Brings summons for an eighteen-penny rate
And gains the praises of the parish state,
Or seizes goods and from the burthened clown
Extorts for extra trouble half a crown,
Himself a beggar that may shortly take
A weekly pittance from the rates they make.
But the old proverb suits the subject well:
Mount such on horseback and they'll ride to hell.
Within the church where they on sabbath-days
Mock God with outward blasphemy of praise,
Making His house a Pharisee's at best,
God's for one day and Satan's all the rest,
The parson oft scarce puts his sermon by
Ere, 'neath his pulpit and with mighty cry,
The clerk announces—what? commandments meet?
No—when the parish vestry next shall meet,
To fleece the poor and rob with vile command
Want of its bread, too feeble to withstand,
Although its aching heart too often knows
Knaves call it debtor where it nothing owes;
For in these vestries, cunning, deep as night,
Plans deeds that would be treason to the light;
And tho' so honest in its own disguise,
'Tis but plain robbery in another's eyes;
For the whole set just as they please can plan,
And what one says all sanction to a man;
Their cheating knavery like contagion runs,
And thus the father's card becomes the son's;
Both play one game to cheat us in the lump,
And the son's turn-up shows the father's trump.

Here shines the man of morals, Farmer Finch,
Smooth-tongued and fine, an angel every inch
In outward guise, and never known as yet
To run in taverns, brothels, or in debt;
In public life all punctual, honest, true,
And flattery gives his graces double due;
For pity's gifts are never public made,

But there his name and guinea is displayed.
A Sunday never comes, or foul or fair,
That misses him at church throughout the year.
The priest himself boasts as the man's reward
That he ne'er preached a sermon but he heard.
Such is the man in public; all agree
That saints themselves no better men could be.
But now of private life let's take the view:
In that same church and in that very pew
Where he each Sabbath sings and reads and prays,
He joins the vestry upon common days,
Cheating the poor with levies doubly laid
On their small means, that wealth may be defrayed;
To save his own and others', his compeers,
He robs the poor whom he has robbed for years,
Making the house of prayer the house of sin
And placing Satan as high priest within.
Such is this good, church-going, godly man,
This man of morals on deception's plan;
So knaves by cant steer free from sin's complaints,
And flattery's cunning coins them into saints.
Oppression often mourns the vile abuse
And flies to justice, deemed of little use;
For 'tis well known that justice winks at crimes,
A saying that's in season at all times;
Or why should the poor sinning, starving clown
Meet jail and hanging for a stolen crown,
While wealthy thieves with knavery's bribes endued
Plunder their millions and are not pursued;
Nay, at the foot of Tyburn's noted tree,
They do deserving deeds and still go free;
Where others suffer for some pigmy cause,
They all but murder and escape the laws,
Skulking awhile in bribery's dirty den,
Then start new guilt and pass as honest men.
Gold is a mighty substitute—it buys
The fool sufficient credit to seem wise,
The coward laurels, virtue unto bawds,
A mask for villainy and fame for lords;

Buys knaves an office, traitors trust and power;
Buys lies and oaths, and breaks them every hour;
Buys cant its flattery, hypocrites their paint,
Making a very devil seem a saint;
Buys asses panegyrics and what not,
And makes man worshipped and leaves God forgot;
In fact, buys all and everything, forsooth,
But two poor outcasts—honesty and truth.

Tho' Justice Terror, who the peace preserves,
Meets more of slander than his deed deserves—
A blunt, opinionated, odd, rude man,
Severe and selfish in his every plan—
Tho' pleading want oft meets with harsh replies,
And truth's too often listened to as lies,
Although he reigns with much caprice and whim,
The poor can name worse governors than him.
His gifts at Christmas time are yearly given,
No doubt as toll fees on the road to heaven.
Tho' to complaints his aid is oft denied,
Tho' said too oft to shun the weaker side,
Yet when foul wrongs are uttered in his ear
Farmers themselves meet reprimands severe.
Poor trembling maids, too, learn his looks to dread,
By sad forced errands to his mansion led;
His worship's lectures are so long and keen,
They're dreaded now as penance once has been.
Tho' it is said (what will not rumour say?)
There e'en were seasons when the priest was gay,
That now and then in manhood's lusty morn
His maids turned mothers and were never sworn,
Yet still he reigns, whatever faults they find,
A blunt, odd, rude, good picture of his kind;
Who preaches partial for both church and king
And runs reform down as a dangerous thing.
Ranters and Methodists, his open foes,
In person and in sermons he'll oppose,
And now and then his sermon's length prolongs
To guard his flock against deceitful tongues,

And takes much trouble on a sabbath-day
To lecture drunkards and drive boys from play;
And tho' from year to year unknown to use,
To keep his peace and Sunday from abuse,
Beside the circling cross upon the hill
The dancing-stocks maintain their station still;
And as derision and decaying time
Weaken their triumph o'er abuse and crime,
The priest, still mindful of his ruling cares,
Renews their reign in threatening repairs.
Laws or religion, be what they will,
Self will not yield but stickles to it still;
And still he rules, in every baffling plan
The same headstrong, opinionated man.

But now grown old in reading Sunday's prayers
And keeping village morals in repairs,
Till e'en his very spectacles refuse
To see the largest print that age can choose,
He seeks a curate to supply his place,
A kinsman of his worship's sacred race,
Who wears his priesthood with a trader's skill
And makes religion learn to make her bill;
Who, ere he cures his sheep of their disease,
Like lawyer studies o'er the church's fees,
Who ekes new claims on custom's ancient price,
When reason ruled and priests were not so nice,
And sets on registers his raising mark
That used to fetch their sixpence to the clerk,
And from the aye-inquiring, staring clown
Extorts the monstrous charge of half a crown;
And if a wanderer leaves his wants to roam
And dies on other ills he meets from home,
His churchyard common for a bed is lost,
And forfeits must be paid by double cost;
And marriage pays its earnest for a bride,
Offering the fees before the knot is tied,
And new-made mother that with thanks repairs
Seeks God's kind love and pays the priest for prayers.

Such is the substitute put on to keep
The close-shorn remnant of his worship's sheep;
And by and by hopes at his friend's decay
To be sole shepherd and receive full pay.
And is religion grown so commonplace
To place self-interest foremost in the race
And leave poor souls in Satan's claws confined,
Crawling like crabs a careless pace behind?

 Excuse the priest, he's prest with weighty cares;
And tho' the pauper dies without his prayers,
What if such worthless sheep slip into hell
For want of prayers before the passing-bell?
The priest was absent—'twas a daily song—
Yet none except the vulgar thought it wrong.
Perhaps when death-beds might his aid desire,
His horse was sick and might a drink require,
Or friends for just necessities might claim
His shooting skill to track the fields for game;
And when they needed partridges or hares
The parish pauper could not look for prayers;
Or if he did indulge the foolish whim,
What cared the priest?—die and be damned for him!
And he had land to shepherd where the wheat
In a sly way the church's profit beat;
Tho' he kept one to manage of his kin,
Yet self was foreman when the gain dropt in.

 And dwells no memory in the days gone by,
No name whose loss is worth a present sigh?
Yes—there was one who priesthood's trade profest,
'One whom the wretched and the poor knew best';
And in yon house that neighbours near the show
Of parish huts, a melancholy row,
That like to them a stubble covering wears,
Decayed the same and needing like repairs
—Superior only was the mansion known
Instead of mud by having walls of stone—
There lived the vicar once in days gone by

When pride and fashion did not rank so high,
Ere poor religion threw her weeds away
To mix in circles of the worldly gay,
Ere hunting parsons in the chase begun,
And added salaries kept their dog and gun,
Ere sheep were driven from the shepherd's door,
And pleasure swallowed what might feed the poor;
In that same time whose loss was keenly felt,
The good old vicar in this mansion dwelt.
Plain as the flock dependent on his cares
For weekday comforts and for Sunday prayers,
He'd no spare wealth to follow fashion's whim,
And if he had she'd little joy for him.
He kept no horse the hunting's sports to share,
He fed no dogs to run the harmless hare;
He'd naught to waste while hunger sought his shed,
And while he had it they ne'er wanted bread.
His chiefest pleasure charity possest
In having means to make another blest;
Little was his and little was required;
Could he do that, 'twas all the wealth desired.
Tho' small the gift, 'twas given with greatest will,
And blessings o'er it made it greater still;
On want's sad tale he never closed his door,
He gave them something and he wished it more;
The beggar's heart, dismantled of its fears,
Leaped up and thanked him for his crust with tears.
The vicar's greensward pathways, once his pride,
His woodbine bowers that used his doors to hide,
The yard and garden roads—his only farms—
And all his stock—the hive bees' yearly swarms—
Are swept away; their produce and their pride
Were doomed to perish when their owner died.
Fresh faces came with little taste or care,
And joyed to ruin what was his to rear;
His garden plants and blossoms all are fled,
And docks and nettles blossom in their stead.
Before the door, where pinks and roses stood,
The hissing goose protects her summer brood,

And noisy hogs are free to wallow o'er
What once was gravelled and kept clean before.
The corner seat where weary hinds had rest,
The snug fireside that welcomed many a guest,
These are decayed as comforts will decay,
As winter's sunshine or as flowers in May;
These all are past as joys are born to pass,
Where life's a shadow and where flesh is grass;
E'en memory's lingering features time shall rot,
And this good man is nearly now forgot,
Save on his tomb and some few hearts beside,
Grey-headed men, left children when he died,
Who from their parents all his goodness knew
And learned to feel it as they older grew.
Yon cot, when in its glory and its pride,
Maintained its priest and half the poor beside;
These are the times that plainness must regret,
These are the times that labour feels as yet,
Ere mock-improvement's plans enclosed the moor,
And farmers built a workhouse for the poor.
The cottage now, with neither lawn nor park,
Instead of vicar keeps the vicar's clerk;
Wolves may devour, oppression's fiends may reign,
None's nigh to listen when the poor complain.
Too high religion looks her flocks to watch,
Or stoop from pride to dwell in cots of thatch.
Too much of pleasure in her mansion dwells
To hear the troubles which the pauper tells,
To turn a look on sorrow's thorny ways
Like good Samaritans of former days,
To heal in mercy when foul wrongs pursue
And weep o'er anguish as she once would do.
Distress may languish and distress may die,
There's none that hears can help them when they cry.
Compassion cannot stoop, nor pride allow
To pass that way with oil or honey now.
Still there are some whose actions merit praise,
The lingering breathings of departed days;
Tho' in this world of vainness thinly sown,

Yet there are some whom fashion leaves alone;
Who, like their Master, plain and humble go,
And strive to follow in his steps below;
Who in the wilderness as beacons stand
To pilgrims journeying to the promised land,
To give instructions to inquiring souls,
To cheer the weak above the world's controls,
To lend their charge and wanderers back restore,
To rest the weary and relieve the poor.

Ah, sure it was a melancholy day
That called the good man from his charge away.
Those poor lorn outcasts, born to many cares,
That shared his table, welcome as his prayers,
To them the bells worse tidings never gave
Than those which called their guardian to the grave;
They'd no more harvests now of hopes to reap;
E'en children wept to see their mothers weep,
And pulled their gowns to ask a question—when
He'd wake and come and give them pence again.
'He'll not sleep there for ever, sure he won't;
'Who'll feed and clothe us if the vicar don't?'
Thus lisped the babes, and while their parents sighed,
Muttering their blessings by the pasture-side,
Warm repetitions of their griefs were given,
And they hoped too to meet their friend in heaven.

Beside the charnel well in humble guise,
A small stone noteth where the vicar lies;
Where age, slow journeying on the sabbath-day,
Oft potters up to wipe the tear away,
And show inquiring youth, with mournful pride,
That good man's name that once its wants supplied,
To hear it read and bring back days to view,
And feel his goodness and his loss anew;
Blessing his name and praying as they weep
To be full soon companion of his sleep,
To share with hin the churchyard's lonely peace,
Where pride forgets its scorn and troubles cease;

Where poverty's sad reign of cares is o'er,
And tells its wants to be denied no more,
The last lorn hope and refuge that appears
Thro' the dull gloom of life's declining years.

Shoved as a nuisance from pride's scornful sight,
In a cold corner stands in woeful plight
The shuttered workhouse of the parish poor,
And towards the north wind opes its creaking door.
A makeshift shed for misery, no thought
Urged plans for comfort when the work was wrought,
No garden spot was left dull want to cheer
And make the calls of hunger less severe
With wholesome herbs that summer might supply;
'Twas not contrived for want to live, but die;
A forced concern to satisfy the law
Built want this covering o'er his bed of straw.
E'en that cheap blessing that's so freely given
To all that live beneath the face of heaven,
The light of day, is not allowed to win
A smiling passage to the glooms within;
No window opens on the southern sky—
A luxury deemed to pride's disdainful eye.
Here dwell the wretched, lost to hopeless strife,
Reduced by want to skeletons in life,
Despised by all; e'en age, grown bald and grey,
Meets scoffs from wanton children in their play,
Who laugh at misery by misfortune bred
And point scorn's finger at the mouldering shed.
The tottering tenant urges no reply,
Turns his white head and chokes the passing sigh,
And seeks his shed and hides his heart's despair,
For pity lives not as a listener there.

Old Farmer Thrifty reigns from year to year
Their tyrant king, yclept an overseer;
A sad proud knave who by a cunning plan
Blindfolds his faults and seems an honest man.
He rarely barters when he buys or sells,

But sets a price, and there his honour dwells;
He rails at cheating knaves for knavery's sake,
And ne'er asks double what he means to take,
Scorns open ways which lesser rogues pursue,
An outside Christian but at heart a Jew.
Old men will tell you when the boy was small
How he blacked shoes and waited at the Hall;
Thro' all the names that wait on wealth and pride,
From shoe-black vile to valet dignified,
He rose successfully without a fall,
And owned the cunning power to please in all.
At length power blessed him with its highest stretch,
Which good men's merits might despair to reach;
No longer doomed in servitude to wait,
Next to the squire he managed his estate,
Yclept a steward; strangers made their bow,
And the squire took him as an equal now,
While to neglect his former steward fell
For no one crime unless 'twas acting well.
And soon the tyrant threw the mask aside,
When wealth thronged in and power was gratified;
He raised the rents of all the tenants round,
And then distressed them as in duty bound,
And then asked leave of the contented squire
To rent the farm, and had his heart's desire.
The storm at first must burst upon the poor,
That urged want's curses as they passed his door;
He viewed their comforts with a jealous heart
And raised their rents and bade their hopes depart;
Yet, loath to leave, their cows were sold for rent,
And the next year left nothing but complaint.
'Twas just as wished; his plans were quickly known;
Each spot was seized and added to his own.
Others resigned and the half-starving poor
Laid down their sufferings at their master's door.
Such whispers urged the easy squire to shift,
And Steward Thrifty then was turned adrift;
But not before his purse was filled with pelf,
For knaves work quick and ne'er lose sight of self;

His nest was feathered ere his fame was old,
And land was bought when farms were cheaply sold.
He now retires at ease and sells his grain
And strives to be an honest rogue in vain;
With big round belly and sleek double chin,
He reads the news and smokes and drinks his gin,
And studies all the week o'er gain's affairs,
And once a week at chapel reads his prayers,
And seems as striving former deeds to mend,
Mild to a foe and coaxing to a friend.
But to the poor his ways are still severe;
Dwindled in office to an overseer,
Still deaf to want that seeks him to be fed,
He gives them curses in the lieu of bread;
Or scoffing at their hopes, tells them they're free
To seek a law as tyrannized as he.
He pleads bad times when justice chides his ways,
Tho' justice' self is ill-deserving praise;
And are bad times the cause of such despair?
Go ask the wretches who inhabit there
If past good times their hopes had ever blest
And left them thus so wretched and distrest;
Ask if their griefs can better times recall;
Their startled tears tell plenty as they fall,
And pity's heart can easy comprehend
That Farmer Thrifty never was their friend.
Art thou a man, thou tyrant o'er distress?
Doubtless thy pride would scorn to think thee less;
Then scorn a deed unworthy of that name,
And live deserving of a better fame;
Hurt not the poor whom fate forbade to shine,
Whose lots were cast in meaner ways than thine;
Infringe not on the comforts they possess,
Nor bid scant hope turn hopeless in distress.
Drive not poor freedom from its niggard soil;
Its independence is their staff for toil;
Take that away which as their right they call,
And thou'rt a rogue that beggars them of all;
They sink in sorrow as a race of slaves,

And their last hope lives green upon their graves.
Still lives unsung a swarm of petty knaves,
Numerous as wasps to sting and torture slaves;
The meanest of the mean, a servile race,
Who, like their betters, study to be base;
Whose dunghill pride grows stiff in dirty state,
And, tho' so little, apes the little-great.
The workhouse keeper, as old Thrifty's man,
Transacts the business on the tyrant's plan,
Supplies its tenants with their scanty food,
And tortures misery for a livelihood,
Despised and hated by the slaves he wrongs,
And e'en too low for satire's scourging songs.

A thing all consequence here takes the lead,
Reigning knight-errant o'er this dirty breed;
A bailiff he, and who so great to brag
Of law and all its terrors as Bumtagg;
Fawning a puppy at his master's side
And frowning like a wolf on all beside;
Who fattens best where sorrow worst appears
And feeds on sad misfortune's bitterest tears?
Such is Bumtagg the bailiff, to a hair,
The worshipper and demon of despair,
Who waits and hopes and wishes for success
At every nod and signal of distress,
Happy at heart, when storms begin to boil,
To seek the shipwreck and to share the spoil.
Brave is this Bumtagg, match him if you can,
For there's none like him living save his man.
As every animal assists his kind,
Just so are these in blood and business joined;
Yet both in different colours hide their art,
And each as suits his ends transacts his part.
One keeps the heart-bred villain full in sight,
The other cants and acts the hypocrite,
Smoothing the deed where law sharks set their gin
Like a coy-dog to draw misfortune in.
But both will chuckle o'er their prisoners' sighs

And are as blest as spiders over flies.
Such is Bumtagg, whose history I resign,
As other knaves wait room to stink and shine;
And, as the meanest knave a dog can brag,
Such is the lurcher that assists Bumtagg.

Born with the changes time and chance doth bring,
A shadow reigns, yclept a woodland king,
Enthroned mid thorns and briers, a clownish wight,
My Lord's chief woodman in his title's height.
The bugbear devil of the boys is he,
Who once for swine picked acorns 'neath the tree,
And starving terror of the village brood
Who gleaned their scraps of fuel from the wood;
When parish charity was vainly tried
'Twas their last refuge—which is now denied.
Small hurt was done by such intrusions there,
Claiming the rotten as their harmless share,
Which might be thought in reason's candid eye
As sent by providence for such supply;
But Turks imperial of the woodland bough
Forbid their trespass in such trifles now,
Threatening the dithering wretch that hence proceeds
With jail and whipping for his shameless deeds,
Well pleased to bid their feeblest hopes decay,
Driving them empty from the woods away,
Cheating scant comfort of its pilfered blaze,
That doubtless warmed him in his beggar days.
Thus knaves in office love to show their power
And unoffending helplessness devour,
Sure on the weak to give their fury vent
Where there's no strength injustice to resent;
As dogs let loose on harmless flocks at night,
Such feel no mercy where they fear no bite.

Others of this small fry as mean, as base,
May live unknown, a pigmy reigning race,
And sink to hell from whence their knavery came,
As nameless tribes, unworthy of a name,

Left on the dunghill, where they reigned, to rot,
Hated while living and when dead forgot.
Here ends the song—let jealousy condemn,
And deem reproofs they merit aimed at them;
When pride is touched and evil conscience bit,
Each random throw will seem a lucky hit;
If common sense its ears and eyes may trust,
Each picture's faithful and each censure just.
So let them rail—the proverb's truth is known,
'Where the cap fits, they'll wear it as their own.'
Full many knaves sharp satire's wounds have met,
Who live on aqua fortis dying yet;
In burning ink their scarecrow memories dwell,
Left to the torture of life's earthly hell,
As marked and lasting as the thief's burnt brand,
Who lives and dies with 'Villain' on his hand.

SECTION II

WINTER winds cold and blea
Chilly blows o'er the lea;
Wander not out to me
Jenny so fair.
Wait in thy cottage free—
I will be there

How sweet can courting prove,
How can I kiss my love
Muffled in hat and glove
From the chill air?
Quaking beneath the grove
What love is there?

Wait in thy cushioned chair
Wi' thy white bosom bare;
Kisses are sweetest there
Leave it for me;
Free from the chilly air
I will meet thee

Lay by thy woollen vest,
Wrap no cloak o'er thy breast
Where my hand oft hath pressed
Pin nothing there.
Where my head droops to rest
Leave its bed bare.

AUTUMN

SIREN of sullen moods and fading hues,
Yet haply not incapable of joy,
Sweet Autumn! I thee hail
With welcome all unfeigned;

And oft as morning from her lattice peeps
To beckon up the sun, I seek with thee
　　To drink the dewy breath
　　Of fields left fragrant then,

In solitudes, where no frequented paths
But what thy own foot makes betray thy home,
　　Stealing obtrusive there
　　To meditate thy end:

By overshadowed ponds, in woody nooks,
With ramping sallows lined, and crowding sedge,
　　Which woo the winds to play,
　　And with them dance for joy;

And meadow pools, torn wide by lawless floods,
Where water-lilies spread their oily leaves,
　　On which, as wont, the fly
　　Oft battens in the sun;

Where leans the mossy willow half-way o'er,
On which the shepherd crawls astride to throw
　　His angle clear of weeds
　　That crowd the water's brim;

Or crispy hills, and hollows scant of sward,
Where step by step the patient lonely boy
　　Hath cut rude flights of stairs
　　To climb their steepy sides;

Then track along their feet, grown hoarse with noise,
The crawling brook, that ekes its weary speed,
　　And struggles through the weeds
　　With faint and sullen brawl.

These haunts I long have favoured, more as now
With thee thus wandering, moralizing on,
　　Stealing glad thoughts from grief,
　　And happy, though I sigh.

Sweet Vision, with the wild dishevelled hair,
And raiment shadowy of each wind's embrace,
    Fain would I win thine harp
    To one accordant theme;

Now not inaptly craved, communing thus
Beneath the curdled arms of this stunt oak,
    While pillowed on the grass,
    We fondly ruminate

O'er the disordered scenes of woods and fields,
Ploughed lands, thin travelled with half-hungry sheep,
    Pastures tracked deep with cows,
    Where small birds seek for seed:

Marking the cow-boy that so merry trills
His frequent, unpremeditated song,
    Wooing the winds to pause,
    Till echo brawls again;

As on with plashy step and clouted shoon
He roves, half indolent and self-employed,
    To rob the little birds
    Of hips and pendent haws,

And sloes, dim covered as with dewy veils,
And rambling bramble-berries, pulp and sweet,
    Arching their prickly trails
    Half o'er the narrow lane:

Noting the hedger front with stubborn face
The dank blea wind, that whistles thinly by
    His leathern garb, thorn-proof,
    And cheek red-hot with toil.

While o'er the pleachy lands of mellow brown,
The mower's stubbling scythe clogs to his foot
    The ever eking wisp,
    With sharp and sudden jerk,

Till into formal rows the russet shocks
Crowd the blank field to thatch time-weathered barns,
     And hovels rude repair,
     Stript by disturbing winds.

See! from the rustling scythe the haunted hare
Scampers circuitous, with startled ears
     Prickt up, then squat, as by
     She brushes to the woods,

Where reeded grass, breast-high and undisturbed,
Forms pleasant clumps, through which the soothing winds
     Soften her rigid fears,
     And lull to calm repose.

Wild sorceress! me thy restless mood delights
More than the stir of summer's crowded scenes,
     Where, jostled in the din,
     Joy palled my ear with song;

Heart-sickening for the silence that is thine,
Not broken inharmoniously, as now
     That lone and vagrant bee
     Booms faint with weary chime.

Now filtering winds thin winnow through the woods
In tremulous noise, that bids, at every breath,
     Some sickly cankered leaf
     Let go its hold, and die.

And now the bickering storm, with sudden start,
In flirting fits of anger carps aloud,
     Thee urging to thine end,
     Sore wept by troubled skies.

And yet, sublime in grief, thy thoughts delight
To show me visions of most gorgeous dyes,
     Haply forgetting now
     They but prepare thy shroud;

Thy pencil dashing its excess of shades,
Improvident of waste, till every bough
  Burns with thy mellow touch
  Disorderly divine.

Soon must I view thee as a pleasant dream
Droop faintly, and so sicken for thine end,
  As sad the winds sink low
  In dirges for their queen;

While in the moment of their weary pause,
To cheer thy bankrupt pomp, the willing lark
  Starts from his shielding clod,
  Snatching sweet scraps of song.

Thy life is waning now, and silence tries
To mourn, but meets no sympathy in sounds,
  As stooping low she bends,
  Forming with leaves thy grave;

To sleep inglorious there mid tangled woods,
Till parch-lipped summer pines in drought away,
  Then from thine ivied trance
  Awake to glories new.

SUMMER IMAGES

Now swarthy summer, by rude health embrowned,
  Precedence takes of rosy-fingered spring;
And laughing joy, with wild flowers pranked and crowned,
  A wild and giddy thing,
And health robust, from every care unbound,
  Come on the zephyr's wing,
      And cheer the toiling clown.

Happy as holiday-enjoying face,
  Loud tongues, and 'merry as a marriage bell,'
Thy lightsome step sheds joy in every place;
  And where the troubled dwell,

Thy witching smiles wean them of half their cares;
　　And from thy sunny spell,
　　　　They greet joy unawares.

Then with thy sultry locks all loose and rude,
　　And mantle laced with gems of garish light,
Come as of wont; for I would fain intrude,
　　And in the world's despite,
Share the rude mirth that thy own heart beguiles,
　　If haply so I might
　　　　Win pleasure from thy smiles.

Me not the noise of brawling pleasure cheers,
　　In nightly revels or in city streets,
But joys which soothe, and not distract the ears,
　　That one at leisure meets
In the green woods, and meadows summer-shorn,
　　Or fields, where bee-fly greets
　　　　The ears with mellow horn.

The green-swathed grasshopper on treble pipe
　　Sings there, and dances in mad-hearted pranks;
There bees go courting every flower that's ripe,
　　On baulks and sunny banks;
And droning dragon-fly on rude bassoon
　　Attempts to give God thanks
　　　　In no discordant tune.

The speckled thrush, by self-delight imbued,
　　There sings unto himself for joy's amends,
And drinks the honey-dew of solitude.
　　There happiness attends
With inbred joy until the heart o'erflow,
　　Of which the world's rude friends,
　　　　Naught heeding, nothing know.

There the gay river, laughing as it goes,
  Plashes with easy wave its flaggy sides,
And to the calm of heart, in calmness shows
  What pleasure there abides,
To trace its sedgy banks, from trouble free:
  Spots solitude provides
    To muse, and happy be.

There ruminating 'neath some pleasant bush,
  On sweet silk grass I stretch me at mine ease,
Where I can pillow on the yielding rush;
  And, acting as I please,
Drop into pleasant dreams; or musing lie,
  Mark the wind-shaken trees,
    And cloud-betravelled sky,

And think me how some barter joy for care,
  And waste life's summer-health in riot rude,
Of nature nor of nature's sweets aware;
  Where passions vain and rude
By calm reflection softened are and still;
  And the heart's better mood
    Feels sick of doing ill.

There I can live, and at my leisure seek
  Joys far from cold restraints—not fearing pride—
Free as the winds, that breathe upon my cheek
  Rude health, so long denied.
Here poor integrity can sit as ease,
  And list self-satisfied
    The song of honey-bees;

And green lane traverse, heedless where it goes,
  Naught guessing, till some sudden turn espies
Rude battered finger-post, that stooping shows
  Where the snug mystery lies;
And then a mossy spire, with ivy crown,
  Clears up the short surprise,
    And shows a peeping town.

I see the wild flowers, in their summer morn
  Of beauty, feeding on joy's luscious hours;
The gay convolvulus, wreathing round the thorn,
  Agape for honey showers;
And slender kingcup, burnished with the dew
  Of morning's early hours,
      Like gold yminted new;

And mark by rustic bridge, o'er shallow stream,
  Cow-tending boy, to toil unreconciled,
Absorbed as in some vagrant summer dream;
  Who now, in gestures wild,
Starts dancing to his shadow on the wall,
  Feeling self-gratified,
      Nor fearing human thrall:

Then thread the sunny valley laced with streams,
  Or forests rude, and the o'ershadowed brims
Of simple ponds, where idle shepherd dreams,
  And streaks his listless limbs;
Or trace hay-scented meadows, smooth and long,
  Where joy's wild impulse swims
      In one continued song.

I love at early morn, from new-mown swath,
  To see the startled frog his route pursue,
And mark while, leaping o'er the dripping path,
  His bright sides scatter dew;
And early lark that from its bustle flies
  To hail his matin new;
      And watch him to the skies:

And note on hedgerow baulks, in moisture sprent,
  The jetty snail creep from the mossy thorn,
With earnest heed and tremulous intent,
  Frail brother of the morn,
That from the tiny bents and misted leaves
  Withdraws his timid horn,
      And fearful vision weaves:

Or swallow heed on smoke-tanned chimney-top,
    Wont to be first unsealing morning's eye,
Ere yet the bee hath gleaned one wayward drop
    Of honey on his thigh;
To see him seek morn's airy couch to sing,
    Until the golden sky
        Bepaint his russet wing:

And sawning boy by tanning corn espy,
    With clapping noise to startle birds away,
And hear him bawl to every passer-by
    To know the hour of day;
And see the uncradled breeze, refreshed and strong,
    With waking blossoms play,
        And breathe aeolian song.

I love the south-west wind, or low or loud,
    And not the less when sudden drops of rain
Moisten my pallid cheek from ebon cloud,
    Threatening soft showers again,
That over lands new ploughed and meadow grounds,
    Summer's sweet breath unchain,
        And wake harmonious sounds.

Rich music breathes in summer's every sound;
    And in her harmony of varied greens,
Woods, meadows, hedgerows, cornfields, all around
    Much beauty intervenes,
Filling with harmony the ear and eye;
    While o'er the mingling scenes
        Far spreads the laughing sky.

And wind-enamoured aspen—mark the leaves
    Turn up their silver lining to the sun,
And list! the brustling noise, that oft deceives,
    And makes the sheep-boy run:
The sound so mimics fast-approaching showers,
    He thinks the rain begun,
        And hastes to sheltering bowers.

But now the evening curdles dank and grey,
  Changing her watchet hue for sombre weed;
And moping owls, to close the lids of day,
  On drowsy wing proceed;
While chickering crickets, tremulous and long,
  Light's farewell inly heed,
        And give it parting song.

The pranking bat its flighty circlet makes;
  The glow-worm burnishes its lamp anew
O'er meadows dew-besprent; and beetle wakes
  Inquiries ever new,
Teasing each passing ear with murmurs vain,
  As wanting to pursue
        His homeward path again.

Hark to the melody of distant bells
  That on the wind with pleasing hum rebounds
By fitful starts, then musically swells
  O'er the dun stilly grounds;
While on the meadow bridge the pausing boy
  Listens the mellow sounds,
        And hums in vacant joy.

Now homeward-bound, the hedger bundles round
  His evening faggot, and with every stride
His leathern doublet leaves a rustling sound.
  Till silly sheep beside
His path start tremulous, and once again
  Look back dissatisfied,
        Then scour the dewy plain.

How sweet the soothing calm that smoothly stills
  O'er the heart's every sense its opiate dews,
In meek-eyed moods and ever balmy trills!
  That softens and subdues,
With gentle quiet's bland and sober train,
  Which dreamy eve renews
        In many a mellow strain.

I love to walk the fields; they are to me
    A legacy no evil can destroy;
They, like a spell, set every rapture free
    That cheered me when a boy.
Play—pastime—all time's blotting pen concealed,
    Comes like a new-born joy,
        To greet me in the field.

For nature's objects ever harmonize
    With emulous taste, that vulgar deed annoys;
It loves in quiet moods to sympathize,
    And meet vibrating joys
O'er nature's pleasant things; nor will it deem
    Pastime the muse employs
        A vain, obtrusive theme.

THE ETERNITY OF NATURE

LEAVES from eternity are simple things
To the world's gaze—whereto a spirit clings
Sublime and lasting.   Trampled under foot,
The daisy lives, and strikes its little root
Into the lap of time: centuries may come,
And pass away into the silent tomb,
And still the child, hid in the womb of time,
Shall smile and pluck them when this simple rhyme
Shall be forgotten, like a churchyard stone,
Or lingering lie unnoticed and alone.
When eighteen hundred years, our common date,
Grow many thousands in their marching state,
Ay, still the child, with pleasure in his eye,
Shall cry—the daisy! a familiar cry—
And run to pluck it, in the self-same state
As when Time found it in his infant date;
And, like a child himself, when all was new,
Might smile with wonder, and take notice too,
Its little golden bosom, frilled with snow,

Might win e'en Eve to stoop adown, and show
Her partner, Adam, in the silky grass
This little gem that smiled where pleasure was,
And loving Eve, from Eden followed ill,
And bloomed with sorrow, and lives smiling still,
As once in Eden under heaven's breath,
So now on earth, and on the lap of death
It smiles for ever.—Cowslips of gold bloom,
That in the pasture and the meadow come,
Shall come when kings and empires fade and die;
And in the closen, as Time's partners, lie
As fresh two thousand years to come as now,
With those five crimson spots upon their brow.
The little brooks that hum a simple lay
In green unnoticed spots, from praise away,
Shall sing when poets in time's darkness hid
Shall lie like memory in a pyramid,
Forgetting yet not all forgot, though lost
Like a thread's end in ravelled windings crost.
The little humble-bee shall hum as long
As nightingales, for Time protects the song;
And Nature is their soul, to whom all clings
Of fair or beautiful in lasting things.
The little robin in the quiet glen,
Hidden from fame and all the strife of men,
Sings unto Time a pastoral, and gives
A music that lives on and ever lives.
Spring and autumnal years shall bloom, and fade,
Longer than songs that poets ever made.
Think ye not these, Time's playthings, pass proud skill?
Time loves them like a child, and ever will;
And so I seek them in each bushy spot,
And sing with them when all else notice not,
And feel the music of their mirth agree
With that sooth quiet that bestirs in me.
And if I touch aright that quiet tone,
That soothing truth that shadows forth their own,
Then many a year to come, in after-days,
Shall still find hearts to love my quiet lays.

Thus cheering mirth with thoughts sung not for fame,
But for the joy that with their utterance came,
That inward breath of rapture urged not loud—
Birds, singing lone, fly silent past a crowd—
In these same pastoral spots, which childish time
Makes dear to me, I wander out and rhyme;
What hour the dewy morning's infancy
Hangs on each blade of grass and every tree,
And sprents the red thighs of the humble-bee,
Who 'gins betimes unwearied minstrelsy;
Who breakfasts, dines, and most divinely sups,
With every flower save golden buttercups—
On whose proud bosoms he will never go,
But passes by with scarcely 'How do ye do?'
Since in their showy, shining, gaudy cells
Haply the summer's honey never dwells.
All nature's ways are mysteries! Endless youth
Lives in them all, unchangeable as truth.
With the odd number five, her curious laws
Play many freaks, nor once mistake the cause;
For in the cowslip-peeps this very day
Five spots appear, which Time wears not away,
Nor once mistakes in counting—look within
Each peep, and five, nor more nor less, are seen.
So trailing bindweed, with its pinky cup,
Five leaves of paler hue go streaking up;
And many a bird, too, keeps the rule alive,
Laying five eggs, nor more nor less than five.
But flowers, how many own that mystic power,
With five leaves ever making up the flower!
The five-leaved grass, mantling its golden cup
Of flowers—five leaves make all for which I stoop.
The bryony, in the hedge, that now adorns
The tree to which it clings, and now the thorns,
Owns five-starred pointed leaves of dingy white;
Count which I will, all make the number right.
The spreading goose-grass, trailing all abroad
In leaves of silver green about the road—
Five leaves make every blossom all along.

I stoop for many, none are counted wrong.
'Tis Nature's wonder, and her Maker's will,
Who bade earth be, and order owns him still,
As that superior Power, who keeps the key
Of wisdom and of might through all eternity.

INSECTS

THESE tiny loiterers on the barley's beard,
And happy units of a numerous herd
Of playfellows, the laughing summer brings,
Mocking the sunshine in their glittering wings,
How merrily they creep, and run, and fly!
No kin they bear to labour's drudgery,
Smoothing the velvet of the pale hedge-rose;
And where they fly for dinner no one knows—
The dew-drops feed them not—they love the shine
Of noon, whose sun may bring them golden wine.
All day they're playing in their Sunday dress—
Till night goes sleep, and they can do no less;
Then, to the heath-bell's silken hood they fly,
And like to princes in their slumbers lie,
Secure from night, and dropping dews, and all,
In silken beds and roomy painted hall.
So merrily they spend their summer day,
Now in the cornfields, now the new-mown hay,
One almost fancies that such happy things,
With coloured hoods and richly burnished wings,
Are fairy folk, in splendid masquerade
Disguised, as if of mortal folk afraid,
Keeping their merry pranks a mystery still,
Lest glaring day should do their secrets ill.

THE VOICE OF NATURE

THERE is a language wrote on earth and sky
By God's own pen in silent majesty;
There is a voice that's heard and felt and seen
In spring's young shades and summer's endless green;
There is a book of poesy and spells

In which that voice in sunny splendour dwells;
There is a page in which that voice aloud
Speaks music to the few and not the crowd;
Though no romantic scenes my feet have trod,
The voice of nature as the voice of God
Appeals to me in every tree and flower,
Breathing his glory, magnitude and power.
In nature's open book I read, and see
Beauty's rich lesson in this seeming-pea;
Crowds see no magic in the trifling thing;
Pshaw! 'tis a weed, and millions came with spring.
I hear rich music wheresoe'er I look,
But heedless worldlings chide the brawling brook;
And that small lark between me and the sky
Breathes sweetest strains of morning's melody;
Yet by the heedless crowd 'tis only heard
As the small warbling of a common bird
That o'er the plough teams hails the morning sun;
They see no music from such magic won.
Yet I see melody in nature's laws,
Or do I dream?—still wonder bids me pause:
I pause, and hear a voice that speaks aloud:
'Tis not on earth nor in the thundercloud;
The many look for sound—'tis silence speaks,
And song like sunshine from her rapture breaks.
I hear it in my bosom ever near;
'Tis in these winds, and they are everywhere.
It casts around my vision magic spells
And makes earth heaven where poor fancy dwells.
I read its language, and its speech is joy;
So, without teaching when a lonely boy,
Each weed to me did happy tidings bring,
And laughing daisies wrote the name of spring,
And God's own language unto nature given
Seemed universal as the light of heaven
And common as the grass upon the plain,
That all may read and meet with joy again,
Save the unheeding heart that, like the tomb,
Shuts joy in darkness and forbids its bloom.

PASTORAL POESY

TRUE poesy is not in words,
  But images that thoughts express,
By which the simplest hearts are stirred
  To elevated happiness.

Mere books would be but useless things
  Where none had taste or mind to read,
Like unknown lands where beauty springs
  And none are there to heed.

But poesy is a language meet,
  And fields are every one's employ;
The wild flower 'neath the shepherd's feet
  Looks up and gives him joy;

A language that is ever green,
  That feelings unto all impart,
As hawthorn blossoms, soon as seen,
  Give May to every heart.

An image to the mind is brought,
  Where happiness enjoys
An easy thoughtlessness of thought
  And meets excess of joys.

And such is poesy; its power
  May varied lights employ,
Yet to all minds it gives the dower
  Of self-creating joy.

And whether it be hill or moor,
  I feel where'er I go
A silence that discourses more
  That any tongue can do.

Unruffled quietness hath made
  A peace in every place,

And woods are resting in their shade
  Of social loneliness.

The storm, from which the shepherd turns
  To pull his beaver down,
While he upon the heath sojourns,
  Which autumn pleaches brown,

Is music, ay, and more indeed
  To those of musing mind
Who through the yellow woods proceed
  And listen to the wind.

The poet in his fitful glee
  And fancy's many moods
Meets it as some strange melody,
  A poem of the woods,

And now a harp that flings around
  The music of the wind;
The poet often hears the sound
  When beauty fills the mind.

So would I my own mind employ,
  And my own heart impress,
That poesy's self's a dwelling joy
  Of humble quietness.

FAIRY THINGS

GREY lichens, mid thy hills of creeping thyme,
Grow like to fairy forests hung with rime;
And fairy money-pots are often found
That spring like little mushrooms out of ground,
Some shaped like cups and some in slender trim
Wineglasses like, that to the very rim
Are filled with little mystic shining seed;
We thought our fortunes promising indeed,
Expecting by and by ere night to find
Money ploughed up of more substantial kind.

Acres of little yellow weeds,
The wheat-field's constant blooms,
That ripen into prickly seeds
For fairy curry-combs,
To comb and clean the little things
That draw their nightly wain;
And so they scrub the beetle's wings
Till he can fly again.

And flannel felt for the beds of the queen
From the soft inside of the shell of the bean,
Where the gipsies down in the lonely dells
Had littered and left the plundered shells.

TO PATTY

FAIR was thy bloom when first I met
    Thy summer's maiden-blossom;
And thou art fair and lovely yet
    And dearer to my bosom.
Oh, thou wert once a wilding flower,
    All garden flowers excelling,
And still I bless the happy hour
    That led me to thy dwelling.

Though nursed by field and brook and wood,
    And wild in every feature,
Spring ne'er unsealed a fairer bud,
    Nor formed a blossom sweeter.
Of all the flowers the spring hath met,
    And it has met with many,
Thou art to me the fairest yet
    And loveliest of any.

Though ripening summers round thee bring
    Buds to thy swelling bosom,
That wait the cheering smiles of spring

To ripen into blossom;
These buds shall added blessings be
　　To make our loves sincerer:
For as their flowers resemble thee,
　　They'll make thy memory dearer.

And though thy bloom shall pass away,
　　By winter overtaken,
Thoughts of the past will charms display,
　　And many joys awaken.
When time shall every sweet remove,
　　And blight thee on my bosom—
Let beauty fade—to me, my love,
　　Thou'lt ne'er be out of blossom!

BALLAD

THE spring returns, the pewit screams
　　Loud welcomes to the dawning,
Though harsh and ill as now it seems,
　　'Twas music last May morning.
The grass so green, the daisy gay
　　Wakes no joy in my bosom,
Although the garland, last May-day,
　　Wore not a finer blossom.

For by this bridge my Mary sat,
　　And praised the screaming plover
As first to hail the day when I
　　Confessed myself her lover;
And at that moment stooping down
　　I plucked a daisy blossom,
Which smilingly she called her own
　　May-garland for her bosom.

And in her breast she hid it there
　　As true love's happy omen;
Gold had not claimed a safer care—

I thought Love's name was Woman.
I claimed a kiss, she laughed away,
    I sweetly sold the blossom,
I thought myself a king that day,
    My throne was Beauty's bosom.

I little thought an evil hour
    Was bringing clouds around me,
And, least of all, that little flower
    Would turn a thorn to wound me.
She showed me, after many days,
    Though withered, how she prized it;
Then she inclined to wealthy praise,
    And my poor love—despised it.

Aloud the whirring pewit screams,
    The daisy blooms as gaily;
But where is Mary?—Absence seems
    To ask that question daily.
Nowhere on earth where joy can be,
    To glad me with her pleasure;
Another name she owns—to me
    She is as stolen treasure.

When lovers part, the longest mile
    Leaves hope of some returning;
Though mine's close by, no hopes the while
    Within my heart are burning.
One hour would bring me to her door;
    Yet sad and lonely hearted,
If seas between us both should roar,
    We were not farther parted.

Though I could reach her with my hand
    Ere sun the earth goes under,
Her heart from mine—the sky and land
    Are not more far asunder.
The wind and clouds, now here, now there,
    Hold not such strange dominion
As woman's cold perverted will
    And soon estranged opinion.

NATURE'S HYMN TO THE DEITY

ALL nature owns with one accord
The great and universal Lord:
The sun proclaims him through the day,
The moon when daylight drops away,
The very darkness smiles to wear
The stars that show us God is there,
On moonlight seas soft gleams the sky,
And, 'God is with us,' waves reply.

Winds breathe from God's abode, 'We come,'
Storms louder own God is their home,
And thunder yet with louder call,
Sounds, 'God is mightiest over all';
Till earth, right loath the proof to miss,
Echoes triumphantly, 'He is,'
And air and ocean makes reply,
'God reigns on earth, in air and sky.'

All nature owns with one accord
The great and universal Lord:
Insect and bird and tree and flower—
The witnesses of every hour—
Are pregnant with his prophecy
And, 'God is with us,' all reply.
The first link in the mighty plan
Is still—and all upbraideth man.

SONNETS

LORD BYRON

A SPLENDID sun hath set!—when shall our eyes
Behold a morn so beautiful arise
As that which gave his mighty genius birth,
And all eclipsed the lesser lights on earth!
His first young burst of twilight did declare
Beyond that haze a sun was rising there;
As when the morn, to usher in the day,
Speeds from the east in sober garb of grey
At first, till warming into wild delight,
She casts her mantle off and shines in light.
The labour of small minds an age may dream,
And be but shadows on time's running stream;
While genius, in an hour, makes what shall be,
The next, a portion of eternity.

MEMORY

I WOULD not that my being all should die
   And pass away with every common lot;
I would not that my humble dust should lie
   In quite a strange and unfrequented spot,
   By all unheeded and by all forgot,
With nothing save the heedless winds to sigh,
   And nothing but the dewy morn to weep
About my grave, far hid from the world's eye:
I fain would have some friend to wander nigh,
   And find a path to where my ashes sleep—
Not the cold heart that merely passes by
   To read who lies beneath, but such as keep
Past memories warm with deeds of other years,
And pay to Friendship some few friendly tears.

DEATH OF BEAUTY

Now thou art gone, the fairy rose is fled,
That erst gay Fancy's garden did adorn.
Thine was the dew on which her folly fed,
The sun by which she glittered in the morn.
Now thou art gone, her pride is withered;
In dress of common weeds she doth array,
And vanity neglects her in its play.
Thou wert the very index of her praise,
Her borrowed bloom was kindled from thy rays:
Like dancing insects that the sun allures,
She little heeded it was gained from thee.
Vain joys! what are they now their sun's away?
What but poor shadows that blank night obscures,
As the grave hides what would dishonoured be?

FAME

WHAT's future fame? a melody loud playing
  In crowds where one is wanting, whose esteeming
Would love to hear it best; a sun displaying
  A solitary glory, whose bright beaming,
Smiling on withered flowers and leaves decaying,
  Lingers behind its world; a crown vain gleaming
Around a shade whose substance death hath banished;
  A living dream o'er which hope once was dreaming;
A busy echo on each lip delaying,
  When he that woke it into life is vanished;
A picture that from all hearts praise is stealing;
  A statue towering over glory's game,
That cannot feel, while he that was all feeling
  Is past, and gone, and nothing but a name.

TO CHARLES LAMB

FRIEND Lamb, thou choosest well, to love the lore
   Of our old bygone bards, whose racy page
Rich mellowing time makes sweeter than before
The blossom left; for the long-garnered store
   Of fruitage is right luscious in its age,
Although to fashion's taste austere.   What more
   Can be expected from the popular rage
For tinsel gauds that are to gold preferred?
   Me much it grieved; for I did long presage
Vain fashion's foils had every heart deterred
   From the warm homely phrase of other days,
Until thy muse's ancient voice I heard.
And now right fain, yet fearing, honest bard,
   I pause to greet thee with so poor a praise.

ENGLAND, 1830

THESE vague allusions to a country's wrongs,
   Where one says 'Ay' and others answer 'No'
In contradiction from a thousand tongues,
   Till like to prison-cells her freedoms grow
Becobwebbed with these oft-repeated songs
   Of peace and plenty in the midst of woe—
And is it thus they mock her year by year,
   Telling poor truth unto her face she lies,
Declaiming of her wealth with gibe severe,
   So long as taxes drain their wished supplies?
And will these jailers rivet every chain
   Anew, yet loudest in their mockery be,
To damn her into madness with disdain,
   Forging new bonds and bidding her be free?

THE SHEPHERD'S TREE

HUGE elm, with rifted trunk all notched and scarred,
  Like to a warrior's destiny, I love
To stretch me often on thy shadowed sward,
  And hear the laugh of summer leaves above;
Or on thy buttressed roots to sit, and lean
  In careless attitude, and there reflect
On times and deeds and darings that have been—
  Old castaways, now swallowed in neglect,
While thou art towering in thy strength of heart,
  Stirring the soul to vain imaginings
In which life's sordid being hath no part.
  The wind of that eternal ditty sings
Humming of future things, that burn the mind
To leave some fragment of itself behind.

SWORDY WELL

I'VE loved thee, Swordy Well, and love thee still.
Long was I with thee, tending sheep and cow,
In boyhood ramping up each steepy hill
To play at 'roly-poly' down; and now,
A man, I trifle on thee, cares to kill,
Haunting thy mossy steeps to botanize
And hunt the orchis tribes, where nature's skill
Doth, like my thoughts, run into phantasies,
Spider and bee all mimicking at will,
Displaying powers that fool the proudly wise,
Showing the wonders of great nature's plan
In trifles insignificant and small,
Puzzling the power of that great trifle, man,
Who finds no reason to be proud at all.

FARE-THEE-WELL

HERE's a sad good-bye for thee, my love,
  To friends and foes a smile:
I leave but one regret behind,
  That's left with thee the while,
But hopes that fortune is our friend
  Already pays the toil.

Force bids me go, your friends to please.
  Would they were not so high!
But be my lot on land or seas,
  It matters not where by,
For I shall keep a thought for thee,
  In my heart's core to lie.

Winter shall lose its frost and snow,
  The spring its blossomed thorn,
The summer all its bloom forgo,
  The autumn hound and horn
Ere I will lose that thought of thee,
  Or ever prove forsworn.

The dove shall change a hawk in kind,
  The cuckoo change its tune,
The nightingale at Christmas sing,
  The fieldfare come in June—
Ere I do change my love for thee
  These things shall change as soon.

So keep your heart at ease, my love,
  Nor waste a joy for me:
I'll ne'er prove false to thee, my love,
  Till fish drown in the sea,
And birds forget to fly, my love,
  And then I'll think of thee.

The red-cock's wing may turn to grey,
　　The crow's to silver white,
The night itself may be for day,
　　And sunshine wake at night:
Till then—and then I'll prove more true
　　Than nature, life, and light.

Though you may break your fondest vow,
　　And take your heart from me,
And though my heart should break to hear
　　What I may never see,
Yet never canst thou break the link
　　That binds my love to thee.

So fare-thee-well, my own true love;
　　No vow from thee I crave,
But thee I never will forgo,
　　Till no spark of life I have,
Nor will I ever thee forget
　　Till we both lie in the grave.

LOVE'S RIDDLE

'UNRIDDLE this riddle, my own Jenny love,
　　Unriddle this riddle for me,
And if ye unriddle the riddle aright,
　　A kiss your prize shall be,
And if ye riddle the riddle all wrong,
　　Ye'll treble the debt to me:

'I'll give thee an apple without any core;
I'll give thee a cherry where stones never be;
I'll give thee a palace without any door,
And thou shall unlock it without any key;
I'll give thee a fortune that kings cannot give,
　　Nor any one take from thee.'

'How can there be apples without any core?
How can there be cherries where stone never be?
How can there be houses without any door?
Or doors I may open without any key?
How canst thou give fortunes that kings cannot give,
    When thou art no richer than me?'

'My head is the apple without any core;
In cherries in blossom no stones ever be;
My mind is love's palace without any door,
Which thou canst unlock, love, without any key.
My heart is the wealth, love, that kings cannot give,
    Nor any one take it from thee.

'So there are love's riddles, my own Jenny love,
    Ye cannot unriddle to me,
And for one kiss you've so easily lost
    I'll make ye give seven to me.
To kiss thee is sweet, but 'tis sweeter by far
    To be kissed, my dear Jenny, by thee.

'Come pay me the forfeit, my own Jenny love;
    Thy kisses and cheeks are akin,
And for thy three sweet ones I'll give thee a score
    On thy cheeks, and thy lips, and thy chin.'
She laughed while he gave them, as much as to say,
    ''Twere better to lose than to win.'

THE BANKS OF IVORY

'Twas on the banks of Ivory, 'neath the hawthorn-scented shade,
Early one summer's morning, I met a lovely maid;
Her hair hung o'er her shoulders broad, her eyes like suns did
    shine,
And on the banks of Ivory, oh, I wished the maid was mine.
Her face it wore the beauty of heaven's own broken mould;
The world's first charm seemed living still; her curls like hanks
    of gold

Hung waving, and her eyes glittered timid as the dew,
When by the banks of Ivory I swore I loved her true.

'Kind sir,' she said, 'forsake me, while it is no pain to go,
For often after kissing and such wooing there comes woe;
And woman's heart is feeble; oh, I wish it were a stone;
So by the banks of Ivory I'd rather walk alone.

'For learned seems your gallant speech, and noble is your
　　trim,
And thus to court an humble maid is just to please your whim;
So go and seek some lady fair, as high in pedigree,
Nor stoop so low by Ivory to flatter one like me.'

'In sooth, fair maid, you mock at me, for truth ne'er harboured
　　ill;
I will not wrong your purity; to love is all my will:
My hall looks over yonder groves; its lady you shall be,
For on the banks of Ivory I'm glad I met with thee.'

He put his hands unto his lips, and whistled loud and shrill,
And thirty-six well-armed men came at their master's will.
Said he, 'I've flattered maids full long, but now the time is past,
And the bonny halls of Ivory a lady own at last.

'My steed's back ne'er was gracèd for a lady's seat before;
Fear not his speed; I'll guard thee, love, till we ride o'er the
　　moor,
To seek the priest, and wed, and love until the day we die.'
So she that was but poor before is Lady Ivory.

THE MAID OF OCRAM: *or*, LORD GREGORY

GAY was the Maid of Ocram
  As lady e'er might be
Ere she did venture past a maid
  To love Lord Gregory.
Fair was the Maid of Ocram
  And shining like the sun
Ere her bower key was turned on two
  Where bride-bed lay for none.

And late at night she sought her love—
  The snow slept on her skin—
'Get up,' she cried, 'thou false young man,
  And let thy true love in.'
And fain would he have loosed the key
  All for his true love's sake,
But Lord Gregory then was fast asleep,
  His mother wide awake.

And up she threw the window sash,
  And out her head put she:
'And who is that which knocks so late
  And taunts so loud to me?'
'It is the Maid of Ocram,
  Your own heart's next akin;
For so you've sworn, Lord Gregory,
  To come and let me in.

'Oh, pause not thus, you know me well,
  Haste down my way to win.
The wind disturbs my yellow locks,
  The snow sleeps on my skin.'
'If you be the Maid of Ocram,
  As much I doubt you be,
Then tell me of three tokens
  That passed with you and me.'

'Oh, talk not now of tokens
　　Which you do wish to break;
Chilled are those lips you've kissed so warm,
　　And all too numbed to speak.
You know when in my father's bower
　　You left your cloak for mine,
Though yours was naught but silver twist
　　And mine the golden twine.'

'If you're the lass of Ocram,
　　As I take you not to be,
The second token you must tell
　　Which passed with you and me.'
'Oh, know you not, oh, know you not
　　'Twas in my father's park,
You led me out a mile too far
　　And courted in the dark?

'When you did change your ring for mine
　　My yielding heart to win,
Though mine was of the beaten gold,
　　Yours but of burnished tin,
Though mine was all true love without,
　　Yours but false love within?

'Oh, ask me no more tokens
　　For fast the snow doth fall.
'Tis sad to strive and speak in vain,
　　You mean to break them all.'
'If you are the Maid of Ocram,
　　As I take you not to be,
You must mention the third token
　　That passed with you and me.'

''Twas when you stole my maidenhead;
　　That grieves me worst of all.'
'Begone, you lying creature, then
　　This instant from my hall,

Or you and your vile baby
　　Shall in the deep sea fall;
For I have none on earth as yet
　　That may me father call.'

'Oh, must none close my dying feet,
　　And must none close my hands,
And may none bind my yellow locks
　　As death for all demands?
You need not use no force at all,
　　Your hard heart breaks the vow;
You've had your wish against my will
　　And you shall have it now.

'And must none close my dying feet,
　　And must none close my hands,
And will none do the last kind deeds
　　That death for all demands?'
'Your sister, she may close your feet,
　　Your brother close your hands,
Your mother, she may wrap your waist
　　In death's fit wedding-bands;
Your father, he may tie your locks
　　And lay you in the sands.'

'My sister, she will weep in vain,
　　My brother ride and run,
My mother, she will break her heart;
　　And ere the rising sun
My father will be looking out—
　　But find me they will none.
I go to lay my woes to rest,
　　None shall know where I'm gone.
God must be friend and father both,
　　Lord Gregory will be none.'

Lord Gregory started up from sleep
　　And thought he heard a voice
That screamed full dreadful in his ear,
　　And once and twice and thrice.

Lord Gregory to his mother called:
  'O mother dear,' said he,
'I 've dreamt the Maid of Ocram
  Was floating on the sea.'

'Lie still, my son,' the mother said,
  ''Tis but a little space,
And half an hour has scarcely passed
  Since she did pass this place.'
'O cruel, cruel mother,
  When she did pass so nigh
How could you let me sleep so sound
  Or let her wander by?
Now if she's lost my heart must break—
  I'll seek her till I die.'

He sought her east, he sought her west,
  He sought through park and plain;
He sought her where she might have been
  But found her not again.
'I cannot curse thee, mother,
  Though thine's the blame,' said he,
'I cannot curse thee, mother,
  Though thou'st done worse to me.
Yet do I curse thy pride that aye
  So tauntingly aspires;
For my love was a gay knight's heir,
  And my father wed a squire's.

'And I will sell my park and hall;
  And if ye wed again
Ye shall not wed for titles twice
  That made ye once so vain.
So if ye will wed, wed for love,
  As I was fain to do;
Ye've gi'n to me a broken heart,
  And I'll give naught to you.

'Your pride has wronged your own heart's blood;
   For she was mine by grace,
And now my lady-love is gone
   None else shall take her place.
I'll sell my park and sell my hall
   And sink my titles too;
Your pride's done wrong enough as now
   To leave it more to do.

'She owneth none that owned them all
   And would have graced them well;
None else shall take the right she missed
   Nor in my bosom dwell.'
And then he took and burnt his will
   Before his mother's face,
And tore his patents all in two,
   While tears fell down apace—
But in his mother's haughty look
   Ye naught but frowns might trace.

And then he sat him down to grieve,
   But could not sit for pain;
And then he laid him on the bed
   And ne'er got up again.

A FINE OLD BALLAD

FARE you well, my own true love,
And fare you well for a while;
And I will be sure to return back again
If I go ten thousand miles, my dear,
   If I go ten thousand miles.

Ten thousand mile's a long long way,
When from me you are gone;
You'll leave me here to lament and sigh
But never shall hear me moan, my dear,
   But never shall hear me moan.

To hear you moan I cannot bear,
Or cure you of your disease;
I shall be sure to return back again
When all your friends are pleased, my dear,
   When all your friends are pleased.

If my friends should never be pleased—
They're grown so lofty and high—
I will never prove false to the girl I love
Till the stars they fall from the sky, my love,
   Till the stars they fall from the sky.

Oh, if the stars never fall from the sky
Nor the rocks never melt in the sun,
I never will prove false to the girl I love
Till all these things are done, my dear,
   Till all these things are done.

Don't you see yon little turtle-dove
That sits on yonder tree,
Making a moan for the loss of her love
As I will do for thee, my dear,
   As I will do for thee?

The blackest crow that ever flies
Shall change his colour white,
And if ever I prove false to thee, my love,
The day shall turn to night, my dear,
   The day shall turn to night.

But if these things ne'er come to pass
So long as we both do live,
I ne'er will prove false, my love, to thee
Till we're both laid in one grave, my dear,
   Till we're both laid in one grave.

POEMS WRITTEN IN THE MANNER OF THE OLDER POETS

TO JOHN MILTON [1]

'From his honoured friend, William Davenant'

POET of mighty power, I fain
Would court the muse that honoured thee,
And, like Elisha's spirit, gain
    A part of thy intensity;
And share the mantle which she flung
Around thee, when thy lyre was strung.

Though faction's scorn at first did shun
With coldness thy inspirèd song,
Though clouds of malice passed thy sun,
    They could not hide it long;
Its brightness soon exhaled away
Dank night, and gained eternal day.

The critics' wrath did darkly frown
Upon thy muse's mighty lay;
But blasts that break the blossom down
    Do only stir the bay;
And thine shall flourish, green and long,
With the eternity of song.

Thy genius saw, in quiet mood,
Gilt fashion's follies pass thee by,
And, like the monarch of the wood,
    Towered o'er it to the sky,
Where thou couldst sing of other spheres,
And feel the fame of future years,

Though bitter sneers and stinging scorns
Did throng the muse's dangerous way,
Thy powers were past such little thorns,
    They gave thee no dismay;

[1] Published in the *Sheffield Iris*, 16 May 1826.

The scoffer's insult passed thee by,
Thou smild'st and mad'st him no reply.

Envy will gnaw its heart away
To see thy genius gather root;
And as its flowers their sweets display
    Scorn's malice shall be mute;
Hornets that summer warmed to fly,
Shall at the death of summer die.

Though friendly praise hath but its hour,
And little praise with thee hath been;
The bay may lose its summer flower,
    But still its leaves are green;
And thine, whose buds are on the shoot,
Shall only fade to change to fruit.

Fame lives not in the breath of words,
In public praises' hue and cry;
The music of these summer birds
    Is silent in a winter sky,
When thine shall live and flourish on,
O'er wrecks where crowds of fames are gone.

The ivy shuns the city wall,
When busy clamorous crowds intrude,
And climbs the desolated hall
    In silent solitude;
The time-worn arch, the fallen dome,
Are roots for its eternal home.

The bard his glory ne'er receives
Where summer's common flowers are seen,
But winter finds it when she leaves
    The laurel only green;
And time from that eternal tree
Shall weave a wreath to honour thee;

A sunny wreath for poets meet,
From Helicon's immortal soil,
Where sacred time with pilgrim feet
    Walks forth to worship, not to spoil,

A wreath which fame creates and bears,
And deathless genius only heirs.

Naught but thy ashes shall expire;
Thy genius, at thy obsequies,
Shall kindle up its living fire
    And light the muse's skies;
Ay, it shall rise, and shine, and be
A sun in song's posterity.

THE GIPSY'S SONG [1]

THE gipsy's life is a merry life,
    And ranting boys we be;
We pay to none or rent or tax,
    And live untithed and free.
None care for us, for none care we,
    And where we list we roam,
And merry boys we gipsies be,
    Though the wild woods are our home.

And come what will brings no dismay;
    Our minds are ne'er perplext;
For if to-day's a swaly day,
    We meet with luck the next.
And thus we sing and kiss our mates,
    While our chorus still shall be—
Bad luck to tyrant magistrates,
    And the gipsies' camp still free.

To mend old pans and bottom chairs
    Around the towns we tramp,
Then a day or two our purse repairs,
    And plenty fills our camp;
And our song we sing, and our fiddles sound
    Their catgut harmony,
While echo fills the woods around
    With gipsy liberty.

[1] Fathered on an unknown, Tom Davies; published in the *European Magazine*, 1825.

The green grass is our softest bed,
  The sun our clock we call,
The nightly sky hangs overhead,
  Our curtains, house, and all.
Tho' houseless while the wild winds blow,
  Our joys are uncontrolled;
We barefoot dance through winter's snow,
  When others die with cold.

Our maidens they are fond and free,
  And lasting are their charms;
Brown as the berry on the tree,
  No sun their beauty harms:
Their beauties are no garden blooms,
  That fade before they flower;
Unsheltered where the tempest comes,
  They smile in sun and shower.

And they are wild as the woodland hare,
  That feeds on the evening lea;
And what care we for ladies fair,
  Since ours are fond and free?
False hearts hide in a lily skin,
  But ours are coarse and fond;
No parson's fetters link us in—
  Our love's a stronger bond.

Tho' wild woods are our house and home,
  'Tis a home of liberty;
Free as the summer clouds we roam,
  And merry boys we be.
We dance and sing the year along,
  And loud our fiddles play;
And no day goes without its song,
  While every month is May.

The hare that haunts the fallow ground,
  And round the common feeds;
The fox that tracks the woodland bounds,
  And in the thicket breeds;

These are the neighbours where we dwell,
    And all the guests we see,
That share and love the quiet well
    Of gipsy liberty.

The elements are grown our friends,
    And leave our huts alone;
The thunderbolt, that shakes and rends
    The cotter's house of stone,
Flies harmless by the blanket roof,
    Where the winds may burst and blow,
For our camps, tho' thin, are tempest-proof,
    We reck not rain and snow.

May the lot we've met our lives befall,
    And nothing worse attend;
So here's success to gipsies all,
    And every gipsy's friend.
And while the ass that bears our camp
    Can find a common free,
Around old England's heaths we'll tramp
    In gipsy liberty.

THE NIGHTINGALE'S NEST

UP this green woodland-ride let's softly rove,
And list the nightingale—she dwells just here.
Hush! let the wood-gate softly clap, for fear
The noise might drive her from her home of love;
For here I've heard her many a merry year—
At morn, at eve, nay, all the livelong day,
As though she lived on song.   This very spot,
Just where that old man's beard all wildly trails
Rude arbours o'er the road and stops the way—
And where that child its bluebell flowers hath got,
Laughing and creeping through the mossy rails—
There have I hunted like a very boy,
Creeping on hands and knees through matted thorn
To find her nest and see her feed her young.
And vainly did I many hours employ:
All seemed as hidden as a thought unborn.
And where those crimping fern-leaves ramp among
The hazel's under-boughs, I've nestled down
And watched her while she sung; and her renown
Hath made me marvel that so famed a bird
Should have no better dress than russet brown.
Her wings would tremble in her ecstasy,
And feathers stand on end, as 'twere with joy,
And mouth wide open to release her heart
Of its out-sobbing songs.   The happiest part
Of summer's fame she shared, for so to me
Did happy fancies shapen her employ;
But if I touched a bush or scarcely stirred,
All in a moment stopt.   I watched in vain:
The timid bird had left the hazel bush,
And at a distance hid to sing again.
Lost in a wilderness of listening leaves,
Rich ecstasy would pour its luscious strain,

[1] These poems about birds have been grouped together because most of them belong to a series of rough drafts written in a separate notebook, 1825–30.

Till envy spurred the emulating thrush
To start less wild and scarce inferior songs;
For while of half the year care him bereaves,
To damp the ardour of his speckled breast,
The nightingale to summer's life belongs,
And naked trees and winter's nipping wrongs
Are strangers to her music and her rest.
Her joys are evergreen, her world is wide—
Hark! there she is as usual—let's be hush—
For in this blackthorn-clump, if rightly guessed,
Her curious house is hidden. Part aside
These hazel branches in a gentle way
And stoop right cautious 'neath the rustling boughs,
For we will have another search to-day
And hunt this fern-strewn thorn-clump round and round;
And where this reeded wood-grass idly bows,
We'll wade right through, it is a likely nook:
In such like spots and often on the ground,
They'll build, where rude boys never think to look.
Ay, as I live! her secret nest is here,
Upon this whitethorn stump! I've searched about
For hours in vain. There! put that bramble by—
Nay, trample on its branches and get near.
How subtle is the bird! she started out,
And raised a plaintive note of danger nigh,
Ere we were past the brambles; and now, near
Her nest, she sudden stops—as choking fear
That might betray her home. So even now
We'll leave it as we found it: safety's guard
Of pathless solitudes shall keep it still.
See there! she's sitting on the old oak bough,
Mute in her fears; our presence doth retard
Her joys, and doubt turns every rapture chill.
Sing on, sweet bird! may no worse hap befall
Thy visions than the fear that now deceives.
We will not plunder music of its dower,
Nor turn this spot of happiness to thrall;
For melody seems hid in every flower
That blossoms near thy home.   These harebells all

Seem bowing with the beautiful in song;
And gaping cuckoo,[3] with its spotted leaves,
Seems blushing with the singing it has heard.
How curious is the nest! no other bird
Uses such loose materials, or weaves
Its dwelling in such spots: dead oaken leaves
Are placed without and velvet moss within,
And little scraps of grass, and—scant and spare,
Of what seem scarce materials—down and hair;
For from men's haunts she nothing seems to win.
Yet nature is the builder, and contrives
Homes for her children's comfort even here,
Where solitude's disciples spend their lives
Unseen, save when a wanderer passes near
Who loves such pleasant places.   Deep adown
The nest is made, a hermit's mossy cell.

Snug lie her curious eggs in number five,
Of deadened green, or rather olive-brown;
And the old prickly thorn-bush guards them well.
So here we'll leave them, still unknown to wrong,
As the old woodland's legacy of song.

THE BLACKCAP

THE blackcap is a singing bird,
   A nightingale in melody;
Last March in Open Wood I heard
   One sing that quite astonished me;
I took it for the nightingale—
   It jug-jugged just the same as he—
So creeping through the mossy rail
   I in the thicket got to see:

When one small bird of saddened green,
   Black head, and breast of ashy grey,
In ivied oak tree scarcely seen,
   Stopt all at once and flew away;
And since, in hedgerow's dotterel trees,

I've oft this tiny minstrel met,
Where ivy flapping to the breeze
   Bear ring-marked berries black as jet;
But whether they find food in these
   I've never seen or known as yet.

THE MISSEL-THRUSH'S NEST

In early March, before the lark
Dare start, beside the huge oak tree,
Close fixed agen the powdered bark,
The mavis' nest I often see;
And mark, as wont, the bits of wool
Hang round about its early bed;
She lays six eggs in colours dull,
Blotched thick with spots of burning red.

THE REDCAP

The redcap is a painted bird
   And beautiful its feathers are;
In early spring its voice is heard
   While searching thistles brown and bare;
It makes a nest of mosses grey
   And lines it round with thistle-down;
Five small pale spotted eggs they lay
   In places never far from town.

I've seen them build on eldern bough
   And tip-top of our russeting,
But never did I see till now
   A bird's nest in a garland hing;
In this old princifeather tree,
   As hiding from the sudden showers,
The redcap's nest delighteth me,
   Hid in a bunch of lilac flowers.

THE LARK'S NEST

FROM yon black clump of wheat that grows
   More rank and higher than the rest,
A lark—I marked her as she rose—
   At early morning left her nest.
Her eggs were four of dusky hue,
   Blotched brown as is the very ground,
With tinges of a purply hue
   The larger ends encircling round.

Behind a clod how snug the nest
   Is in a horse's footing fixed!
Of twitch and stubbles roughly dressed,
   With roots and horsehair intermixed.
The wheat surrounds it like a bower,
   And like to thatch each bowing blade
Throws off the frequent falling shower
   —And here's an egg this morning laid!

THE FLIGHT OF BIRDS

THE crow goes flopping on from wood to wood,
The wild duck wherries to the distant flood,
The starnels hurry o'er in merry crowds,
And overhead whew by like hasty clouds;
The wild duck from the meadow-water plies
And dashes up the water as he flies;
The pigeon suthers by on rapid wing,
The lark mounts upward at the call of spring.
In easy flights above the hurricane
With doubled neck high sails the noisy crane.
Whizz goes the pewit o'er the ploughman's team,
With many a whew and whirl and sudden scream;
And lightly fluttering to the tree just by,
In chattering journeys whirls the noisy pie;
From bush to bush slow swees the screaming jay,
With one harsh note of pleasure all the day.

THE FERN-OWL'S NEST

THE weary woodman, rocking home beneath
His tightly banded faggot, wonders oft,
While crossing over the furze-crowded heath,
To hear the fern-owl's cry, that whews aloft
In circling whirls, and often by his head
Whizzes as quick as thought and ill at rest,
As through the rustling ling with heavy tread
He goes, nor heeds he tramples near its nest,
That underneath the furze or squatting thorn
Lies hidden on the ground; and teasing round
That lonely spot, she wakes her jarring noise
To the unheeding waste, till mottled morn
Fills the red east with daylight's coming sound
And the heath's echoes mock the herding boys.

THE REED-BIRD

A LITTLE slender bird of reddish brown
With frequent haste pops in and out the reeds,
And on the river frequent flutters down
As if for food; and so securely feeds
Her little brood, that in their ambush needs
Her frequent journeys, hid in thickest shade
Where danger never finds a path to throw
A fear on comfort's nest, securely made
In woods of reeds round which the waters flow;
Save by a jilted stone that boys will throw,
Or passing rustle of the fisher's boat.
It is the reed-bird, prized for pleasant note.
Ah, happy songster, man can seldom share
A spot so hidden from the haunts of care.

THE WREN

WHY is the cuckoo's melody preferred,
  And nightingale's rich songs so madly praised
In poets' rhymes? Is there no other bird
  Of nature's minstrelsy, that oft hath raised
One's heart to ecstasy and mirth as well?
  I judge not how another's taste is caught,
With mine are other birds that bear the bell,
  Whose song hath crowds of happy memories brought:
Such the wood robin, singing in the dell,
  And little wren, that many a time hath sought
Shelter from showers, in huts where I did dwell
  In early spring, the tenant of the plain,
Tenting my sheep; and still they come to tell
  The happy stories of the past again.

THE THRUSH'S NEST

WITHIN a thick and spreading hawthorn bush
  That overhung a mole-hill large and round,
I heard from morn to morn a merry thrush
  Sing hymns to sunrise, while I drank the sound
With joy; and, often an intruding guest,
  I watched her secret toils from day to day—
How true she warped the moss to form a nest,
  And modelled it within with wood and clay;
And by and by, like heath-bells gilt with dew,
  There lay her shining eggs, as bright as flowers,
Ink-spotted over shells of greeny blue;
  And there I witnessed, in the sunny hours,
A brood of nature's minstrels chirp and fly,
Glad as that sunshine and the laughing sky.

POEMS WRITTEN AT NORTHBOROUGH
1832–5

REMEMBRANCES

Summer's pleasures they are gone like to visions every one,
And the cloudy days of autumn and of winter cometh on.
I tried to call them back, but unbidden they are gone
Far away from heart and eye and for ever far away.
Dear heart, and can it be that such raptures meet decay?
I thought them all eternal when by Langley Bush I lay,
I thought them joys eternal when I used to shout and play
On its bank at 'clink and bandy,' 'chock' and 'taw' and 'duck-
    ing-stone,'
Where silence sitteth now on the wild heath as her own
Like a ruin of the past all alone.

When I used to lie and sing by old Eastwell's boiling spring,
When I used to tie the willow boughs together for a swing,
And fish with crooked pins and thread and never catch a thing,
With heart just like a feather, now as heavy as a stone;
When beneath old Lea Close Oak I the bottom branches broke
To make our harvest cart like so many working folk,
And then to cut a straw at the brook to have a soak.
Oh, I never dreamed of parting or that trouble had a sting,
Or that pleasures like a flock of birds would ever take to wing,
Leaving nothing but a little naked spring.

When jumping time away on old Crossberry Way,
And eating haws like sugarplums ere they had lost the may,
And skipping like a leveret before the peep of day
On the roly-poly up and downs of pleasant Swordy Well,
When in Round Oak's narrow lane as the south got black again
We sought the hollow ash that was shelter from the rain,
With our pockets full of peas we had stolen from the grain;
How delicious was the dinner-time on such a showery day!
Oh, words are poor receipts for what time hath stole away,
The ancient pulpit trees and the play.

When for school o'er Little Field with its brook and wooden brig,
Where I swaggered like a man though I was not half so big,
While I held my little plough though 'twas but a willow twig,
And drove my team along made of nothing but a name,
'Gee hep' and 'hoit' and 'woi'—oh, I never call to mind
These pleasant names of places but I leave a sigh behind,
While I see the little mouldiwarps hang sweeing to the wind
On the only aged willow that in all the field remains,
And nature hides her face while they're sweeing in their chains
And in a silent murmuring complains.

Here was commons for their hills, where they seek for freedom
    still,
Though every common's gone and though traps are set to kill
The little homeless miners—oh, it turns my bosom chill
When I think of old Sneap Green, Puddock's Nook and Hilly
    Snow,
Where bramble bushes grew and the daisy gemmed in dew
And the hills of silken grass like to cushions to the view,
Where we threw the pismire crumbs when we'd nothing else to
    do,
All levelled like a desert by the never-weary plough,
All vanished like the sun where that cloud is passing now
And settled here for ever on its brow.

Oh, I never thought that joys would run away from boys,
Or that boys would change their minds and forsake such summer
    joys;
But alack, I never dreamed that the world had other toys
To petrify first feeling like the fable into stone,
Till I found the pleasure past and a winter come at last,
Then the fields were sudden bare and the sky got overcast,
And boyhood's pleasing haunts, like a blossom in the blast,
Was shrivelled to a withered weed and trampled down and done,
Till vanished was the morning spring and set the summer sun,
And winter fought her battle strife and won.

By Langley Bush I roam, but the bush hath left its hill,
On Cowper Green I stray, 'tis a desert strange and chill,
And the spreading Lea Close Oak, ere decay had penned its will,
To the axe of the spoiler and self-interest fell a prey,
And Crossberry Way and old Round Oak's narrow lane
With its hollow trees like pulpits I shall never see again,
Enclosure like a Buonaparte let not a thing remain,
It levelled every bush and tree and levelled every hill
And hung the moles for traitors—though the brook is running
    still
It runs a naked stream, cold and chill.

Oh, had I known as then joy had left the paths of men,
I had watched her night and day, be sure, and never slept agen,
And when she turned to go, oh, I'd caught her mantle then,
And wooed her like a lover by my lonely side to stay;
Ay, knelt and worshipped on, as love in beauty's bower,
And clung upon her smiles as a bee upon a flower,
And gave her heart my posies, all cropt in a sunny hour,
As keepsakes and pledges all to never fade away;
But love never heeded to treasure up the may,
So it went the common road to decay.

THE SECRET

I LOVED thee, though I told thee not,
    Right earlily and long,
Thou wert my joy in every spot,
    My theme in every song.

And when I saw a stranger face
    Where beauty held the claim,
I gave it like a secret grace
    The being of thy name.

And all the charms of face or voice
    Which I in others see
Are but the recollected choice
    Of what I felt for thee.

SONG'S ETERNITY

WHAT is song's eternity?
   Come and see.
Can it noise and bustle be?
   Come and see.
Praises sung or praises said
   Can it be?
Wait awhile and these are dead—
   Sigh, sigh;
Be they high or lowly bred
   They die.

What is song's eternity?
   Come and see.
Melodies of earth and sky,
   Here they be.
Song once sung to Adam's ears
   Can it be?
Ballads of six thousand years
   Thrive, thrive;
Songs awakened with the spheres
   Alive.

Mighty songs that miss decay,
   What are they?
Crowds and cities pass away
   Like a day.
Books are writ and books are read;
   What are they?
Years will lay them with the dead—
   Sigh, sigh;
Trifles unto nothing wed,
   They die.

Dreamers, list the honey-bee;
   Mark the tree
Where the bluecap, 'tootle tee,'
   Sings a glee

Sung to Adam and to Eve—
　　Here they be.
When floods covered every bough,
　　Noah's ark
Heard that ballad singing now;
　　Hark, hark,

'Tootle tootle tootle tee'—
　　Can it be
Pride and fame must shadows be?
　　Come and see—
Every season owns her own;
　　Bird and bee
Sing creation's music on;
　　Nature's glee
Is in every mood and tone
　　Eternity.

The eternity of song
　　Liveth here;
Nature's universal tongue
　　Singeth here
Songs I've heard and felt and seen
　　Everywhere;
Songs like the grass are evergreen:
　　The giver
Said 'Live and be'—and they have been,
　　For ever.[1]

γε

WITH GARMENTS FLOWING

COME, come, my love, the bush is growing,
　　The linnet sings the tune again
He sung when thou with garments flowing
　　Went talking with me down the lane,
Dreaming of beauty ere I found thee,
　　And musing by the bushes green;
The wind, enamoured, streaming round thee
　　Painted the visions I had seen.

[1] The last stanza appears by itself in another MS.

I guessed thy face without the knowing
   Was beautiful as e'er was seen;
I thought so by thy garments flowing
   And gait as airy as a queen;
Thy shape, thy size, could not deceive me;
   Beauty seemed hid in every limb;
And then thy face, when seen, believe me,
   Made every former fancy dim.

Yes, when thy face in beauty brightened
   The music of a voice divine,
Upon my heart thy sweetness lightened;
   Life, love, that moment, all were thine;
All I imagined musing lonely,
   When dreaming 'neath the greenwood tree,
Seeming to fancy visions only,
   Breathed living when I met with thee.

I wander oft, not to forget thee
   But just to feel those joys again,
When by the hawbush stile I met thee
   And heard thy voice adown the lane
Return me its good-humoured greeting;
   And oh, what music met my ear!
And then thy looks of wonder meeting,
   To see me come and talk so near!

Thy face that held no sort of scorning,
   Thy careless jump to reach the may;
That bush—I saw it many a morning
   And hoped to meet thee many a day;
Till winter came and stripped the bushes,
   The thistle withered on the moors,
Hopes sighed like winds along the rushes—
   I could not meet thee out of doors.

But winter's gone and spring is going
   And by thy own fireside I've been,
And told thee, dear, with garments flowing
   I met thee when the spring was green;

When travellers through snow-deserts rustle,
  Far from the strife of humankind,
How little seems the noise and bustle
  Of places they have left behind!

And on that long-remembered morning
  When first I lost this heart of mine,
Fame, all I'd hoped for, turned to scorning
  And love and hope lived wholly thine;
I told thee, and with rapture glowing
  I heard thee more than once declare,
That down the lane with garments flowing
  Thou with the spring wouldst wander there.

COUNTRY LETTER

DEAR brother Robin, this comes from us all
With our kind love, and could Gip write and all
Though but a dog he'd have his love to spare,
For still he knows, and by your corner chair
The moment he comes in he lies him down
And seems to fancy you are in the town.
This leaves us well in health, thank God for that!
For old acquaintance Sue has kept your hat
Which mother brushes ere she lays it by
And every Sunday goes upstairs to cry.
Jane still is yours till you come back agen
And ne'er so much as dances with the men;
And Ned the woodman every week comes in
And asks about you kindly as our kin;
And he with this and goody Thompson sends
Remembrances with those of all our friends.
Father with us sends love until he hears
And mother she has nothing but her tears,
Yet wishes you like us in health the same
And longs to see a letter with your name,
So, loving brother, don't forget to write.

Old Gip lies on the hearth stone every night;
Mother can't bear to turn him out of doors
And never noises now of dirty floors;
Father will laugh but lets her have her way,
And Gip for kindness get a double pay.
So Robin write and let us quickly see
You don't forget old friends no more than we,
Nor let my mother have so much to blame
To go three journeys ere your letter came.

POEMS WRITTEN AT NORTHBOROUGH
1835–7

BADGER

When midnight comes a host of dogs and men
Go out and track the badger to his den,
And put a sack within the hole, and lie
Till the old grunting badger passes by.
He comes and hears—they let the strongest loose.
The old fox hears the noise and drops the goose.
The poacher shoots and hurries from the cry,
And the old hare half wounded buzzes by.
They get a forkèd stick to bear him down
And clap the dogs and take him to the town,
And bait him all the day with many dogs,
And laugh and shout and fright the scampering hogs.
He runs along and bites at all he meets:
They shout and hollo down the noisy streets.

He turns about to face the loud uproar
And drives the rebels to their very door.
The frequent stone is hurled where'er they go;
When badgers fight, then every one's a foe.
The dogs are clapt and urged to join the fray;
The badger turns and drives them all away.
Though scarcely half as big, demure and small,
He fights with dogs for hours and beats them all.
The heavy mastiff, savage in the fray,
Lies down and licks his feet and turns away.
The bulldog knows his match and waxes cold,
The badger grins and never leaves his hold.
He drives the crowd and follows at their heels
And bites them through—the drunkard swears and reels.

The frighted women take the boys away,
The blackguard laughs and hurries on the fray.
He tries to reach the woods, an awkward race,
But sticks and cudgels quickly stop the chase.
He turns agen and drives the noisy crowd
And beats the many dogs in noises loud.
He drives away and beats them every one,

And then they loose them all and set them on.
He falls as dead and kicked by boys and men,
Then starts and grins and drives the crowd agen;
Till kicked and torn and beaten out he lies
And leaves his hold and cackles, groans, and dies.

THE VIXEN

AMONG the taller wood with ivy hung,
The old fox plays and dances round her young.
She snuffs and barks if any passes by
And swings her tail and turns prepared to fly.
The horseman hurries by, she bolts to see,
And turns agen, from danger never free.
If any stands she runs among the poles
And barks and snaps and drives them in the holes.
The shepherd sees them and the boy goes by
And gets a stick and progs the hole to try.
They get all still and lie in safety sure,
And out again when everything's secure,
And start and snap at blackbirds bouncing by
To fight and catch the great white butterfly.

THE LOUT (I)

No sort of learning ever hurts his head;
He buys a song and never hears it read;
He gets the tune and never heeds the words;
His pocket, too, a penny oft affords
To buy a book, no matter what about,
And there he keeps it till he wears it out.
In every job he's sure to have a share,
And shouts to haste his speed he cannot bear.
He seldom seeks the house in leisure hour,
But finds the haystack in a sudden shower,
And hid from all he there contrives to lie,
Rain how it will, to keep his garments dry.
He owns one suit and wears it all the week,
A dirty slop as dingy as his cheek.

THE STUDENT

He always tells a story plain and plump,
And talks so loud he almost makes you jump;
He asks a question and his learning shows,
And takes his pocket-book to show he knows;
The village all his learning will allow,
And every boy he passes makes his bow;
To such a man all will their manners show
And if he is not proud he might be so;
He meets with many but has naught to say
And never talks with any by the way;
Some say that study makes the man so pale,
He shuns the toper and refuses ale,
And takes a quiet journey every day
And seems to gather knowledge by the way.

THE MOLE-CATCHER

Tattered and ragg'd, with greatcoat tied in strings,
And collared up to keep his chin from cold,
The old mole-catcher on his journey sings,
Followed by shaggy dog infirm and old,
Who potters on and keeps his steady pace;
He is so lame he scarce can get abroad
But hopples on and growls at anything;
Yet silly sheep will scarcely leave the road.
With stick and spud he tried the new-made hills
And bears his cheating traps from place to place;
Full many are the miners that he kills.
His trotting dog oft looks him in the face;
And when his toils are done he tries to play
And finds a quicker pace and barks him on his way.

MOUSE'S NEST

I FOUND a ball of grass among the hay
And progged it as I passed and went away;
And when I looked I fancied something stirred,
And turned agen and hoped to catch the bird—
When out an old mouse bolted in the wheats
With all her young ones hanging at her teats;
She looked so odd and so grotesque to me,
I ran and wondered what the thing could be,
And pushed the knapweed bunches where I stood;
Then the mouse hurried from the craking brood.
The young ones squeaked, and as I went away
She found her nest again among the hay.
The water o'er the pebbles scarce could run
And broad old cesspools glittered in the sun.

POEMS WRITTEN AT HIGH BEECH, EPPING, 1837–41, AND AT NORTHBOROUGH, 1841

THE FRIGHTENED PLOUGHMAN

I WENT in the fields with the leisure I got;
The stranger might smile but I heeded him not;
The hovel was ready to screen from a shower,
And the book in my pocket was read in an hour.

The bird came for shelter, but soon flew away;
The horse came to look, and seemed happy to stay;
He stood up in quiet, and hung down his head,
And seemed to be hearing the poem I read.

The ploughman would turn from his plough in the day
And wonder what being had come in his way,
To lie on a mole-hill and read the day long
And laugh out aloud when he'd finished his song.

The pewit turned over and stooped o'er my head
Where the raven croaked loud like the ploughman ill-bred,
But the lark high above charmed me all the day long,
So I sat down and joined in the chorus of song.

The foolhardy ploughman I well could endure;
His praise was worth nothing, his censure was poor;
Fame bade me go on, and I toiled the day long,
Till the fields where he lived should be known in my song.

A WALK IN THE FOREST

I LOVE the Forest and its airy bounds,
Where friendly Campbell takes his daily rounds;
I love the breakneck hills, that headlong go,
And leave me high, and half the world below;
I love to see the Beech Hill mounting high,
The brook without a bridge, and nearly dry.
There's Buckhurst Hill, a place of furze and clouds,
Which evening in a golden haze enshrouds;
I hear the cows go home with tinkling bell,
And see the woodman in the forest dwell,
Whose dog runs eager where the rabbit's gone;
He eats the grass, then kicks and hurries on;
Then scrapes for hoarded bone, and tries to play,
And barks at larger dogs and runs away.

MAID OF WALKHERD

MAID of Walkherd, meet agen,
By the wilding in the glen,
By the oak against the door,
Where we often met before;
By thy bosom's heaving snow,
By thy fondness none shall know,
Maid of Walkherd, meet agen
By the wilding in the glen.

By thy hand of slender make,
By thy love I'll ne'er forsake,
By thy heart I'll ne'er betray,
Let me kiss thy fears away!
I will live and love thee ever,
Leave thee and forsake thee never;
Though far in other lands to be,
Yet never far from love and thee.

ON THE NEGLECT OF TRUE MERIT

FASHION and Folly always follow fame,
Which Merit, slowly paced, is slow to claim.
The gaudy and the mean, men love to praise,
But quiet Merit lives for other days.
There's pleasant Cruikshank, hearty Rippingille,
And quiet Hilton of diviner skill,
There's simple Etty, never vain or proud,
Are left as common men among the crowd:
But Fame keeps watch and looks for other days,
And Merit claims for them diviner praise;
The others left behind have naught to claim,
And Merit wonders how they got to fame;
For Merit still will live above the mean,
And Cruikshank is what Hogarth would have been.

CHILD HAROLD [1]

[1] Seventy-seven nine-line stanzas with twenty-three songs and ballads interspersed are printed here under this title. Clare began his *Child Harold* in the early spring of 1841, while he was at Dr Matthew Allen's asylum, in Epping Forest. He was inspired to this, though his poem has nothing in common with Byron's beyond title and stanza, after Cyrus Redding lent him Byron's poems. One rough draft of at least thirty stanzas and some ballads, not in consecutive order, is mixed up with a rough draft of *Don Juan* in a small pocket-book among the Northampton MSS. Clare used this notebook during his escape from Epping on 20th July 1841, and he used it before his return to Northborough. That autumn and winter at Northborough, during his five months' stay with his wife and family, he made a copy of *Child Harold* (MS. 6, Northampton). He entitled forty-one stanzas and some fifteen songs and ballads *Child Harold*, made abundantly clear that songs were to intersperse stanzas, but did not use by any means all the stanzas of the small book, MS.8. His 'fair' copy is without any indication that it is complete. Did he intend the whole poem to be seasonal, beginning in spring, through summer and autumn, to end, as the last stanza headed 'Child Harold' does end, in winter? The seasons may be indicative of spring, summer, autumn and winter of his own life and of human life in general. We have therefore placed earlier 'spring' stanzas and all stanzas that from clear internal evidence were written whilst Clare was still at Epping towards the beginning of the poem. This means that the stanza order of his incomplete 'fair' copy is not always kept. The sequence here given is not at all incontrovertible: stanza 30, numbered 27 by Clare(?) in the pocket-book, should perhaps come earlier; stanza 2 of MS. 6 upsets some of the numbering in MS. 8; and 2 and 3 in the small MS. 8 have been placed after the Thunderstorm poem. They belong to his journey home from High Beech five days after the storm. No purpose seems served by placing stanzas obviously written in the spring of 1841 *after* the lines 'Written in a Thunderstorm', dated 'July'.

The poem emerges as an important, metrically varied and beautiful *résumé* of the poet's life. It is also about constancy, the importance of love, especially first love, about failure, about loneliness, about hope and about poetry.

Child Harold is one of the few late poems of which we have Clare's own manuscript: it has been printed here with only Clare's occasional dash or comma for punctuation and with his own, only rarely inadequate, spelling—as close as we could come to the manuscript.

MANY are poets—though they use no pen
To show their labours to the shuffling age
Real poets must be truly honest men
Tied to no mongrel laws on flatterys page

No zeal have they for wrong or party rage
The life of labour is a rural song
That hurts no cause—nor warfare tries to wage
Toil like the brook in music wears along—
Great little minds claim right to act the wrong

Summer morning is risen
& to even it wends
& still I'm in prison
Without any friends

I had joys assurance
Though in bondage I lie
—I am left still in durance
Unwilling to sigh

Still the forest is round me
Where the trees bloom in green
As if chains ne'er had bound me
Or cares had ne'er been

Nature's love is eternal
In forest & plain
Her course is diurnal
To blossom again

For home & friends vanished
I have kindness not wrath
For in days care has banished
My heart possessed both

My hopes are all hopeless
My skys have no sun
Winter fell in youth's mayday
& still freezes on

But love like the seed is
In the heart of a flower
It will blossom with truth
In a prosperous hour

True love is eternal
For God is the giver
& love like the soul will
Endure——& for ever

& he who studies natures volume through
& reads it with a pure unselfish mind
Will find Gods power all round in every view
As one bright vision of the almighty mind
His eyes are open though the world is blind
No ill from him creations works deform
The high & lofty one is great & kind
Evil may cause the blight & crushing storm——
His is the sunny glory & the calm.

Song

The sun has gone down with a veil on his brow
While I in the forest sit musing alone
The maiden has been oer the hills for her cow
While my hearts affections are freezing to stone
Sweet Mary I wish that the day was my own
To live in a cottage with beauty & thee
The past I will not as a mourner bemoan
For abscence leaves Mary still dearer to me

How sweet are the glooms of the midsummer even
Dark night in the bushes seems going to rest
& the bosom of Mary with fancys is heaving
Where my sorrows & feelings for seasons were blest
Nor will I repine though in love we're divided
She in the Lowlands & I in the glen
Of these forest beeches——by nature we're guided
& I shall find rest in her bosom agen

How soft the dew falls on the leaves of the beeches
How fresh the wild flowers seem to slumber below
How sweet are the lessons that nature still teaches
For truth is her tidings wherever I go

From schooldays of boyhood her image was cherished
In manhood sweet Mary was fairer than flowers
Nor yet has her name or her memory perished
Though abscence like winter oer happiness lowers

Though cares still will gather like clouds in my sky
Though hopes may grow hopeless & fetters recoil
While the sun of existence sheds light in my eye
I'll be free in a prison & cling to the soil
I'll cling to the spot where my first love was cherished
Where my heart nay my soul unto Mary I gave
& when my last hope of existence is perished
Her memory will shine like a sun on my grave

Green bushes & green trees where fancy feeds [4]
On the retiring solitudes of May
Where the sweet foliage like a volume reads
& weeds are gifts too choice to throw away
How sweet the evening now succeeds the day
The velvet hillock forms a happy seat
The whitethorn bushes bend with snowey may
Dwarf furze in golden blooms & violets sweet
Make this wild scene a pleasure grounds retreat

Mary thou ace of hearts thou muse of song
The pole star of my being & decay
Earth's coward foes my shattered bark may wrong
Still thourt the sunrise of my natal day
Born to misfortunes—where no sheltering bay
Keeps off the tempest—wrecked where'er I flee
I struggle with my fate—in trouble strong
Mary thy name loved long still keeps me free
Till my lost life becomes a part of thee

Love is the mainspring of existence—It
Becomes a soul wherebye I live to love
On all I see that dearest name is writ

Falsehood is here—but truth has life above
Where every star that shines exists in love
Skys vary in their clouds—the seasons vary
From heat to cold—change cannot constant prove
The south is bright—but smiles can act contrary—
My guide star gilds the north—& shines with Mary

Now come the balm and breezes of the spring
Not with the pleasures of my early days
Where Nature seemed one endless song to sing
Of joyous melody & happy praise
Ah would they come again—but life betrays
Quicksands & gulphs & storms that howl & sting
All quiet into madness & delays—
Care hides the sunshine with its raven wing
& hell glooms sadness oer the songs of Spring

Like satan's war cry first in paradise
When love lay sleeping on the flowery slope
Like virtue waking in the arms of vice
Or deaths sea bursting in the midst of hope
Sorrows will stay—& pleasures will elope
In the uncertain certainty of care
Joys bounds are narrow but a wider scope
Is left for trouble which our life must bear
Of which all human life is more or less the heir

My mind is dark & fathomless & wears
The hues of hopeless agony & hell
No plummet ever sounds the souls affairs
There death eternal never sounds the knell
There love imprisoned sounds the long farewell
& still may sigh in thoughts no heart hath penned
Alone in loneliness where sorrows dwell
& hopeless hope hopes on & meets no end
Wastes without springs & homes without a friend

Song

Say what is Love—to live in vain
To live & die & live again

Say what is Love—is it to be
In prison still & still be free

Or seem as free—alone & prove
The hopeless hopes of real Love

Does real Love on earth exist
Tis like a sunbeam on the mist

That fades & nowhere will remain
& nowhere is oertook again

Say what is Love—a blooming name
A rose leaf on the page of fame

That blooms then fades—to cheat no more
& is what nothing was before

Say what is Love—what e'er it be
It centres Mary still with thee

Where is the orphan child without a friend
That knows no fathers care or mothers love
No leading hand his infant steps defend
& none to notice but his God above
No joys are seen his little heart to move
Care turns all joys to dross & nought to gold
& he in fancys time may still disprove
Growing to cares & sorrows manifold
Bud of the waste a lamb without a fold

No mothers love or fathers care have they
Left to the storms of fate like creatures wild
They live like blossoms in the winters day

E'en Nature frowns upon the orphan child
On whose young face a mother never smiled
Foolhardy care increasing with his years
From friends & joys of every kind exiled
Even old in care the infant babe appears
& many a mother meets its face in tears

The dog can find a friend & seeks his side
The ass can know its owner & is fed
But none are known to be the orphans guide
Toil breaks his sleep & sorrow makes his bed
No mothers hand holds out the sugared bread
To fill his little hand—he hears no song
To please his pouting humours—Love is dead
With him & will be all his whole life long
Lone child of sorrow & perpetual wrong

But Providence that grand eternal calm
Is with him like the sunshine in the sky
Nature our kindest mother void of harm
Watches the orphans lonely infancy
Strengthening the man when childhoods cares are bye
She nurses still young unreproached distress
& hears the lonely infants every sigh
Who finds at length to make its sorrows less
Mid earths cold curses that is One to bless

Sweet rural maids made beautiful by health
Brought up where Natures calm encircles all
Where simple love remains as sterling wealth
Where simple habits early joys recall
Of youthful feelings which no wiles enthrall
The happy milkmaid in her mean array
Fresh as the new blown rose outblooms them all
E'en queens might sigh to be as blest as they
While milkmaids laugh & sing their cares away

How doth those scenes which rural mirth endears
Revise old feelings that my youth hath known

& Paint the fadedest blooms of earlier years
& soften feelings petrified to stone
Joy fled & care proclaimed itself my own
Farewells I took of joys in earliest years
& found the greatest bliss to be alone
My manhood was eclipsed but not in fears
Hell came in curses but she laughed at tears

But memory left sweet traces of her smiles
Which I remember still & still endure
The hopes of first love my heart beguiles
Time brought birth pain & pleasure but no cure
Sweet Bessey maid of health & fancies pure
How did I love thee once—still unforgot
But promises in love are never sure
& where we met how dear is every spot
& though we parted still I murmur not

For loves however dear must meet with clouds
& ties made tight yet loose & may be parted
Springs first young flowers the winter often shrouds
& loves first hopes are very often thwarted
E'en mine beat high & then fell broken hearted
& sorrow mourned in verse to reconcile
My feelings to my fate though lone & parted
Loves enemies are like the scorpion vile
That oer its ruined hopes will hiss & smile

Ballad

The blackbird has built in the pasture agen
& the thorn oer the pond shows a delicate green
Where I strolled with Patty adown in the glen
& spent summer evenings & Sundays unseen
How sweet the hill brow
& the low of the cow
& the sunshine that gilded the bushes so
When evening brought dews Natures thirst to allay

& clouds seemed to nestle round hamlets & farms
While in the green bushes we spent the sweet day
& Patty sweet Patty was still in my arms

The love bloom that redded upon her sweet lips
The love light that glistened within her sweet eye
The singing bees there that the wild honey sips
From wild blossoms seemed not so happy as I
How sweet her smile seemed
While the summer sun gleamed
& the laugh of the Spring shadowed joys from on high
While the birds sung about us & cattle grazed round
& beauty was blooming oer hamlets & farms
How sweet steamed the inscence of dew from the ground
While Patty sweet Patty sat locked in my arms

Yet Love lives on in every kind of weather
In heats & colds in sunshine & in glooms
Winter may blight & stormy clouds may gather
Nature invigorates & love will bloom
It fears no sorrow in a life to come
But lives within itself from year to year
As doth the wild flower in its own perfume
As in the Lapland snows Spring's blooms appear
So true Love blooms & blossoms everywhere

Ballad

The rose of the world was dear Mary to me
In the days of my boyhood & youth
I told her in songs where my heart wished to be
My songs were the language of Truth

I told her in looks when I gazed in her eyes
That Mary was dearest to me
I told her in words in the language of sighs
Where my whole hearts affections would be

I told her in love that all nature was true
I convinced her that nature was kind
But love in his trials had labour to do
& Mary would be in the mind

Mary met me in spring where the speedwell knots grew
& the kingcups were shining like flame
I chose her all colours red yellow & blue
But my love was one hue & the same

Spring summer & winter & all the year through
In the sunshine the shower & the blast
I told the same tale & she knew it all true
& Mary's my blossom at last

Good is of heaven still the first akin
Twas born in paradise & left its home
For desert lands stray hearts to nurse & win
Though pains like plagues pursue them where they roam
Its Joys are evergreen & blooms at home
The sailor rocking on the giddy mast
The soldier when the cannons cease to boom
& every heart its doubts or dangers past
Beats on its way for love & home at last

Nature thou truth of heaven if heaven be true
Falsehood may tell her ever changing lie
But nature's truth looks green in every view
& love in every landscape glads the eye
How beautiful these sloping thickets lie
Woods on the hills & plains all smooth & even
Through which we see the ribboned evening skie
Though winter here in floods & snows was driven
Spring came like God & turned it all to heaven

There is a Tale for every day to hear
For every heart to feel & tongue to tell
The daughters anxious dread the lovers fear
Pains that in cots & palaces may dwell

Not short & passing like the friends farewell
Where tears may fall & leave a smile beneath
Eternal grief rings in the passing bell
Tis not the sobs of momentary breath
Ties part for ever in the tale of death

Where are my friends & childern Where are They
The childern of two mothers born in joy
One roof has held them—all have been at play
Beneath the pleasures of a mothers eye
And are my late hopes blighted need I sigh
Hath care commenced his long perpetual reign
The spring & summer hath with me gone by
Hope views the bud a flower & not in vain
Long is the night that brings no morn again

The dew falls on the weed & on the flower
The rose & thistle bathe their heads in dew
The lowliest heart may have its prospering hour
The saddest bosom meet its wishes true
E'en I may joy love & happiness renew
Though not the sweets of my first early days
When one sweet face was all the loves I knew
& my soul trembled in her eyes to gaze
Whose very censure seemed intended praise

A soul within the heart that loves the more
Giving to pains & fears eternal life
Burning the flesh till it consumed the core
So love is still the eternal calm of strife
Thou soul within a soul thou life of life
Thou essence of my hopes & fears & joys
M—y my dear first love & early wife
& still the flower my inmost soul enjoys
Thy love's the bloom no canker worm destroys

Flow on my verse though barren thou mayst be
Of thought—Yet sing & let thy fancys roll
In early days thou swept a mighty sea

All calm in troublous deeps & spurned control
Thou fire & iceberg to an aching soul
& still an angel in my gloomy way
Far better opiate than the draining bowl
Still sing my muse to drive cares fiends away
Nor heed what loitering listener hears the lay

My themes be artless cots & happy plains
Though far from man my wayward fancies flee
Of fields & woods rehearse in willing strains
& I mayhap may feed on joys with thee
This cowslip field this sward my pillow be
So I may sleep the sun into the west
My cot this awthorn [1] hedge this spreading tree
Mary & Martha once my daily guests
& still as mine both wedded loved & blest

I rest my wearied life in these sweet fields
Reflecting every smile in nature's face
& much of joy this grass—these hedges yield
Not found in citys where crowds daily trace
Scant pleasures there hath no abiding place
The star-gemmed early morn the silent even
With pleasures that our broken hopes deface
To love too well leaves nought to be forgiven
The Gates of Eden is the bounds of Heaven

The apathy that fickle love wears through
The doubts & certaintys are still akin
Its every joy has sorrow in the view
Its holy truth like Eve's beguiling sin
Seems to be losses even while we win
Tormenting joys & cheating into wrong
& still we love—& fall into the Gin
My sun of love was short—& clouded long
& now its shadow fills a feeble song

[1] Clare often spelt hawthorn without the initial h.

Song

I saw her in my spring's young choice
Ere loves hopes looked upon the crowd
Ere loves first secrets found a voice
Or dared to speak the name aloud

I saw her in my boyish hours
A Girl as fair as heaven above
When all the world seemed strewn with flowers
& every pulse & look was love

I saw her when her heart was young
I saw her when my heart was true
When truth was all the themes I sung
& love the only nurse I knew

Ere infancy had left her brow
I seemed to love her from her birth
& thought her then as I do now
The dearest angel upon earth

O she was more than fair—divinely fair
Can language paint the soul in those blue eyes
Can fancy read the feelings painted there
—Those hills of snow that on her bosom lies—
Or beauty speak for all those sweet replies
That through love's visions like the sun is breaking
Waking new hopes & fears & stifled sighs
From first love's dreams my love is scarcely waking
The wounds might heal but still the heart is aching

Her looks was like the spring her very voice
Was springs own music more than song to me—
Choice of my boyhood nay my souls first choice
From her sweet thralldom I am never free
Yet here my prison is a spring to me
Past memories bloom like flowers where e'er I rove

My very bondage though in snares—is free
I love to stretch me in this shadey grove
& muse upon the memories of love

The paigles bloom in showers in grassy close (5)
How sweet to be among their blossoms led
& hear sweet Nature to herself discourse
While pale the moon is rising [1] overhead
& hear the grazeing cattle softly tread
Cropping the hedgerows newly leafing thorn—
Sounds soft as visions murmured oer in bed
At dusky eve or sober silent morn
For such delights 'twere happy man was born

Hail Solitude still peace & Lonely good
Thou spirit of all joys to be alone
My best of friends these glades & this green wood
Where nature is herself & loves her own
The hearts hid anguish here I make it known
& tell my troubles to the gentle wind
Friends cold neglects have froze my heart to stone
& wrecked the voyage of a quiet mind
With wives & friends & every hope disjoined

Wrecked of all hopes save one—to be alone
Where Solitude becomes my wedded mate
Sweet Forest with rich beauties overgrown
Where Solitude is queen & reigns in state
Hid in green trees I hear the clapping gate
& voices calling to the rambling cows
I laugh at Love & all its idle fate
The Present hour is all my lot alows
An age of sorrow springs from lovers vows

Sweet is the song of Birds for that restores
The soul to harmony the mind to love
Tis natures song of freedom out of doors

[1] Could be 'bering'.—MS. 8.

Forest beneath free winds & clouds above
The Thrush & Nightingale & timid dove
Breathe music round me where the gipseys dwell
Pierced hearts left burning in the doubts of love
Are desolate where crowds & cities dwell—
The splendid palace seems the gates of hell

Song [1] (a)

I've wandered many a weary mile
—Love in my heart was burning—
To seek a home in Marys smile
But cold is lifes sojourning
The cold ground was a feather-bed
Truth never acts contrary
I had no home above my head
My home was love & Mary

I had no home in early youth
When my first love was thwarted
But if her heart still beats with truth
We'll never more be parted
& changing as her love may be
My own shall never vary
Nor night nor day I'm never free
But sigh for abscent Mary

Nor night nor day nor sun nor shade
Week month nor rolling year
Repairs the breach wronged love hath made
There madness—misery here
Lifes lease was lengthened by her smiles
—Are truth & love contrary
No ray of hope my fate beguiles—
I've lost love home & Mary

Song [1] (b)

Here's where Mary loved to be
& here are flowers she planted
Here are books she loved to see
& here, the kiss she granted

Here on the wall with smiling brow
Her picture used to cheer me
Both walls & rooms are naked now
No Marys nigh to hear me

The church spire still attracts my eye
& leaves me broken hearted
Though grief hath worn their channels dry
I sigh o'er days departed

The churchyard where she used to play
My feet could wander hourly
My school walks there was every day
Where she made winter flowery

But where is angel Mary now
Loves secrets none disclose 'em
Her rosey cheek & broken vow
Live in my aching bosom

My life hath been one love—no blot it out
My life hath been one chain of contradictions—
Madhouses Prisons wh-re shops—never doubt
But that my life hath had some strong convictions
That such was wrong—religion makes restrictions
I would have followed—but life turned a bubble

---

[1] Clare's note in his incomplete fair copy, MS. 6, Northampton, runs:
'a and b   The above songs were written directly after my return home to
Northborough last Friday evening   the rest of the stanzas & songs were
written on Epping Forest Essex.'

& clumb the giant stile of maledictions
They took me from my wife & to save trouble
I wed again & made the error double

Yet abscence claims them both & keeps them too
& locks me in a shop in spite of law
Among a low lived set & dirty crew
Here let the Muse oblivions curtain draw
& let man think—for God hath often saw
Things here too dirty for the light of day
For in a madhouse there exists no law—
Now stagnant grows my too refined clay
I envy birds their wings to flye away

How servile is the task to please alone
Though beauty woo & love inspire the song
Mere painted beauty with her heart of stone
Thinks the world worships while she flaunts along
The flower of sunshine butterflye of song
Give me the truth of heart in womans life
The love to cherish one—& do no wrong
To none—O peace of every care & strife
Is true love in an estimable wife

How beautifull this hill of fern swells on
So beautifull the chappel peeps between
The hornbeams—with its simple bell—Alone
I wander here hid in a palace green
Mary is abscent—but the forest queen
Nature is with me—morning noon & gloaming
I write my poems in these paths unseen
& when among these brakes & beeches roaming
I sigh for truth & home & love & woman

I sigh for one & two—& still I sigh
For many are the whispers I have heard
From beautys lips—loves soul in many an eye

255

Hath pierced my heart with such intense regard
I looked for joy & pain was the reward
I think of them I love each girl & boy
Babes of two mothers—on this velvet sward
& nature thinks—in her so sweet employ
While dews fall on each blossom weeping joy

Here is the chappel yard enclosed with pales
& oak trees nearly top its little bell
Here is the little bridge with guiding rail
That leads me on to many a pleasant dell
The fern owl chitters like a startled knell
To nature—yet tis sweet at evening still—
A pleasant road curves round the gentle swell
Where nature seems to have her own sweet will
Planting her beech & thorn about the sweet fern hill

I have had many loves—& seek no more
These solitudes my last delights shall be
The leaf hid forest—& the lonely shore
Seem to my mind like beings that are free
Yet would I had some eye to smile on me
Some heart where I could make a happy home in
Sweet Susan that was wont my love to be
& Bessey of the glen—for I've been roaming
With both at morn & noon & dusky gloaming

Cares gather round—I snap their chains in two
& smile in agony & laugh in tears
Like playing with a deadly serpent—who
Stings to the death—there is no room for fears
Where death would bring me happiness—his sheers
Kills cares that hiss to poison many a vein
The thought to be extinct my fate endears
Pale death the grand phisician cures all pain
The dead rest well—who lived for joys in vain

Written in a Thunderstorm July 15 1841

The heavens are wrath—the thunders rattling peal
Rolls like a vast volcano in the sky
Yet nothing starts the apathy I feel
Nor chills with fear eternal destiny

My soul is apathy—a ruin vast
Time cannot clear the ruined mass away
My life is hell—the hopeless die is cast
& manhoods prime is premature decay

Roll on ye wrath of thunders—peal on peal
Till worlds are ruins & myself alone
Melt heart & soul cased in obdurate steel
Till I can feel that nature is my throne

I live in love sun of undying light
& fathom my own heart for ways of good
In its pure atmosphere day without night
Smiles on the plains the forest & the flood

Smile on ye elements of earth & sky
Or frown in thunders as ye frown on me
Bid earth & its delusions pass away
But leave the mind as its creator free

This twilight seems a veil of gause & mist
Trees seem dark hills between the earth & sky
Winds sob awake & then a gusty hist
Fanns through the wheat like serpents gliding bye
I love to stretch my length 'tween earth & sky
& see the inky foliage oer me wave
Though shades are still my prison where I lie
Long use grows nature which I easy brave
& think how sweet cares rest within the grave

Remind me not of other years or tell
My broken hopes of joys they are to meet
While thy own falsehood rings the loudest knell
To one fond heart that aches too cold to beat
Mary how oft with fondness I repeat
That name alone to give my troubles rest
The very sound though bitter seemeth sweet—
In my loves home & thy own faithless breast
Truth's bonds are broke & every nerve distrest

Life is to me a dream that never wakes
Night finds me on this lengthening road alone
Love is to me a thought that ever aches
A frost bound thought that freezes life to stone
Mary in truth & nature still my own
That warms the winter of my aching breast
Thy name is joy nor will I life bemoan—
Midnight when sleep takes charge of nature's rest
Finds me awake & friendless—not distrest

Tie all my cares up in thy arms O sleep
& give my weary spirits peace & rest
I'm not an outlaw in this midnight deep
If prayers are offered from sweet womans breast
One & one only makes my being blest
& fancy shapes her form in every dell
On that sweet bosom I've had hours of rest
Though now through years of abscence doomed to dwell
Day seems my night & night seems blackest hell

England my country though my setting sun
Sinks in the ocean gloom & dregs of life
My muse can sing my Marys heart was won
& joy was heaven when I called her wife
The only harbour in my days of strife
Was Mary when the sea roil'd mountains high
When joy was lost & every sorrow rife
To her sweet bosom I was wont to flye
To undeceive by truth life's treacherous agony

Friend of the friendless from a host of snares
From lying varlets & from friendly foes
I sought the quiet truth to ease my cares
& on the blight of reason found repose
But when the strife of nature ceased her throes
& other hearts would beat for my return
I trusted fate to ease my world of woes
Seeking love's harbour—where I now sojourn
—But hell is heaven could I cease to mourn

For her for one whose very name is yet
My hell or heaven & will ever be
Falsehood is doubt—but I can ne'er forget
Oaths virtuous falsehood volunteered to me
To make my soul new bonds which God made free
God's gift is love & do I wrong the giver
To place affections wrong from Gods decree
—No when farewell upon my lips did quiver
& all seemed lost—I loved her more than ever

I loved her in all climes beneath the sun
Her name was like a jewel in my heart
Twas heavens own choice—& so God's will be done
Love ties that keep unbroken cannot part
Nor can cold abscence sever or desert
That simple beauty blessed with matchless charms
Oceans have rolled between us—not to part
E'en Icelands snows true love's delirium warms
For there I've dreamed—& Mary filled my arms

Song

O Mary sing thy songs to me
Of love & beautys melody
My sorrows sink beneath distress
My deepest griefs are sorrowless
So used to glooms & cares am I

My tearless troubles seem as joy
O Mary sing thy songs to me
Of love & beautys melody

'To be beloved is all I need
'& them I love are loved indeed'
The soul of woman is my shrine
& Mary made my songs divine
O for that time that happy time
To hear thy sweet piano chime
In music so divine & clear
That woke my soul in heaven to hear

But heaven itself without thy face
To me would be no resting place
& though the world was one delight
No joy would live but in thy sight
The soul of woman is my shrine
Then Mary make those songs divine
For music love & melody
Breath all of thee & only thee

Song

Lovely Mary when we parted
I ne'er felt so lonely hearted
As I do now in field & glen
When hope says 'we shall meet agen'
& by yon spire that points to heaven
Where my earliest vows were given
By each meadow field & fen
I'll love thee till we meet agen

True as the needle to the pole
My life I love thee heart & soul
Wa'n't thy love in my heart enrolled
Though love was fire 'twould soon be cold

By thine eye of heavens own blue
My heart for thine was ever true
By sun & moon & sea & shore
My life I love thee more & more

& by that hope that lingers last
For heaven when life's hell is past
By time the present past & gone
I loved thee—& I loved thee on
Thy beauty made youth's life divine
Till my soul grew a part of thine
Mary I mourn no pleasures gone—
The past hath made us both as one

Now melancholly autumn comes anew
With showery clouds & fields of wheat tanned brown
Along the meadow banks I peace pursue
& see the wild flowers gleaming up & down
Like sun & light—the ragworts golden crown
Mirrors like sunshine when sunbeams retire
& silver yarrow—there's the little town
& oer the meadows gleams that slender spire
Reminding me of one—& waking fond desire

I love thee nature in my inmost heart
Go where I will thy truth seems from above
Go where I will thy landscape forms a part
Of heaven—e'en these fens where wood nor grove
Are seen—their very nakedness I love
For one dwells nigh that secret hopes prefer
Above the race of women—like the dove
I mourn her abscence Fate that would deter
My hate of all things strengthens love for her

Thus saith the great & high & lofty one
Whose name is holy—home eternity
In the high & holy place I dwell alone
& with them also that I wish to see
Of contrite humble spirits—from sin free

Who trembles at my word—& good receive
—Thou high & lofty one—O give to me
Truths low estate & I will glad believe
If such I am not—such I'm feign to live

That form from boyhood loved & still loved on
That voice that look that face of one delight
Loves register for years months weeks—time past & gone
Her looks was ne'er forgot or out of sight
—Mary the muse of every song I write
Thy cherished beauty never leaves my own
Though cares chill winter doth my manhood blight
& freeze like Niobe my thoughts to stone—
Our lives are two—our end and aim is one

Ballad

Sweet days while God your blessings send
I call your joys my own
& if I have an only friend
I am not left alone

She sees the fields the trees the spires
Which I can daily see
& if true love her heart inspires
Life still has joys for me

She sees the wild flower in the dells
That in my rambles shine
The sky that oer her homestead dwells
Looks sunny over mine

The cloud that passes where she dwells
In less than half an hour
Darkens around these orchard dells
Or melts a sudden shower

The wind that leaves the sunny south
& fans the orchard tree

Might steal the kisses from her mouth
& waft her voice to me

O when will autumn bring the news
Now harvest browns the fen
That Mary as my vagrant muse
& I shall meet agen

Tis pleasant now days hours begin to pass
To dewy eve to walk down narrow close
& feel ones feet among refreshing grass
& hear the insects in their homes discourse
& startled blackbird fly from covert close
Of white thorn hedge with wild fears fluttering wings
& see the spire & hear the clock toll hoarse
& whisper names—& think oer many things
That love hurds up in truths imaginings

Fame blazed upon me like a comets glare
Fame waned & left me like a fallen star
Because I told the evil what they are
& truth & falsehood never wished to mar
My Life hath been a wreck & I've gone far
For peace & truth—& hope—for home & rest
Like Edens gates—fate throws a constant bar—
Thoughts may o'ertake the sunset in the west
—Man meets no home within a woman's breast

Though they are blazoned in the poets song
As all the comforts which our lifes contain
I read & sought such joys my whole life long
& found the best of poets sung in vain
& still I read & sighed & sued again
& lost no purpose where I had the will
I almost worshipped when my toils grew vain
Finding no antidote my pains to kill
I sigh a poet & a lover still

Song

Dying gales of sweet even
How can you sigh so
Though the sweet day is leaving
& the sun sinketh low
How can you sigh so
For the wild flower is gay
& her dew gems all glow
For the abscence of day

Dying gales of sweet even
Breathe music from toil
Dusky eve is loves heaven
& meets beautys smile
Love leans on the stile
Where the rustic brooks flow
Dying gales all the while
How can you sigh so

Dying gales round a prison
To fancy may sigh
But day here hath risen
Over prospects of joy
Here Mary would toy
When the sun it got low
Even gales whisper joy
& never sigh so

Labour lets man his brother
Retire to his rest
The babe meets its mother
& sleeps on her breast
The sun in the west
Has gone down in the ocean
Dying gales gently sweep
O'er the hearts ruffled motion
& sing it to sleep

Song

The spring may forget he reigns in the sky
& winter again hide her flowers in the snow
The summer may thirst when her fountains are dry
But I'll think of Mary wherever I go
The bird may forget that her nest is begun
When the snow settles white on the new budding tree
& nature in tempests forget the bright sun
But I'll ne'er forget her—that was plighted to me

How could I—How should I—that loved her so early
Forget—when I've sung of her beauty in song
How could I forget—what I've worshipped so dearly
From boyhood to manhood—& all my life long
As leaves to the branches in summer comes duly
& blossoms will bloom on the stalk & the tree
To her beauty I'll cling—& I'll love her as truly
& think of sweet Mary wherever I be

Song

No single hour can stand for naught
No moment hand can move
But calendars an aching thought
Of my first lonely love

Where silence doth the loudest call
My secrets to betray
As moonlight holds the night in thrall
As suns reveal the day

I hide it in the silent shades
Till silence finds a tongue
I make its grave where time invades
Till Time becomes a song

I bid my foolish heart be still
But hopes will not be chid
My heart will beat—& burn—& chill
First love will not be hid

When summer ceases to be green
& winter bare & blea—
Death may forget what I have been
But I must cease to be

When words refuse before the crowd
My Mary's name to give
The muse in silence sings aloud
& there my love will live

Now harvest smiles embrowning all the plain
The sun of heaven oer its ripeness shines
'Peace-plenty' has been sung nor sung in vain
As all bring forth the makers grand designs
—Like gold that brightens in some hidden mines
His nature is the wealth that brings increase
To all the world—his sun for ever shines
—He hides his face & troubles they increase
He smiles—the sun looks out in wealth & peace

In cant & mystery there lurks a wrong
Poisonous as fangs within the Serpent's head
The subtlest one to Priestcraft does belong
They humbug till the living turn the dead
Hypocricy the highest holds her head
In Pulpit placed with fair & smirking face
With tongues new oiled & hearts as cold as lead
The priests descending into hells embrace
The surplice [1] leaves & shows a harlot's face

[1] Clare has 'surplus'.—MS. 10, p. 91.

This life is made of lying & grimace
This world is filled with whoring & decieving
Hypocrisy ne'er masks an honest face
Storys are told—but seeing is believing
& I've seen much from which there's no retrieving
I've seen deceptions take the place of truth
I've seen knaves flourish—& the country grieving
Lies was the current gospel in my youth
& now a man—I'm further off from truth

Song

They near read the heart
Who would read it in mine
That love can desert
The first truth on his shrine
Though in Lethe I steep it
& sorrows prefer
In my hearts core I keep it
& keep it for her

For her & her only
Through months & through years
I've wandered thus lonely
In sorrow & fears
My sorrows I smother
Though troubles anoy
In this world & no other
I cannot meet joy

No peace nor yet pleasure
Without her will stay
Life looses its treasure
When Mary's away
Though the nightingale often
In sorrow may sing
—Can the blast of the winter
Meet bloom of the spring

Thou first best & dearest
Though dwelling apart
To my heart still the nearest
Forever thou art
& thou wilt be the dearest
Though our joys may be o'er
& to me thou art nearest
Though I meet thee no more

Song

Did I know where to meet thee
Thou dearest in life
How soon would I greet thee
My true love & wife
How soon would I meet thee
At close of the day
Though cares would still cheat me
If Mary would meet me
I'd kiss her sweet beautys & love them away

& when evening discovers
The sun in the west
I long like true lovers
To lean on thy breast
To meet thee my dearest
—Thy eyes beaming blue
Abscent [1] pains the severest
Feel Mary the dearest
& if Mary's abscent—how can I be true

How dull the glooms cover
This meadow & fen
Where I as a lover
Seek Mary agen
But silence is teazing
Wherever I stray
There's nothing seems pleasing
Or aching thoughts easing
Though Mary lives near me—she seems far away

O would these gales murmur
My love in her ear
Or a birds note inform her
While I linger here
But nature contrary
Turns night into day
No bird—gale—or fairy
Can whisper to Mary
To tell her who seeks her—while Mary's away

Dull must that being be who sees unmoved
The scenes & objects that his childhood knew—
The schoolyard & the maid he early loved
The sunny wall where long the old Elms grew
The grass that e'en till noon retains the dew
Beneath the wallnut shade I see them still
Though not such fancys do I now pursue
Yet still the picture turns my bosom chill
& leaves a void—nor love nor hope may fill

After long abscence how the mind recalls
pleasing associations of the past
Haunts of his youth—thorn hedges & old walls
& hollow trees that sheltered from the blast
& all that map of boyhood overcast
With glooms & wrongs & sorrows not his own
That oer his brow like the scathed lightning passed
That turned his spring to winter & alone
Wrecked name & fame & all—to solitude unknown

So on he lives in glooms & living death
A shade like night forgetting & forgot
Insects that kindle in the springs young breath
Take hold of life & share a brighter lot
Than he the tennant of the hall & Cot
The princely palace too hath been his home
& Gipseys camp where friends would know him not
In midst of wealth a beggar still to roam
Parted from one whose heart was once his home

& yet not parted—still loves hope illumes
& like the rainbow brightest in the storm
It looks for joy beyond the wreck of tombs
& in lifes winter keeps loves embers warm
The oceans roughest tempest meets a calm
Care's thickest cloud shall break in sunny joy
O'er the parched waste showers yet shall fall like balm
& she the soul of life for whom I sigh
Like flowers shall cheer me when the storm is bye

Song

O Mary dear three springs have been
Three summers too have blossomed here
Three blasting winters crept between
Though abscence is the most severe
Another summer blooms in green
But Mary never once was seen

I've sought her in the fields & flowers
I've sought her in the forest groves
In avenues & shaded bowers
& every scene that Mary loves
E'en round her home I seek her here
But Mary's abscent everywhere

'Tis autumn & the rustling corn
Goes loaded on the creaking wain
I seek her in the early morn
But cannot meet her face again
Sweet Mary she is abscent still
& much I fear she ever will

The autumn morn looks mellow as the fruit
& ripe as harvest—every field & farm
Is full of health & toil—yet never mute
With rustic mirth & peace the day is warm

The village maid with gleans upon her arm
Brown as the hazel nut from field to field
Goes cheerily—the valleys native charm—
I seek for charms that autumn best can yield
In mellowing wood & timedy-bleaching field

Song

'Tis autumn now & nature's scenes
The pleachy fields & yellowing tree
Looses their blooming hues & greens
But nature finds no change in me
The fading woods the russet grange
The hues of nature may desert
But nought in me shall find a change
To wrong the angel of my heart
For Mary is my angel still
Through every month & every ill

The leaves they loosen from the branch
& fall upon the gusty wind
But my hearts silent love is staunch
& nought can tear her from my mind
The flowers are gone from dell & bower
Though crowds from summers lap was given
But love is an eternal flower
Like purple amaranths in heaven
To Mary first my heart did bow
& if she's true she keeps it now

Just as the summer keeps the flower
Which springs conscealed in hoods of gold
Or unripe harvest met the shower
& made earth's blessings manifold
Just so my Mary lives for me
A silent thought for months & years
The world may live in revelry
Her name my lonely quiet cheers
& cheer it will whate'er may be
While Mary lives to think of me

Sweet comes the misty mornings in September
Among the dewy paths how sweet to stray
Greensward or stubbles as I well remember
I once have done—the mist curls thick & gray
As cottage smoke—like net work on the spray
Or seeded grass the cobweb draperies run
Beaded with pearls of dew at early day
& o'er the pleachy stubbles peeps the sun
The lamp of day when that of night is done

What mellowness these harvest days unfold
In the strong glances of the midday sun
The homesteads very grass seems changed to gold
The light in golden shadows seems to run
& tinges every spray it rests upon
With that rich harvest hue of sunny joy
Nature life's sweet companion cheers alone
The hare starts up before the shepherd boy
& partridge coveys wir on russet wings of joy

The meadow flags now rustle bleached & dank
& misted oer with down as fine as dew
The sloe & dewberry shine along the bank
Where weeds in blooms luxuriance lately grew
Red rose the sun & up the moorhen flew
From bank to bank the meadow arches stride
Where foamy floods in winter tumbles through
& spread a restless ocean foaming wide
Where now the cow boys sleep nor fear the coming tide

About the meadows now I love to sit
On banks bridge walls & rails as when a boy
To see old trees bend o'er the flaggy pit
With huge roots bare that time does not destroy
Where sits the angler at his days employ
& there Ivy leaves the bank to climb
The tree—& now how sweet to weary joy
—Aye nothing seems so happy & sublime
As Sabbath bells & their delightfull chime

Sweet solitude thou partner of my life
Thou balm of hope & every pressing care
Thou soothing silence oer the noise of strife
These meadow flats & trees—the autumn air
Mellows my heart to harmony—I bear
Lifes burthen happily—these fenny dells
Seem Eden in this Sabbath rest from care
My heart with love's first early memory swells
To hear the music of those village bells

For in that hamlet lives my rising sun
Whose beams hath cheered me all my lorn life long
My heart to nature there was early won
For she was nature's self—& still my song
Is her through sun & shade through right & wrong
On her my memory for ever dwells
The flower of Eden—evergreen of song
Truth in my heart the same love story tells—
—I love the music of those village bells

Song

Here's a health unto thee bonny lassie O
Leave the thorns o' care wi' me
& whatever I may be
Here's happiness to thee
Bonny lassie O

Here's joy unto thee bonny lassie O
Though we never meet again
I well can bear the pain
If happiness is thine
Bonny lassie O

Here is true love unto thee bonny lassie O
Though abscence cold is ours
The spring will come wi' flowers
& love will wait for thee
Bonny lassie O

So here's love unto thee bonny lassie O
Aye wherever I may be
Here's a double health to thee
Till life shall cease to love
Bonny lassie O

The blackbird startles from the homestead hedge
Raindrops & leaves fall yellow as he springs
Such images are natures sweetest pledge
For me there's music in his rustling wings
'Prink prink' he cries & loud the robin sings
The small hawk like a shot drops from the sky
Close to my feet for mice & creeping things
Then swift as thought again he suthers bye
& hides among the clouds from the pursuing eye

The lightnings vivid flashes rend the cloud
That rides like castled crags along the sky
& splinters them to fragments—while aloud
The thunder, heaven's artillery vollies bye
Trees crash earth trembles—beast prepare to flye
Almighty what a crash—yet man is free
& walks unhurt while danger seems so nigh—
Heaven's archway now the rainbow seems to be
That spans the eternal round of earth & sky & sea

A shock a moment in the wrath of God
Is long as hell's eternity to all
His thunderbolts leave life but as the clod
Cold & inanimate—their temples fall
Beneath his frown to ashes—the eternal pall
Of wrath sleeps o'er the ruins where they fell
& nought of memory may their creeds recall
The sin of Sodom was a moments yell
Fire's deathbed theirs their first grave the last hell

The towering willow with its pliant boughs
Sweeps its grey foliage to the autumn wind
The level grounds where oft a group of cows

274

Huddled together close—or propped behind
An hedge or hovel ruminate & find
The peace—as walks & health & I pursue
For natures every place is still resigned
To happiness—new life's in every view
& here I comfort seek & early joys renew

The lake that held a mirror to the sun
Now curves with wrinkles in the stillest place
The autumn wind sounds hollow as a gun
& water stands in every swampy place
Yet in these fens peace harmony & grace
The attributes of nature are allied
The barge with naked mast in sheltered place
Beside the brig close to the bank is tied
While small waves plashes by its bulky side

Song

The floods come o'er the meadow leas
The dykes & full & brimming
Field furrows reach the horses knees
Where wild ducks oft are swimming
The skyes are black the fields are bare
The trees their coats are loosing
The leaves are dancing in the air
The sun its warmth refusing

Brown are the flags & fading sedge
& tanned the meadow plains
Bright yellow is the osier hedge
Beside the brimming drains
The crows sit on the willow tree
The lake is full below
But still the dullest thing I see
Is self that wanders slow

The dullest scenes are not so dull
As thoughts I cannot tell
The brimming dykes are not so full
As my hearts silent swell
I leave my troubles to the winds
With none to share a part
The only joy my feeling finds
Hides in an aching heart

Abscence in love is worse than any fate
Summer is winter's desert & the spring
Is like a ruined city desolate
Joy dies & hope retires on feeble wing
Nature sinks heedless—birds unheeded sing
'Tis solitude in citys—crowds all move
Like living death—though all to life still cling—
The strangest [1] bitterest thing that life can prove
Is woman's undisguise of hate & love

I think of thee: A Song

I think of thee at early day
& wonder where my love can be
& when the evening shadows grey
O how I think of thee

Along the meadow banks I rove
& down the flaggy fen
& hope my first & early love
To meet thee once agen

I think of thee at dewy morn
& at the sunny noon
& walks with thee—now left forlorn
Beneath the silent moon

[1] or 'strongest'.

I think of thee I think of all
How blest we both have been—
The sun looks pale upon the wall
& autumn shuts the scene

I can't expect to meet thee now
The winter floods begin
The wind sighs through the naked bough
Sad as my heart within

I think of thee the seasons through
In spring when flowers I see
In winters lorn & naked view
I think of only thee

While life breaths on this earthly ball
What e'er my lot may be
Wether in freedom or in thrall
Mary I think of thee

Tis winter & the fields are bare & waste
The air one mass of 'vapour clouds & storms'
The suns broad beams are buried & oercast
& chilly glooms the midday light deforms
Yet comfort now the social bosom warms
Friendship of nature which I hourly prove
Even in this winter scene of frost & storms
Bare fields the frozen lake & leafless grove
Are natures grand religion & true love

Song

In this cold world without a home
Disconsolate I go
The summer looks as cold to me
As winters frost & snow
Though winters scenes are dull & drear
A colder lot I prove
No home had I through all the year
But Marys honest love

But Love inconstant as the wind
Soon shifts another way
No other home my heart can find
Life wasting day by day
I sigh & sit & sit & sigh
For better days to come
For Mary was my hope & joy
Her truth & heart my home

Her truth & heart was once my home
& May was all the year
But now through seasons as I roam
Tis winter everywhere
Hopeless I go through care & toil
No friend I e'er possest
To reccompence for Marys smile
& the love within her breast

My love was ne'er so blest as when
It mingled with her own
Told often to be told agen
& every feeling known
But now loves hopes are all bereft
A lonely man I roam
& abscent Mary long hath left
My heart without a home [5]

POEMS WRITTEN IN NORTHAMPTON[1] ASYLUM, 1842–64

[1] From this point, since Clare's original manuscripts have not come to light, the text follows that of Knight, on the assumption thát Knight and his successors at St Andrew's were in closest contact with Clare and therefore their careful text best approximates to what Clare wrote. But this is not proven; and the second Northampton transcriber, as well as the Peterborough copyist, may have seen Clare's originals. The Notes on the Text indicate where Knight's transcripts have not been followed.

SPRING COMES

Spring comes and it is May—white as are sheets,
　Each orchard shines beside its little town.
Children at every bush a posy meets,
　Bluebells and primroses—wandering up and down
　To hunt birds' nests and flowers a stone's throw from
　　town,
And hear the blackbird in the coppice sing.
　Green spots appear, like doubling a book down
To find the place agen; and strange birds sing
We have [no] [6] name for in the burst of spring.

The sparrow comes and chelps about the slates
　And pops into her hole beneath the eaves,
While the cock pigeon amorously awaits
　The hen, on barn ridge cooing, and then leaves
　With crop all ruffled; where the sower heaves
The hopper at his side, his beans to sow,
　There he with timid courage harmless thieves,
And whirls around the teams, and then drops low,
While plops the sudden gun, and great the overthrow.

And in the maple bush, there hides the stile,
　And then the gate the hawthorn stands before—
Till close upon't you cannot see't the while;
　'Tis like to ivy creeping o'er a door,
　And green as spring, nor gap is seen before.
And still the path leads on, till 'neath your hand
　The gate waits to be opened, and then claps; the sower
Scatters the seeds of spring beneath his hand—
And then the footpath tracks the elting land.

Tall grows the nettle by the hedgeway side,
　And by the old barn end they shade the wall,
In sunshine nodding to the angry tide

Of winds that winnows by: these one and all
  Make up the harmony of spring, and all
That passes feels a sudden love for flowers,
  They look so green; and when the soft showers fall
They grow so fast.   Dock, burdocks, henbane, all,
Who loves not wild flowers by the old stone wall?

I love the little pond to meet at spring
  When frogs and toads are croaking round its brink,
When blackbirds' yellow bills 'gin first to sing
  And green woodpecker rotten trees to clink.
  I love to see the cattle muse and drink
And water crinkle to the rude March wind:
  While two ash dotterels flourish on its brink,
Bearing key-bunches children run to find—
And water-buttercups they're forced to leave behind.

The red-bagged bee on never-weary wing
  Pipes his small trumpet round the early flowers,
And the white nettles by the hedge in spring
  Hear his low music all the sunny hours,
  Till clouds come on and leave the falling showers.
Herald of spring and music of wild blooms,
  It seems the minstrel of spring's early flowers:
On banks where the red nettle flowers it comes,
And there all the long sunny morning hums.

Bluebells, how beautiful and bright they look,
  Bowed o'er green moss and pearled in morning dew,
Shedding a shower of pearls as soon as shook:
  In every wood-hedge gap they're shining through,
  Smelling of spring and beautifully blue.
Childhood and spring, how beautifully dwells
  Their memories in the woods we now walk through!
Oh, balmy days of spring in whitethorn dells,
How beautiful are woods and their bluebells!

LOVE IS LIFE'S SPRING

LOVE is life's spring, the summer of the soul,
The Eden of earth's happiness, the spring
Of all on earth that's lovely.   No control
Can hinder its conception—'tis the wing
That bears the turtle to its nest in spring.
It is the mainspring that conducts the whole,
The eternal anthem which all nature sings:
And woman is of man the life and soul
As long as earth exists or planets roll.

Love is an April sky of various shades,
Today all sunshine and all showers tomorrow:
Buds early blighted, blossoms born to fade,
And woman stamped with the pale hues of sorrow.
Care keeps her cashbook where none like to borrow;
Tears are as lonely as the lonely dove;
Procrastinated falsehood is hell's horror,
Hope is its fire that kindles from above;
Hate burns hell-deep in chronicles of love.

Yet such is love and of the purest waters,
The secret essence of the living clay
That feeds upon itself and wrongs no daughter
Of Eve; but glides on in its own pure way,
Living as in its own light.   The diamond's ray
Had no reflection upon meaner things;
Impurity takes all its hues away,
While purity its grand impressions brings.
Love is the jewel in the crown of kings.

THE PALE SUN [1]

Pale sunbeams gleam
That nurtur [2] a few flowers
Pilewort & daisey & a sprig o' green
On whitethorn bushes
In the leaf strewn hedge

These harbingers
Tell spring is coming fast
& these the schoolboy marks
& wastes an hour from school
Agen the old pasture hedge

Cropping the daisey
& the pilewort flowers
Pleased with the Spring & all he looks upon
He opes his spelling book
& hides her blossoms there

Shadows fall dark
Like black in the pale sun
& lye the bleak day long
Like black stock under hedges
& bare wind rocked trees

Tis chill but pleasant—
In the hedge bottom lined
With brown seer leaves the last
Year littered there & left
Mopes the hedge sparrow

[1] This poem, Clare's most beautiful attempt at what intrigues every poet, an unrhymed stanza, is given from rough draft (MS. 110, Northampton). In this draft it is entitled 'Spring'. A fair copy with the above title is in America. The poem foreshadows with odd vividness the Imagist movement in poetry that began early in the twentieth century.

[2] *nurtur* (nurture) could be *muster*.—MS.

284

With trembling wings & cheeps
Its welcome to pale sunbeams
Creeping through—& further on
Made of green moss
The nest & green-blue eggs are seen

All token spring & every day
Green & more green hedges & close
& everywhere appears—
Still tis but March
But still that March is Spring

GRAVES OF INFANTS

INFANTS' graves are steps of angels, where
Earth's brightest gems of innocence repose.
God is their parent, and they need no tear;
He takes them to his bosom from earth's woes,
A bud their lifetime and a flower their close.
Their spirits are an Iris of the skies,
Needing no prayers; a sunset's happy close,
Gone are the bright rays of their soft blue eyes;
Flowers weep in dewdrops o'er them, and the gale gently sighs.

Their lives were nothing but a sunny shower,
Melting on flowers as tears melt from the eye.
Their deaths were dewdrops on heaven's amaranth bower,
And tolled on flowers as summer gales went by.
They bowed and trembled, and they left no sigh,
And the sun smiled to show their end was well.
Infants have naught to weep for ere they die;
All prayers are needless, beads they need not tell,
White flowers their mourners are, nature their passing-bell.

June, 1844

COME HITHER

COME hither, ye who thirst;
Pure still the brook flows on;
Its waters are not curst;
Clear from its rock of stone
It bubbles and it boils,

An everlasting rill,
Then eddies and recoils
And wimples clearer still.
Art troubled? then come hither,
And taste of peace for ever.

Art weary? here's the place
For weariness to rest,
These flowers are herbs of grace
To cure the aching breast;

Soft beds these mossy banks
Where dewdrops only weep,
Where Nature 'turns God thanks
And sings herself to sleep.
Art troubled with strife? come hither,
Here's peace and summer weather.

Come hither for pleasure who list—
Here are oak boughs for a shade;
These leaves they will hide from the mist
Ere the sun his broad disk has displayed.
Here is peace if thy bosom be troubled,
Here is rest—if thou'rt weary, sit down—
Here pleasure you'll find it is doubled,
For content is life's only crown.
Disciples of sorrow, come hither,
For no blasts my joys can wither.

Art sick of the naughty world?
There's many been sick before thee;
Then leave these young shoots with their tendrils curled
For the oaks that are mossy and hoary.
Art weary with beating the flood?
Here's a mossy bank—come and sit down:
'Twas Nature that planted this wood,
Unknown to the sins of the town
Full of pride and contention—come hither,
We'll talk of our troubles together.

The world is all lost in commotion,
The blind lead the blind into strife;
Come hither, thou wreck of life's ocean,
Let solitude warm thee to life.
Be the pilgrim of love and the joy of its sorrow,
Be anything but the world's man:
The dark of to-day brings the sun of to-morrow,
Be proud that your joy here began.
Poor shipwreck of life, journey hither,
And we'll talk of life's troubles together.

STANZAS

Wouldst thou but know where nature clings,
   That cannot pass away,
Stand not to look on human things,
   For they shall all decay.
False hearts shall change and rot to dust,
   While truth exerts her powers.
Love lives with nature, not with lust,
   Go, find her in the flowers.

Dost dream o'er faces once so fair,
   Unwilling to forget?
Seek nature in the fields, and there
   The first love's face is met:
The nature-gales are lovers' voices,
   As nature's self can prove;
The wild field-flowers are lovers' choices,
   And nature's self is love.

THE SLEEP OF SPRING

Oh, for that sweet, untroubled rest
   That poets oft have sung!—
The babe upon its mother's breast,
   The bird upon its young,
The heart asleep without a pain—
When shall I know that sleep again?

When shall I be as I have been
   Upon my mother's breast
Sweet nature's garb of verdant green
   To woo my former [9] rest—
Love in the meadow, field, and glen,
And in my native wilds agen?

The sheep within the fallow field,
   The herd upon the green,
The larks that in the thistle shield,
   And pipe from morn to e'en—
Oh for the pasture, fields, [10] and fen!
When shall I see such rest agen?

I love the weeds along the fen,
   More sweet than garden flowers,
For freedom haunts the humble glen
   That blest my happiest hours.
Here prison injures health and me:
I love sweet freedom and the free.

The crows upon the swelling hills,
   The cows upon the lea,
Sheep feeding by the pasture rills,
   Are ever dear to me,
Because sweet freedom is their mate
While I am lone and desolate.

I loved the winds when I was young,
   When life was dear to me;
I loved the song which nature sung,
   Endearing liberty;
I loved the wood, the dales, [11] the stream,
For there my boyhood used to dream.

There toil itself was even play, [12]
   'Twas pleasure e'en to weep;
'Twas joy to think of dreams by day,
   The beautiful of sleep.
When shall I see the wood and plain,
And dream those happy dreams again?

THE NIGHTINGALE

THIS is the month the nightingale, clod-brown,
Is heard among the woodland shady boughs:
This is the time when, in the vale, grass-grown,
The maiden hears at eve her lover's vows,
What time the blue mist round the patient cows
Dim rises from the grass and half conceals
Their dappled hides.   I hear the nightingale,
That from the little blackthorn spinney steals
To the old hazel hedge that skirts the vale,
And still unseen sings sweet.   The ploughman feels
The thrilling music as he goes along,
And imitates and listens; while the fields
Lose all their paths in dusk to lead him wrong,
Still sings the nightingale her soft melodious song.

June 12th, 1844

LOVE'S PAINS

THIS love I canna bear it,
   It cheats me night and day;
This love I canna wear it,
   It takes my peace away.

This love was once a flower,
   But now it is a thorn;
The joy of evening hour
   Turned to a pain ere morn.

This love it was a bud
   And a secret known to me,
Like a flower within a wood,
   Like a nest within a tree.

This love, wrong understood,
   Oft turned my joy to pain.
I tried to throw away the bud,
   But the blossom would remain.

July 13th, 1844

POETS LOVE NATURE

Poets love nature, and themselves are love,
The [(13)] scorn of fools, and mock of idle pride.
The vile in nature worthless deeds approve,
They court the vile and spurn all good beside.
Poets love nature; like the calm of heaven,
Her gifts like heaven's own love [(14)] spread far and wide
In all her works there are no signs of leaven;
Sorrow abashes from her simple pride.
Her flowers, like pleasures, have their season's birth,
And bloom through regions here below [(15)]
They are her very scriptures upon earth,
And teach us simple mirth where'er we go.
Even in prison they can solace me,
For where they bloom God is, and I am free.

LOVE LIES [1] BEYOND THE TOMB

Love lies beyond
The tomb, the earth, which fades like dew!
I love the fond,
The faithful, and the true.

Love lives in sleep,
The happiness of healthy dreams:
Eve's dews may weep,
But love delightful seems.

'Tis seen in flowers,
And in the even's [(16)] pearly dew;
On earth's green hours,
And in the heaven's eternal blue.

'Tis heard in spring
When light and sunbeams, warm and kind,
On angel's wing
Bring love and music to the mind. [(17)]

[1] Knight has 'lives,' but the Peterborough transcriber's 'lies' gives
deeper meaning.

And where is voice,
So young, so beautifully (18) sweet
   As nature's choice,
When (19) spring and lovers meet?

   Love lies beyond
The tomb, the earth, the flowers, and dew.
   I love the fond,
The faithful, young, and true.

O, WERT THOU IN THE STORM

O, WERT thou in the storm,
   How I would shield thee!
To keep thee dry and warm
   A camp I would build thee.

Though the clouds poured again,
   Not a drop should harm thee;
The music of wind and rain
   Rather should charm thee.

O, wert thou in the storm,
   A shed I would build for thee,
To keep thee dry and warm.
   How I would shield thee!

The rain should not wet thee
   Nor thunderclap harm thee;
By thy side I would set me
   To comfort and warm thee.

I would sit by thy side, love,
   While the dread storm was over,
And the wings of an angel
   My charmer would cover.

July 25th, 1844

SONG (10) [1]

O Love is so decieving
Like bees it wears a sting
I thought it true believing
But its no such a thing

They smile but to decieve [2] you
They kiss & then they leave you
Speak truth they wont believe you
Their honey wears a Sting

What's the use o' pretty faces
Ruby Lips & cheeks so red
Flowers grows in pleasant places
So does a maidenhead

The fairest wont believe you
The foulest all decieve you
The many laugh & grieve you
Untill your coffin dead

I'LL COME TO THEE AT EVENTIDE

I'll come to thee at eventide (21)
When the west is streaked wi' grey;
I'll wish the night thy charms to hide
& daylight all away.
I'll come to thee at set o' sun,
Where whitethorns i' the May;
I'll come to thee when work is done
& love thee till the day.

[1] From the small red pocket-book, Northampton MS. 10, in which
Clare wrote his title 'Halfpenny Ballads by John Clare I Vol,' and in
which he advised himself 'Gently John gently John.' This manuscript
contains some letters in code and some of the lists of girls' and women's
names mentioned in the Foreword.

When Daisey stars are all turned green
& all is meadow grass,
I'll wander down the bauk at e'en
& court the bonny Lass.
The green bauks and the rustleing sedge
I'll wander down at e'en,
All slopeing to the water's edge
& in the water green.

& there's the luscious meadow sweet
Beside the meadow drain;
My lassie there I once did meet
Who I wish to meet again.
The water lilies where in flower
The yellow & the white;
I met her there at even's hour
& stood for half the night.

We stood & loved in that green place
When Sunday's sun got low;
Its beams reflected in her face
The fairest thing below.
My sweet Ann Foot, my bonny Ann,
The Meadow bauks are green;
Meet me at even when you can;
Be mine as you have been.

HAYMAKING [11]

AMONG the meadow haycocks
  'Tis beautiful to lie,
When pleasantly the day looks
  And gold like is the sky.

How lovely looks the hay-swath
  When turning to the sun;
How richly looks the dark path
  When the rickings all are done.

There's nothing looks more lovely
    As a meadow field in cock;
There's nothing sounds more sweetly
    As the evening's six o'clock.

There's nothing sounds so welcome
    As their singing at their toil:
Sweet maidens wi' tan'd faces
    And bosoms fit to broil.

And it's beautiful to look on,
    How the hay-cleared meadow lies;
How the sun pours down in welcome heat
    Like gold from yonder skies.

There's a calm upon the level
    When the sun is getting low;
Smooth as a lawn is the green level
    Save where swaths their printings [1] shew.

There the mother makes a journey
    With a babbie at her breast;
While the sun is fit to burn ye
    On the sabath day at rest.

There's nothing like such beauty
    With a woman ere compares;
Unless the love within her arms
    The infant which she heirs.

MARY

IT is the evening hour,
    How silent all doth lie:
The hornèd moon she shows her face
    In the river with the sky.
Just [23] by the path on which we pass,
The flaggy lake lies still as glass.

----

[1] Taylor's copyist has 'pointings,' and Knight's word might easily
be misread thus. But 'pointings' has no meaning.

Spirit of her I love,
 Whispering to me
Stories [24] of sweet visions as I rove,
 Here stop, and crop with me
Sweet flowers that in the still hour grew—
We'll take them home, nor shake off the bright dew.

Mary, or sweet spirit of thee,
 As the bright sun shines to-morrow
Thy dark eyes these flowers shall see,
 Gathered by me in sorrow,
In the still hour when my mind was free
To walk alone—yet wish I walked with thee.

STANZAS

BLACK absence hides [25] upon the past,
 I quite forget thy face;
And memory like the angry blast
 Will love's last smile erase.
I try to think of what has been,
 But all is blank to me;
And other faces pass between
 My early love and thee.

I try to trace thy memory now,
 And only find thy name;
Those inky lashes on thy brow,
 Black hair and eyes the same;
Thy round pale face of snowy dyes,
 There's nothing paints thee there.
A darkness comes before my eyes
 For nothing seems so fair.

I knew thy name so sweet and young;
 'Twas music to my ears,
A silent word upon my tongue,
 A hidden thought for years.
Dark hair and lashes swarthy too,
 Arched on thy forehead pale:
All else is vanished from my view
 Like voices on the gale.

WILT [27] thou go with me, sweet maid,
Say, maiden, wilt thou go with me
Through the valley-depths of shade,
Of night and dark obscurity;
Where the path has lost its way,
Where the sun forgets the day,
Where there's nor life nor light to see,[28]
Sweet maiden, wilt thou go with me?

Where stones will turn to flooding streams,
Where plains will rise like ocean waves,
Where life will fade like visioned dreams
And mountains darken into caves,
Say, maiden, wilt thou go with me
Through this sad non-identity,
Where parents live and are forgot,
And sisters live and know us not?

Say, maiden, wilt thou go with me
In this strange death of life[29] to be,
To live in death and be the same,
Without this life or home or name,
At once to be and not to be—
That was and is not—yet to see
Things pass like shadows, and the sky
Above, below, around us lie?

The land of shadows wilt thou trace,
And look—nor know each other's face; [30]
The present mixed [31] with reason gone,
And past and present all as one?
Say, maiden, can thy life be led
To join the living with [32] the dead?
Then trace thy footsteps on with me;
We're wed to one eternity.

1844?

I AM [33]

I AM—yet what I am none cares or knows,
   My friends forsake me like a memory lost;
I am the self-consumer of my woes,
   They rise and vanish in oblivions [34] host,
Like shadows in love—frenzied stifled throes
And yet I am, and live like vapours tost [35]

Into the nothingness of scorn and noise,
   Into the living sea of waking dreams,
Where there is neither sense of life or [36] joys,
   But the vast shipwreck of my life's esteems;
And e'en the dearest—that I love [37] the best—
Are strange—nay, rather stranger than the rest.

I long for scenes where man has never trod,
   A place where woman never smiled or wept;
There to abide with my Creator, God,
   And sleep as I in childhood sweetly slept:
Untroubling and untroubled where I lie,
The grass below—above the vaulted sky.

A VISION [39]

I LOST the love of heaven above,
   I spurned the lust of earth below,
I felt the sweets of fancied love,
   And hell itself my only foe.

I lost earth's joys, but felt the glow
   Of heaven's flame abound in me,
Till loveliness and I did grow
   The bard of immortality.

I loved, but woman fell away;
   I hid me from her faded fame. [40]
I snatched the sun's eternal ray
   And wrote till earth was but a name.

In every language upon earth,
   On every shore, o'er every sea,
I gave my name immortal birth
   And kept my spirit with the free.

August 2nd, 1844

APRIL

In April time flowers come like dreams;
The nightingales and cuckoos sing;
The may-fly setling [1] on the streams
Makes wrinkles with its russet wing.
The river sedge is sprouting green;
The mare-blobs are in burnished gold;
The daisies spread about the green,
And all is lovely to behold.

The skylark winnows in the air,
And cheers the valley with his song;
The slopes are green, the scene is fair;
The herd-boys whistle all day long;
The ash trees they are full of flower
And fallen ones float on the stream;
The sun through haze like misty shower
Shines warmly on the lovely scene.

The meadows they are emerald green;
The river sparkles with the light;
Like snowstorms are the orchard seen;
The fields are with daisies white;
The buttercups are buds of green
That bye and bye are flowers of Gold;
The fields look warm, the air serene
And all is lovely to behold.

'Tis spring the April of the year,
The holiday of birds and flowers.
Some build ere yet the leaves appear,

---

[1] Knight: could be 'sitting'.

While others wait for safer hours:
Hid in green leaves that shun the shower
They're safe and happy all along;
The meanest weed now finds a flower;
The simplest bird will learn a song.

SONNET

ENOUGH of misery keeps my heart alive
To make it feel more mental agony:
Till even life itself becomes all pain,
And bondage more than hell to keep alive;
And still I live, nor murmur nor complain,
Save that the bonds which hold me may make free
My lonely solitude and give me rest,
When every foe hath ceased to trouble me
On the soft throbbing of a woman's breast;
Where love and truth and feeling live confest.
The little cottage with those bonds of joy
My family—life's blood within my breast
Is not more dear than is each girl and boy
Which time matures and nothing can destroy.

MARY

'TIS April and the morning, love,
  Awakes in balmy dew;
Flowers are the meads adorning, love,
  In yellow white and blue;
And if thy heart is true, my love,
  As true it used to be,
Then leave thy cot and kye, my love,
  And walk the fields with me.

And we will walk the meadow, love,
  And we will walk the grove;
And by the winding river love

We'll walk and talk of love.
And by the whitethorn bushes, love,
Just budding into green
Where the shaded fountain rushes, love,
We'll steal a kiss unseen.

Where the daisey on the brink, my love,
Stands peeping in the flood,
And the blackcap flies to drink, my love,
That whistles in the wood,
Where the crowflower like the sun, my love,
Shines in the grass so green,
Let's go where waters run, my love,
And live and love unseen.

And live and love unseen, my dear,
For one sweet April day—
Drear winter seems to last a year
While Mary is away—
Where we can see and not be seen
By woods or shady grove,
Or by the hawthorn's tender green
Let's meet and live and love.

CONTENT

I'M SILVERLESS and pennyless;
    I've no small coin about me;
And yet I'm not in want's distress—
    The rich may live without me.
Though money makes the married glad,
    And finds the single nappy,
Yet wanting wealth I'm never sad
    While health can make me happy.

For health's the flower of mountain's pride,
    The lily of the valley,
The red rose by the cottage side,
    While sickness keeps the valley.

In poverty there is no shame,
    Industry's not the slave on't,
And self-content's a happy name
    So I whistle o'er the leave on't.

I'm silverless and pennyless,
    And poor enough God knows,
Yet in no pinfold of distress
    Long as I get food and clothes.
The heart that keeps its own command,
    Of little makes the more
Content—and all may understand
    I've no wishes from my door.

THE VIOLET

I WILL not throw away the flower,
    The little violet blue;
I pluck'd it in a lonely hour
    When she I loved was true.

Beside a hedge upon a hill
    All by itself it grew:
A type of her who loves me still
    In scent and colour true,

I'll keep the blossom many hours
    Until it withered be;
A type of sweet and withered flowers
    But most of love and thee.

EVENING

IT IS the silent hour when they who roam
    Seek shelter on the earth or ocean's breast;
It is the hour when travel finds a home
    On deserts or within the cot to rest;
    It is the hour when joy and grief are blest,

And nature finds repose where'er she roves;
　　It is the hour that lovers like the best,
When in the twilight shades or darker groves
The maiden wanders with the swain she loves.

The balmy hour when fond hearts fondly meet,
　　The hour when dew like welcome rest descends
On wild flowers shedding forth their odours sweet,
　　The hour when sleep lays foes as quiet friends,
　　The hour when labour's toilworn journey ends
And seeks the cot for sweet repose till morn,
　　The hour when prayer from all to God ascends—
At twilight's hour love's softiest sighs are born,
When lovers linger 'neath the flowering thorn.

Oh at this hour I love to be abroad
　　Gazing upon the moonlit scene around:
'Looking through Nature up to Nature's God,'
　　Regarding all with reverence profound,
　　The wild flowers studding every inch of ground,
And trees with dews bespangled looking bright
　　As burnished silver while the entrancing sound
Of melody from the sweet bird of night
Fills my whole soul with rapture and delight.

DRINKING SONG [41]

Come along my good fellow,
Let's sit and get mellow,
For sorrow we haven't got leisure;
We've money and time,
And that's just the prime
To enjoy it in comfort & pleasure.
Call for ale, or else wine;
On roast beef we can dine,
And joy we shall have without measure.

The parson may preach
Against ale and beseach
His church folks to head no such liquor;
But in neat sanded rooms,
With young girls in their blooms,
Pray who'd ever think of the vicar?
Then leave that dull dunce;
Let's have sandwich for lunch,
And pull at the tankard or pitcher.

Let the dull parson think
Was he here but to drink
He would say beer was made for to please us.
When man is a-dry,
A good sermon's my eye:
The vicar his task is to tease us.
Tankards foam o'er the rim,
Where the fly loves to swim;
And that is the lecture to please us.

So come my old fellow,
Let's go and get mellow.
For care brings no hour of leisure.
We've money and time,
And just now in prime
To sit down enjoying our pleasure.
'Tis summer's prime hours
And the room smells of flowers:
Now, boys, is the season for leisure.

THE ROUND OAK

THE apple top't oak in the old narrow lane,
And the hedgerow of bramble and thorn
Will n'er throw their green on my visions again,
As they did on that sweet dewy morn:
When I went for spring pooteys and birds' nests to look,

Down the border of bushes ayont the fair spring;
I gathered the palm grass close to the brook,
And heard the sweet birds in thorn-bushes sing.

I gathered flat gravel stones up in the shallows
To make ducks and drakes when I got to a pond.
The reedsparrow's nest it was close to the sallows,
And the wren's in a thorn bush a little beyond;
And there did the stickleback shoot through the pebbles,
As the bow shoots the arrow quick darting unseen,
Till it came to the shallows where the water scarce drebbles,
Then back dart again to the spring-head of green.

The nest of the magpie in the low bush of whitethorn,
And the carrion crow's nest on the tree o'er the spring,
I saw it in march on many a cold morning,
When the arum it bloomed like a beautiful thing;
And the apple top't oak aye as round as a table
That grew just above on the bank by the spring,
Where every saturday noon I was able
To spend half a day and hear the birds sing.

But now there's no holidays left to my choice
That can bring time to sit in thy pleasures again;
Thy limpid brook flows and thy waters rejoice,
And I long for that tree but my wishes are vain.
All that's left to me now I find in my dreams:
For fate in my fortune's left nothing the same;
Sweet apple top't oak that grew by the stream
I loved thy shade once, now I love but thy name.

June 19/46

AUTUMN

THE thistledown's flying, though the winds are all still,
On the green grass now lying, now mounting the hill,
The spring from the fountain now boils like a pot;
Through stones past the counting it bubbles red-hot.

The ground parched and cracked is like overbaked bread,
The greensward all wracked is, bents dried up and dead.
The fallow fields glitter like water indeed,
And gossamers twitter, flung from weed unto weed.

Hill-tops like hot iron glitter bright in the sun,
And the rivers we're eying burn to gold as they run;
Burning hot is the ground, liquid gold is the air;
Whoever looks round sees Eternity there.

AUTUMN

I LOVE the fitful gust that shakes
    The casement all the day,
And from the mossy elm-tree takes
    The faded leaf (42) away,
Twirling it (43) by the window pane
With thousand others down the lane.

I love to see the shaking twig
    Dance till the shut of eve,
The sparrow on the cottage rig,
    Whose chirp would make believe
That spring was just now flirting by
In summer's lap with flowers to lie.

I love to see the cottage smoke
    Curl upwards through the trees,
The pigeons nestled round the cote
    On November days like these;
The cock upon the dunghill crowing,
The mill-sails on the heath a-going.

The feather from the raven's breast
    Falls on the stubble lea,
The acorns near the old crow's nest
    Fall (44) pattering down the tree;
The grunting pigs, that wait for all,
Scramble and hurry where they fall.

THE AUTUMN'S WIND

THE autumn's wind on suthering wings
  Plays round the oak-tree strong
And through the hawthorn hedges sings
  The year's departing song.
There's every leaf upon the whirl
  Ten thousand times an hour,
The grassy meadows crisp and curl
  With here and there a flower.
There's nothing in this world I find
But wakens to the autumn wind.

The chaffinch flies from out the bushes,
  The bluecap 'teehees' on the tree,
The wind sues on in merry gushes
  His murmuring Autumn minstrelsy.
The robin sings his Autumn song
  Upon the crab-tree overhead,
The clouds like smoke slow sail along, [45]
  Leaves rustle like the human tread. [46]
There's nothing suits my musing mind
Like to the pleasant autumn wind.

How many a mile it suthers on
  And stays to dally with the leaves,
And when the first broad blast is gone
  A stronger [47] gust the foliage heaves.
The poplar-tree it turns to gray [48]
  As leaves lift up their undersides, [49]
The birch it [50] dances all the day
  To rippling billows petrified. [51]
There's nothing calms the unquiet mind
Like to the soothing autumn's wind.

Sweet twittering o'er the meadow grass,
  Soft sueing o'er the fallow ground,
The lark starts up as on they pass
  With many a gush and moaning sound.

It fans the feathers of the bird
  And ruffles robin's ruddy breast
As round the hovel's end it swownd [52]
  Then sobs and sighs and goes to rest.
In solitude the musing mind
Must ever love the autumn wind.

October 15th, 1845

THE WINTER'S COME

SWEET chestnuts brown like soling leather turn;
  The larch-trees, like the colour of the sun;
That paled sky in the autumn seem'd to burn,
  What a strange scene before us now does run—
Red, brown, and yellow, russet, black, and dun;
  Whitethorn, wild cherry, and the poplar bare;
The sycamore all withered in the sun.
  No leaves are now upon the birch-tree there:
  All now is stript to the cold wintry air.

See, not one tree but what has lost its leaves—
  And yet the landscape wears a pleasing hue.
The winter chill on his cold bed receives
  Foliage which once hung o'er the waters blue.
Naked and bare the leafless trees repose.
  Blue-headed titmouse now seeks maggots rare,
Sluggish and dull the leaf-strewn river flows;
  That is not green, which was so through the year
Dark chill November draweth to a close.

'Tis winter, and I love to read indoors,
  When the moon hangs her crescent up on high;
While on the window shutters the wind roars,
  And storms like furies pass remorseless by.
How pleasant on a feather-bed to lie,
  Or, sitting by the fire, in fancy soar
With Dante or with Milton to regions high,
  Or read fresh volumes we've not seen before,
  Or o'er old Burton's *Melancholy* pore.

COWPER

COWPER, the poet of the fields
    Who found the muse on common ground—
The homesteads that each cottage shields
    He loved—and made them classic ground.

The lonely house, the rural walk
    He sang so musically true,
E'en now they share the people's talk
    Who love the poet Cowper too.

Who has not read the 'Winter Storm,'
    And does not feel the falling snow
And woodmen keeping noses warm
    With pipes wherever forests grow?

The 'Winter's Walk' and 'Summer's Noon'—
    We meet together by the fire
And think the walks are o'er too soon
    When books are read and we retire.

Who travels o'er those sweet fields now
    And brings not Cowper to his mind?
Birds sing his name in every bough,
    Nature repeats it in the wind.

And every place the poet trod
    And every place the poet sung
Are like the Holy Land of God,
    In every mouth, on every tongue.

DEWDROPS

THE dewdrops on every blade of grass are so much like silver
drops that I am obliged to stoop down as I walk to see if they are
pearls, and those sprinkled on the Ivy-woven beds of primroses
underneath the hazels, whitethorns, and maples are so like gold
beads that I stooped down to feel if they were hard, but they

melted from my finger. And where the dew lies on the primrose, the violet and whitethorn leaves, they are emerald and beryl, yet nothing more than the dews of the morning on the budding leaves; nay, the road grasses are covered with gold and silver beads, and the further we go the brighter they seem to shine, like solid gold and silver. It is nothing more than the sun's light and shade upon them in the dewy morning; every thorn-point and every bramble-spear has its trembling ornament: till the wind gets a little brisker, and then all is shaken off, and all the shining jewelry passes away into a common spring morning full of budding leaves, Primroses, Violets, Vernal Speedwell, Bluebell and Orchis and commonplace objects.

HOUSE OR WINDOW FLIES

THESE little indoor dwellers, in cottages and halls, were always entertaining to me; after dancing in the window all day from sunrise to sunset they would sip of the tea, drink of the beer, and eat of the sugar, and be welcome all summer long. They look like things of mind or fairies, and seem pleased or dull as the weather permits. In many clean cottages and genteel houses, they are allowed every liberty to creep, fly, or do as they like; and seldom or ever do wrong. In fact they are the small or dwarfish portion of our own family, and so many fairy familiars that we know and treat as one of ourselves.

THE BEANFIELD

A BEANFIELD full in blossom smells as sweet
As Araby, or groves of orange flowers;
Black-eyed and white, and feathered to one's feet,
How sweet they smell in morning's dewy hours!
When seething night is left upon the flowers,
And when morn's sun shines brightly o'er the field,
The bean-bloom glitters in the gems of showers,
And sweet the fragrance which the union yields
To battered footpaths crossing o'er the fields.

HESPERUS, the day is gone;
Soft falls the silent dew;
A tear is now on many a flower
And heaven lives in you.

Hesperus, the evening mild
Falls round us soft and sweet:
'Tis like the breathings of a child
When day and evening meet

Hesperus, the closing flower
Sleeps on the dewy ground;
While dews fall in a silent shower
And heaven breathes around

Hesperus, thy twinkling ray
Beams in the blue of heaven,
And tells the traveller on his way
That earth shall be forgiven.

O ONCE I HAD A TRUE LOVE

O ONCE I had a true love And loved her very well,
Untill she got a new love; For my wish I could not tell.
When absent I talked to her And when she might have heard,
Thinking silence best could woo her, I passed without a word.
I hid me from her light, And I hid me from her thoughts too.
I lost my relish for delight And vainly studied ways to woo.

I thought she saw my heart beat: My waistcoat seemed to heave
    and stir;
My eyes that others used to cheat Was ever fond and true to
    her.
She saw me quake unheeding; My eyes they watered dim;
The flower 'True love lies bleeding' Could never talk for him.
I thought she saw my legs shake; She never spoke a word;
I thought she saw my hands quake, Though her hands they
    never stirred.

We silent stood together And we passed without a word;
In spring and winter weather Was nothing seen or heard.
I thought to send a letter, But I never wrote a line;
Another time seemed better To ask her to be mine.
But 'another time' was absent: No silence love could prove;
No word was spoke, no line was sent, And so I lost my love.

TO MISS B.

ODD rot it! what a shame it is
   That love should puzzles grow!
That we the one we seek should miss,
   And change from top to toe!
     The Gilafer's a Gilafer;
      And nature owns the plan;
     And strange a thing it is to me
      A man can't be a man.

I paced the woods and mountain's brow,
   And felt as feels a man.
Love pleased me then that puzzles now,
   E'en do the best I can.
     Nature her same green mantle spread,
      And boundless is her span;
     The same bright sun is o'er my head;
      But I can't be a man.

The turf is green and fair the sky,
   And nature still divine;
And summat lovely fills my eye,
   Just like this love of mine.
     And though I love it may not be;
      For do the best I can,
     'Mong such disordered company
      I cannot be a man.

Through married ties—affection's ties
   And all the ties of love
I struggled to be just and wise,

But just I cannot prove.
　　The Bible says that God is Love;
　　　　I like so wise a plan:
　　But was it ordered from above
　　　　That love was [not] (53) wi' man?

This contradiction puzzles me;
　　And it may puzzle all;
Was Adam thus foredoomed to be
　　Our misery by his fall?
　　　　Eve's fall has been a fall to me;
　　　　　　And do the best I can—
　　　　Woman—I neither love nor see,
　　　　　　And cannot be a man.

MISFORTUNE

HERE's black misfortune hauds me down
And keeps me scant o' gear;
I ever bear her winter frown,
And am poor from year to year.
My pockets penniless remain
In sunshine and in shades;
Muses my requests disdain
Are nought but flirting jades.
I'm scant o' grace and scant o'gear
And pennyless [for] (54) a' the year.

Misfortune is a flirting jade,
Her face a bump o'sin;
Of priest-craft-cant she makes a trade
And takes the simple in.
She makes the rich oppress the poor;
The poor she keeps as slaves;
The pulpit stands at hell's hot door;
She reads them in their graves.
I've stood her gab the whole year round,
And now I'm all but underground.

Sae black misfortune hauds me down
I'm waur than parritch pauir (55)
Though five bare shillings make a crown
I pennyless endure.
While hypocrites are set to preach
And turn the right to wrong,
I'm forced to hear but no beseach:
I tell them in a song.
No Priestcraft balls down me they cram;
I only show them—That I am.

THE RED ROBIN

COCK ROBIN, he got a neat tippet in spring,
And he sat in a shed, and heard other birds sing.
And he whistled a ballad as loud as he could,
And built him a nest of oak leaves by the wood,
And finished it just as the celandine pressed
Like a bright burning blaze, by the edge of its nest,
All glittering with sunshine and beautiful rays,
Like high polished brass, or the fire in a blaze;
Then sung a new song on the edge o' the brere;
And so it kept singing the whole of the year.
Till cowslips and wild roses blossomed and died,
The red robin sang by the old spinney side.

LOVE'S STORY

I DO not love thee
So I'll not deceive thee.
I do not love thee,
Yet I'm loth to leave thee.

I do not love thee
Yet joy's very essence
Comes with thy footstep,
Is complete in thy presence.

I do not love thee
Yet when gone, I sigh
And think about thee
Till the stars all die

I do not love thee
Yet thy bright black eyes
Bring to my heart's soul
Heaven and paradise

I do not love thee
Yet thy handsome ways
Bring me in absence
Almost hopeless days

I cannot hate thee
Yet my love seems debtor
To love thee more
So hating, love thee better.

LOVE OF NATURE

I LOVE thee, nature, with a boundless love,
   The calm of earth, the storm of roaring woods;
The winds breathe happiness where'er I rove,
   There's life's own music in the swelling floods.
My harp (56) is in the thunder-melting clouds,
   The snow-capt mountain, and the rolling sea;
And hear ye not the voice where darkness shrouds
   The heavens? There lives happiness for me.

Death breathes its pleasures when it speaks of him;
   My pulse beats calmer while his lightnings play.
My eye, with earth's delusions waxing dim,
   Clears with the brightness of eternal day.
The elements crash round me: it is he!
   Calmly I hear his voice and never start.
From Eve's posterity I stand quite free,
   Nor feel her curses rankle round my heart.

Love is not here. Hope is, and at his voice—
   The rolling thunder and the roaring sea—
My pulses leap, and with the hills rejoice;
   Then strife and turmoil are at end for me,
No matter where life's ocean leads me on;
   For nature is my mother, and I rest,
When tempests trouble and the sun is gone,
   Like to a weary child upon her breast.

LITTLE TROTTY WAGTAIL

LITTLE trotty wagtail, he went in the rain,
And tittering, tottering sideways he near [57] got straight again,
He stooped to get a worm, and look'd up to catch a fly,
And then he flew away ere his feathers they were dry.

Little trotty wagtail, he waddled in the mud,
And left his little footmarks, trample where he would.
He waddled in the water-pudge, and waggle went his tail,
And chirrup up his wings to dry upon the garden rail.

Little trotty wagtail, you nimble all about,
And in the dimpling water-pudge you waddle in and out;
Your home is nigh at hand, and in the warm pigsty,
So, little Master Wagtail, I'll bid you a good-bye.

August 9th, 1849

CLOCK-A-CLAY

IN the cowslips peeps [58] I lie,
Hidden from the buzzing fly,
While green grass beneath me lies,
Pearled wi' dew like fishes' eyes,
Here I lye, a clock-a-clay,
Waiting for the time o' day.

While grassy forests quake [59] surprise,
And the wild wind sobs and sighs,
My gold home rocks as like to fall,
On its pillar green and tall;
When the pattering [60] rain drives by
Clock-a-clay keeps warm and dry.

Day by day and night by night,
All the week I hide from sight;
In the cowslips peeps I lie,
In rain and dew still warm and dry;
Day and night, and night and day,
Red, black-spotted clock-a-clay.

My home it [61] shakes in wind and showers,
Pale green pillar top't wi' flowers, [62]
Bending at the wild wind's breath,
Till I touch the grass beneath;
Here still [63] I live, lone clock-a-clay,
Watching for the time of day.

THE INVITATION

Come hither, my fair [64] one, my choice one, and rare one,
  And let us be walking the meadows so fair,
Where pilewort and daisies in light and gold blazes, [65]
  And the wind plays so sweet in thy bonny brown hair.

Come in thy maiden eye, lay silk and satin by; [66]
  Come in thy russet or green [67] cotton gown;
Come to the meads, my dear, where flags, [68] sedge, and reeds
    appear,
  Rustling to soft winds and bow up and down. [69]

Come with thy parted hair, bright eyes, and forehead bare;
  Come to the whitethorn that grows in the lane;
On [70] banks of primroses, where sweetness reposes,
  Come, love, and let us be happy again.

Come where the speedwell [71] flowers, come where the
    morning showers
  Pearl on the primrose and speedwell so blue;
Come to that clearest brook that ever runs round the nook
  Where you and I pledged our first love so true.

A THOUGHT

A NIGHT without a morning,
    A trouble without end,
A life of bitter scorning,
    A world without a friend.

June 30th, 1849

CLARE TO HIS WIFE [72]

OH, once I had a true love,
    As blest as I could be:
Young [73] Patty was my turtle-dove,
    And Patty she loved me.
We walked the fields together,
    By wild [74] roses and woodbine,
In summer's sunshine weather,
    And Patty she was mine.

We stopped to gather primroses,
    And violets white and blue,
In pastures and green closes
    All glistening with the dew.
We sat upon green mole-hills,
    Among the daisy flowers,
To hear the small birds' merry trills,
    And share the sunny hours.

The blackbird on her grassy nest
    We would not scare away,
Who nuzzling sat wi' scorchin' [75] breast

On her eggs for half the day.
The chaffinch cheeped on the whitethorn,[76]
   And a pretty nest had she;
The magpie chattered all the morn
   From her perch upon the tree.

And I would go to Patty's cot,
   And Patty came to mine;
Each knew the other's very thought
   As birds at Valentine.
And Patty had a kiss to give,
   And Patty had a smile,
To bid me hope and bid me live,[77]
   At every stopping stile.

We loved one summer quite away,
   And when another came,
The cowslip close and sunny day,
   It found us much the same.
We both looked on the selfsame thing,
   Till both became as one;
The birds did in the hedges sing,
   And happy time went on.

The brambles from the hedge advance,
   In love wi' Patty's eyes:
On flowers, like ladies at a dance,
   Flew scores of butterflies.
I claimed a kiss at every stile,
   And had her kind replies.
The bees did round the woodbine toil,
   Where sweet the small wind sighs.

Then my Patty was a young thing;
   And now she's past her teens;
And we've been married many springs,
   And mixed in many scenes.
And I'll be true for Patty's sake,

And she'll be true for mine;
And I this little ballad make,
   To be her valentine.

October 20th, 1848

WHERE SHE TOLD HER LOVE

I SAW her crop a rose
   Right early in the day,
And I went to kiss the place
   Where she broke the rose away,
And I saw the patten rings
   Where she o'er the stile had gone,
And I love all other things
   Her bright eyes look upon.
If she looks upon the hedge or up the leafing tree,
The whitethorn or the brown oak are the dearest (78) things
   to me.

I have a pleasant hill
   Which I sit upon for hours,
Where she cropt some sprigs of thyme
   And other little flowers;
And she muttered as she did it
   As does beauty in a dream,
And I loved her when she hid it
   On her breast, so like to cream,
Near the brown mole on her neck that to me a diamond shone;
Then my eye was like to fire, and my heart was like a stone. (79)

There is a small green place
   Where cowslips early curled,
Which on sabbath day I trace,
   The dearest in the world.
A little oak spreads o'er it,
   And throws a shadow round,
A green sward close before it,
   The greenest ever found:
There is not a woodland nigh nor is there a green grove,
Yet stood the fair maid nigh me and told me all her love.

TO LIBERTY

O SPIRIT of the wind and sky,
Where doth thy harp neglected lie?
Is there no heart thy bard to be,
To wake that soul of melody?
Is liberty herself a slave?
No! God forbid it! On, ye brave!

I've loved thee as the common air,
And paid thee worship everywhere:
In every soil beneath the sun
Thy simple song my heart has won.
And art thou silent? Still a slave?
And thy sons living? On, ye brave!

Gather on mountain and on plain!
Make gossamer the iron chain!
Make prison walls as paper screen,
That tyrant maskers may be seen!
Let earth as well as heaven be free!
So, on, ye brave, for liberty!

I've loved thy being from a boy;
The Highland hills were once my joy;
Then morning mists did round them lie,
Like sunshine in the happiest sky.
The hills and valley seemed my own,
When Scottish land was freedom's throne.

And Scottish land is freedom's still;
Her beacon fires, on every hill,
Have told, in characters of flame,
Her ancient birthright to her fame.
A thousand hills will speak again,
In fire, that language ever plain

To sycophants and fawning knaves,
That Scotland ne'er was made for slaves!

Each fruitful vale, each mountain throne,
Is ruled by nature's law alone;
And naught but falsehood's poisoned breath
Will urge the claymore from its sheath.

O spirit of the wind and sky,
Where doth thy harp neglected lie?
Is there no harp thy bard to be,
To wake that soul of melody?
Is liberty herself a slave?
No! God forbid it! On, ye brave!

THE DYING CHILD [80]

He could not die when trees were green,
  For he loved the time too well.
His little hands, when flowers were seen,
  Were held for the bluebell,
    As he was carried o'er the green.

His eye glanced at the white-nosed bee;
  He knew those children of the spring:
When he was well and on the lea
  He held one in his hands to sing,
    Which filled his little heart with glee. [81]

Infants, the children of the spring!
  How can an infant die
When butterflies are on the wing,
  Green grass, and such a sky?
    How can they die at spring?

He held his hands for daisies white,
  And then for violets blue,
And took them all to bed at night
  That in the green fields grew,
    As childhood's sweet delight.

And then he shut his little eyes,
　　And flowers would notice not;
Birds' nests and eggs made [82] no surprise,
　　Nor any blossoms got:
　　　　All met with plaintive sighs.[83]

When winter came and blasts did sigh,
　　And bare was [84] plain and tree,
As he for ease in bed did lie
　　His soul seemed with the free,
　　　　He died so quietly.

DEATH

FLOWERS shall hang upon the palls,
Brighter than patterns upon shawls,
And blossoms shall be in the coffin lids,
Sadder than tears on grief's eyelids,[85]
Garlands shall hide pale corpses' faces
When beauty shall rot in charnel places,
Spring flowers shall come in tears of sorrow [86]
For the maiden goes down to her grave to-morrow.

Last week she went walking and stepping along,
Gay as first flowers of spring or the tune of a song;
Her eye was as bright as the sun in its calm,
Her lips they were rubies, her bosom was warm,
And white as the snowdrop that lies on her breast;
Now death like a dream is her bedfellow guest,
And white as the sheets—ay, and paler than they—
Now her face in its beauty has perished to clay.

Spring flowers they shall hang on her pall,
More bright than the pattern that bloom'd on her shawl,
And blooms shall be strewn where the corpse lies hid,
More sad than the tears upon grief's eyelid;
And ere the return of another sweet May
She'll be rotting to dust in the coffined clay,
And the grave whereon the bright snowdrops grow
Shall be the same soil as the beauty below.

　　　　　　　　　　　　　　February 11th, 1847

MARY BYFIELD

'Twas in the morning early,
The dew was on the barley,
    Each spear a string of beads;
Bluecaps intensely blue,
Corn poppies burnt me through,
    Seemed flowers among the weeds.

Her cheeks the rosy brere's bloom,
Her eyes like ripples, lately come
    From gravel-paven spring;
She looked across the red and blue,
Each colour wore a livelier hue,
    While larks popt up to sing.

How lovely hung the barley spears,
Beaded in morning's dewy tears
    Rich green and grey did seem;
The pea more rich than velvet glows,
Sweeter than double the dog-rose,
    A sweet midsummer dream.

The sun gleamed o'er that waving corn
Where her I kissed one dewy morn,
    A shining golden river.
I clasped her in a locked embrace,
And gazing on her bonny face,
    I loved her and for ever.

FIRST LOVE

I ne'er was struck before that hour
    With love so sudden and so sweet.
Her face it bloomed like a sweet flower
    And stole my heart away complete.
My face turned pale as deadly pale,

My legs refused to walk away,
 And when she looked 'what could I ail?'
My life and all seemed turned to clay.

And then my blood rushed to my face
 And took my eyesight quite away.[87]
The trees and bushes round the place
 Seemed midnight at noonday.
I could not see a single thing,
 Words from my eyes did start;
They spoke as chords do from the string
 And blood burnt round my heart.

Are flowers the winter's choice?
 Is love's bed always snow?
She seemed to hear my silent voice
 Not love's appeals [88] to know.
I never saw so sweet a face
 As that I stood before:
My heart has left its dwelling-place
 And can return no more.

HOW CAN I FORGET?

THAT farewell voice of love is never heard again,
Yet I remember it, and think on it with pain;
I see the place she spoke when passing by,
The flowers were blooming as her form drew nigh;
That voice is gone with every pleasing tone,
Loved but one moment, and the next alone.

'Farewell!' the woods repeated as she went
Walking in silence through the grassy bent;
The wild flowers, they ne'er looked so sweet before,
Bowed in farewells to her they'll see no more.
In this same spot the wild flowers bloom the same
In scent and hue and shape, ay, even name;
'Twas here she said farewell, and no one yet
Has so sweet spoken.   How can I forget?

ADIEU

'Adieu, my love, adieu!
Be constant and be true
As the daisies gemmed with dew,
    Bonny maid.'
Dews are on the braken
Which the playful winds are shaking;
Sweet songs the birds are making [89]
    In the shade.

The moss upon the tree
Was as green as green could be,
The clover on the lea
    Ruddy glowed;
Leaves were silver wi' the dew,
Where the tall sow-thistles grew,
And I bade the maid adieu
    On the road.

Then I took myself to sea,
While the little chiming bee
Sung his ballads on the lea,
    Chiming [90] sweet;
And the blue-wing'd butterfly [91]
Was sailing through the sky,
Skimming up and bouncing by
    Near my feet.

I left the little birds,
And sweet lowing o' the herds,
And couldn't find out words,
    Do you see,
To say to them good-bye,
Where the yellow-cups do lye;
So heaving a deep sigh,
    Took to sea.

THE PEASANT POET

He loved the brook's soft sound,
    The swallow swimming by.
He loved the daisy-covered ground,
    The cloud-bedappled sky.
To him the dismal storm appeared
    The very voice of God; [92]
And when the Evening rack was reared
    Stood Moses with his rod.
And everything his eyes surveyed,
    The insects i' the brake,
Were creatures God Almighty made,
    He loved them for His sake—
    A silent man in life's affairs,
        A thinker from a boy,
    A peasant in his daily cares,
        The poet in his joy.

SONG

    The hurly burly wind
    And it whirls the wheat about,
    While it's coming in the ear,
    And the barley's on the sprout;
    It whirls the wheat about me
    In its suit of sunny green;
    And my lassie need not doubt me,
    She's the sweetest ever seen.

    Her hair is of the auburn,
    And her cheek is of the rose;
    And my bonny Sarah Ann is
    The sweetest flower that grows.
    Her lips are like the cherry
    And her skin is lily white;
    Her tongue is ever merry;
    Her smiles are all delight.

The hurly burly wind
And it whirls the wheat about;
The billows swab behind,
And the headaches swirl without.
The bluecaps in the green
Eddy like Butterflies;
And nothing still is seen,
Where e'er we turn our eyes.

My love is like the wild scene;
Her gown is floating free;
And I have like a child been
To seek her company.
And I must like a child be,
In fancys to delight;
So I walk to see the wild bee
And butterfly till night.

SONG

COME weal come woe I care not;
　　Nor fear it not a fly;
Though others ills I bear not
　　They often make me sigh.
I'm poor, but not in nature's choice:
　　Her laws I always own;
I hear her as a mother's voice,
　　And never feel alone.
Come weal come woe I never care;
The ills of life I gladly bear.

The spring has clad the land in green;
　　The daisy opens on the lea;
A golden stud in silver sheen,
　　And spreads her choicest gifts for me.
I scent the violet's breath perfume
　　Beneath the whitethorn leafing shade;
I see and bend me o'er their bloom,

And think upon the lovely maid.
Come weal come woe I never care;
The ills of life I gladly bear.

The knotting bloom is on the thorn;
  The little bird is on its nest;
And I've been happy all the morn
  Leaning on my true love's breast:
A breast as white as any curd,
  And soft as any pillows are,
With voice o' music like the bird—
  And fair. O she was more than fair.
Come weal come woe I never care;
The ills of life I gladly bear.

MY LOVE

MY LOVE is like a pleasant thought,
A first flower of the may;
My Love she is a charm unbought,
Young, beautiful, and gay.
My Love she is a dream of joy,
More living than a dream:
A sweetness nothing would destroy,
The sunlight i' the stream.
My Love is all and more than these,
A pleasant thought that's born to please.

Than summer flowers her face more sweet;
Than morning dews her eye more clear;
The hedge-rose and wild woodbines meet:
In them I pay her worship here.
Wild woodbine's streaky hues o' red,
Hedge-roses' blushing fleshy hue,
Carnations glowing in their bed—
My Love's as fair and sweet and true—
My love's a thought of more than these,
To charm in secret witcheries.

Sweet pleasant thoughts and happy dreams,
My lover's more o' woman's kin;
She's even sweeter than she seems;
And O her heart is warm within.
Warm as the smile upon her lip,
Warm as the turtle in its nest,
As nectar which the wild bees sip,
As moles upon her bonny breast,
Sweeter than all these visions prove
Is her I worship in first Love.

MY LOVE IN DISHABILLE

'TWAS in the month of April when birds all merry sing
I took a walk to Kingsthorpe right early i' the spring;
I took a walk to Kingsthorpe right early i' the day,
And there I met my true love go barefoot by the way.

Her ancles they were handsome and lovely was her feet;
Her face was like an Irish girl's & beautifully sweet;
She passed me like a stranger; I think I see her still:
I could not tell my own true love in such a dishabille.

Her eyes were like two diamonds and a woman all complete;
I could have knelt on both my knees and kissed her very feet;
I loved her where I passed and love her dearly still;
But I could not tell my own true love in such a dishabille.

She passed me by in silence; I passed her by the same;
I could not tell her person; I did not know her name;
But her person I love dearly, and I love her dearly still;
Though I did not know my own true love in rags & dishabille.

I MET A PLEASANT MAIDEN

ON THE seventeenth of April i' the good year forty-one
I met a pleasant maiden & I wished the maid was mine:
She'd cowslips in her basket; she'd sweetbrier in her hand;
Her love I would have ask'd but she would not understand.

I touched her gown in passing & she looked in strange surprise.
The meadow pool spread glassing in the beautiful sunrise;
Her shawl was of the flags so green her gown was brown & red;
Her stockings white as snow were seen & lightsome was her
    tread.

The linnet chirrup in the thorn; the lark sung in the sky;
And bonny was the sunny morn & every road was dry.
I took her by the waist so—all in a pleasant place:
She no denial made at all but smiled upon my face.

I cuddled her in the green grass & sat among the hay,
Till sunshine o'er the hill did pass & daylight went away;
I kissed o'er her bonny face so tender & so true
And left my blessing on the place among the foggy dew.

MY LOVED ONE MY OWN

By THE Moon and Star lightin',
By the still of midnight in
Which waiseys [93] delight in
I love thee alone;
I love thee my dearest,
With feelings, sincerest,
Farthest off thou'rt the nearest,
My loved one my own.

True love canna cheat me;
Falsehood canna beat me;
Yet Mary love meet me—'
I'm sad and alone.
The day's full o' lying,
But the last light is dying,
And o'er the west flying,
There thou still art my own.

The night wind is born brief;
Lady birds i' green corn sleep;
The dews on the thorn leaf:
Dearest, meet, for I'm lone;
I'm lone, love, and weary,
Where the hazels hang near thee;
O come love and cheer me,
And make me thy own.

WHEN I WAS YOUNG

WHEN I was young I fell in love and got but little good on't:
When she passed I turned away;
At first she would, then wouldn't.
I wished to speak & then the sigh
Came first and always stopt it.
Come Silence, tell my wishes then;
I thought so and then dropt it,
And never tried to speak agen.

The path that o'er the cornfield lay,
I met her one day early;
She turned her face another way,
And I walked in the barley.
A lark that moment sought the sky
Close to her gown or nearly;
Her bright eye looked to see him fly,
And then I loved her dearly.

And turns the rosey cheek to clay?
'Tis beauty's face in woman's form,
That steals the senses all away,
That rends the bosom like a storm;
Though mild as evening's sober ray,
The winds they sigh, the dews they weep;
And on the violet's bosom fall:
First love and truth unriddles all.

THE DARK DAYS OF AUTUMN (94)

THE dark days of Autumn grows cloudy & rainy;
The sun pales like sulphur; the shadows grow long:
To me the dull season the sweetest of any;
I love to see yellow leaves fall in my song.
The rush-covered green and thistle-capped mountain,
The dead leaves a-falling and winds singing round,
The willow and ash leaves, they choak up the fountain:
There's health i' the strife o't and joy i' the sound.

I love there to loiter wi' winds blowing round me,
Till the strong eddy's past and the rain gust is over;
Wild pigeons fly over the distance (96) looks downy,
With [   ] (97) willow rows pieces of clover;
Brown pieces o' stubble, ground o' turnips bright green,
The crows flying over the lakes silver light,
Scarce a wild blossom left to enliven the scene:
Rauk and mist are for ever in sight

IT IS LOVE

IT IS love.
There's a mildness i' the air;
The fields are green & fair;
And sunbeams there
From above.
There is singing o' birds;
There is bleating o' herds;
Waters waving like curds;
What is love
But the landscapes o' spring sunny green o' the grove?
And the maid walking there Mary Dove?

Is it love
To admire what God's sending,
Charm on charm never ending,
Ever varying, unspending?

Look above.
Clouds, rocks rough and ragged,
Temples unhewed, and jagged,
Where currish man never begged.
What is love
But nature & truth over ocean & grove?
And that first boyish charm Mary Dove?

It is love.
While grass remains green,
Mary Dove,
And clouds sail in heaven above,
And flowers come wi' spring you'll be love,
Mary Dove.
Burnet buttons growed dark in that hour;
Purple fitch dangled on the thorn bower;
And each little weed had no flower but love.
In that little meadow, like joys from above,
Walks the poet's young fancy, the sweet Mary Dove.

LOST AS STRANGERS AS WE PASS

THE summer rose in love's own hue
Blushes and blooms so fair and free;
I gaze on thee with looks as true;
Thou look'st on me and vacancy.
Canst thou look here and all forget?
The place, the time, is nothing there?
Then pity man who's so beset,
And woman e'er was made so fair.

Thy swelling breast is just the same
As when we met and lov'd so true;
The evening Sun went down in flame,
And shed her shower of pearly dew;
My arm was o'er thy shoulders thrown;
Thy gentle hand was held in mine;
And now I pass to thee unknown,
Thy eye that brightens only mine.

I guess and know and own it not:
We're lost as strangers and we pass;
Though there's green places unforgot,
Where love would clasp my bonny lass.
Aye, clasp her in the fondest arms,
And hold her like a lamp of love:
The same flowers grow in fields and farms;
The same blue sky is arched above.

FRAGMENT (97)

By MUD pools see a gnat stupid nameless fly
Two hairs for sail all on one end sail by
The sprinkling rain blotches the thirsty dust
And makes the little insects hang out of sight
As if their little feet were scalded by 't. . . .

'COME THE BACK WAY DEAR' (98)

Now Granny's gone to bed Steal in the back way;
Ye shall be my favoured lad; I'll be your lass alway.
Come in this happy night, For Granny's fast asleep;
And I'll put out the light, Fear some should come to peep.

So come the back way dear, To love me ye'll be free;
Should ye kick at Granny's chair Till furder ye'll find me;
The fire it may be out, Or there'll maybe be a spark;
For there's nothing half so sweet As kisses in the dark.

Love come the back way in. By the mint and lad's-love tree;
And where my Granny's been I' the next chair feel for me;
The fire's upon the hearth And there'll maybe be a spark;
The crickets sing i' mirth, And the kiss is sweet at dark.

So Roger pulled the string; She from the window flew:
She was a lassie sweet; He was a lover true.
He felt o'er Granny's chair, And felt his heart's delight,
I' kisses sweet and fair, Till morning brought a light.

SONG

I HID MY LOVE (99)

I HID my love when young while (100) I
Couldn't bear the buzzing of a fly;
I hid my love to my despite
Till I could not bear to look at light:
I dare not gaze upon her face
But left her memory in each place;
Where'er I saw a wild flower lie
I kissed and bade my love good-bye.

I met her in the greenest dells,
Where dewdrops pearl the wood bluebells;
The lost breeze kissed her bright blue eye,
The bee kissed and went singing by,
A sunbeam found a passage there,
A gold chain round her neck so fair;
As secret as the wild bee's song
She lay there all the summer long.

I hid my love in field and town
Till e'en the breeze would knock me down;
The Bees seemed singing ballads o'er,
The flyes buzz turned a Lion's roar; (101)
And even silence found a tongue,
To haunt me all the summer long;
The riddle nature could not prove
Was nothing else but secret love.

BORN UPON AN ANGEL'S BREAST (102)

IN crime and enmity they lie
Who sin and tell us love can die,
Who say to us in slander's breath
That love belongs to sin and death.
From Heaven it came on Angel's wing
To bloom on earth, Eternal spring;
In falsehood's enmity they lie
Who sin and tell us love can die.

'Twas born upon an angel's breast.
The softest dreams, the sweetest rest,
The brightest sun, the bluest sky,
Are love's own home and canopy.
The thought that cheers this heart of mine
Is that of Love—Love so divine,
They sin who say in slander's breath
That love belongs to sin and death.

The sweetest voice that lips contain,
The sweetest thought that leaves the brain,
The sweetest feeling of the heart—
There's pleasure even in its smart. [103]
The scent of Rose and Cinnamon
Is not like Love remembered on;
In falsehood's enmity they lie
Who sin and tell us love can die.

FRAGMENT

Vetches both yellow and blue
Grew thick in the meadow-lane;
Isabella's shawl kept off the dew,
As thickly upon her it came.
A thorn bush caught her umbrella,
As though it would bid her to stay;
But the loving and loved Isabella
Went laughing and walking away.

MY EVERLASTING LOVE

My love is like the Gilliflower
  I planted by mysell;
My love is like a Willowflower,
  A blossom wi'out smell.

How sweet & very fair my love,
  Like diamonds are her eyes;

Like dewdrops sparkling from above,
    That on the white rose lies.

Her cheeks are like the red rose tree,
    Her bosom like the white;
Her thoughts from heaven surely be
    To give to man delight.

Her voice is like the Nightingale,
    Her bosom like the dove;
She shall be in this one tale
    My everlasting Love.

OH WHITHER FAIR MAIDEN

'OH WHITHER, fair maiden, so soon in the morning,
In thy High-Lows & stockings as black as a coal?
Oh whither fair maiden in Nature's adorning?
Thy face has bewitch'd me both body and soul.'
'I'm going to the village just o'er the tillage there
Where the weather-cock shines i' the gleam o' the Sun:
Where the Jackdaws a-choir build their nests i' the spire
As soon as the spring has its season begun.'

We pass'd the pale primrose beneath the wild Briar;
The sunbeams were playing in the arc of the sky;
The sweet smelling violet we stopped to admire
That blossomed beneath every hedge we pass'd by.
Behind and before me I looked all around:
I saw no one near when I kiss'd her red cheek;
About her white neck I both my arms wound,
When she blush'd like a fire & was ready to speak.

The lace-work o' spiders was beaded wi' pearls;
The leaves of the clover were silvered wi' dew,
Where I took the white hand o' the innocent girl,
And led her the field and the spinney quite through.
The nuthatches ran down the bark o' the trees;
Ringdoves in the Ivy sat still on their nest;
And round the wet wild flowers whirring were the bees,
All choosing those blossoms which suited them best.

Neath ribb'd maple stovens sweet lies the bluebell,
And Harriett's bosom bent low to the ground
To crop two or three as she liked them so well—
How pleasantly fair all the scenery around.
In sight o' the Cottage we sat on the stile
When I kissed her sweet lips in a thrill o' delight:
I had to return agen two or three mile,
But I promised at parting to meet her that night.

WILT THOU THINK O' ME [104]

Now the spring's coming and wild bees are humming
    Mary think of me;
    When leaves come to the wild wind
    So loved by thee in childhood,
    O then remember me;
    Then think who loved thee dearest,
    And got wild flowers the nearest,
    And claimed the kiss sincerest
    Which Mary still owes me.
    O Mary in spring weather
    Lets both go there together,
    And still remember me:
    Where places are greenest,
    And summer's serenest,
    Wilt thou think o' me?

    The primrose o' the wildwood
    Talk agen to thy childhood,
    Neath the old ivy tree,
    Where the ringdove coos lofty,
    And the winds flutter softly,
    My love, think o' me;
    By the beds o' green mosses
    That the oak root embosses,
    And lichens white glosses,
    Remember thou me.

My love, let's be roaming;
Come to me at gloaming;
I' the Lane let us be:
Where the woodbine is wreathing,
And dogrose is breathing,
Remember thou me.
The cockchafer born
From the dewey whitethorn
Is sounding his horn,
Dear Mary, to thee;
I'll meet thee at gloaming,
I' the fields to be roaming,
Till then think o' me.

MY MINNIE TOLD ALL

My MINNIE told all to my Daddie at e'en,
And my lover was by both denied:
Sae I made him a bed in fields in their green,
And laid mysen close by his side.
The wind it blew brisk and shook all the leaves
Which covered us both as we lay:
For honest true love it never deceives;
Here Minnie & Daddie hae nothing to say.

The Linnet sang o'er us a pleasant gay tune
As ever I heard him before,
While there we lay down by the light of the moon,
And he kissed me quite home to the door.
My Minnie said nay, and my Daddie forbade;
But they could do naething with him:
A whisper by dark is not lost in the shade;
And to kiss one we love is no sin.

The peas are in blossom, & sweet the beans smell;
And the grass where we sat wavered green;
And love in that place not a secret will tell,

Where we were not listened to or seen.
My Minnie said nay, and my Daddie forbade;
But forbidden my Lover won't be;
We meet there at e'en when he's put by the spade;
And will while a leaf's on the tree.

SONG FOR MISS B—— [105]

THE thrush in the firdeal is singing till e'en,
While to the far woods flies the wearisome crow;
The bonny thorn hedge o' the pasture is green,
And green is the moss-bank where primroses grow;
So come to the dewy lane, young handsome maiden;
We'll wander the sheep walks where Ivy trees lean;
The bee buzzes by with his legs heavy laden;
And sweet purple violets nestle in green.

O come, bonny maiden, & I will go with thee,
A-down the footpath way the cowslip nods o'er;
Among the green rushes sweet kisses I'll gie thee;
And the cold world shall trouble our pleasures no more.
Sweet is the song of the thrush i' the wild wood,
While blue misty hastiness [106] gathers around;
And grey look the trees i' the scenes o' thy childhood;
And when the Ox lows how delightful the sound.

The brimstone-hued primrose looks bright on the mossy bank;
Round the stulps of old maple the violets perfume;
At the ivy'd hedge bottom the Arum looks glossy & rank,
While the hedge-sparrow sits on its nest in the gloom.
O come, my sweet maiden, there's nought to confound thee:
The evening is pleasant; the valley is still:
I'll kiss thy soft cheek with my arm clasping round thee,
While the moon shows its horn at the top of the hill.

WRITTEN IN PRISON

I ENVY e'en the fly its gleams of joy
In the green woods; from being but a boy
Among the vulgar and the lowly bred,
I envied e'en the hare her grassy bed.
Inured to strife and hardships from a child,
I traced with lonely step the desert wild;
Sighed o'er bird pleasures, but no nest destroyed;
With pleasure felt the singing they enjoyed;
Saw nature smile on all and shed no tears,
A slave through ages, though a child in years;
The mockery and scorn of those more old,
An Aesop in the world's extended fold.
The fly I envy settling in the sun
On the green leaf, and wish my goal [107] was won.

THE DAISY [108]

THE daisy is a happy flower,
　　And comes at early spring,
And brings with it the sunny hour
　　When bees are on the wing.

It brings with it the butterfly,
　　And early humble-bee;
With the polyanthus' golden eye,
　　And blooming apple-tree;

Hedge-sparrows form [109] the mossy nest
　　In the old garden hedge,
Where schoolboys, in their idle glee,
　　Seek pooties as their pledge.

341

The cow stands browsing all the day
  Over the orchard gate,
And eats her bit of sweet old hay;
  And Goody stands to wait,

Lest what's not eaten the rude wind
  May rise and snatch away
Over the neighbour's hedge behind,
  Where hungry cattle lay.

February 10th, 1860

WELL, HONEST JOHN [110]

WELL, honest John, how fare you now at home?
The spring is come, and birds are building nests;
The old cock-robin to the sty is come,
With olive feathers and its ruddy breast;
And the old cock, with wattles and red comb,
Struts with the hens, and seems to like some best,
Then crows, and looks about for little crumbs,
Swept out by little folks an hour ago;
The pigs sleep in the sty; the bookman comes—
The little boy lets home-close nesting go,
And pockets tops and taws, where daisies blow,
To look at the new number just laid down,
With lots of pictures, and good stories too,
And Jack the Giant-killer's high renown.

February 10th, 1860

EARLY SPRING

THE spring is come, and spring flowers coming too,
  The crocus, patty kay, the rich heartsease;
The polyanthus peeps with blebs of dew,
  And daisy flowers; the buds swell on the trees;
  While o'er the odd flowers swim grandfather bees.
In the old homestead rests the cottage cow;

The dogs sit on their haunches near the pale,
The least one to the stranger growls 'bow-wow,'
    Then hurries to the door and cocks his tail,
To gnaw the unfinished bone; the placid cow
    Looks o'er the gate; the thresher's lumping flail
Is all the noise the spring encounters now.

THE GREEN LANE (111)

A LITTLE lane—the brook runs close beside,
    And spangles in the sunshine, while the fish glide swiftly by;
And hedges leafing with the green springtide;
    From out their greenery the old birds fly,
And chirp and whistle in the morning sun;
    The pilewort glitters 'neath the pale blue sky,
The little robin has its nest begun,
    And grass-green linnets round the bushes fly.
How mild the spring comes in! the daisy buds
    Lift up their golden blossoms to the sky.
How lovely are the pingles and the woods!
    Here a beetle runs—and there a fly
Rests on the arum leaf in bottle-green,
And all the spring in this sweet lane is seen.

1860

BIRDS' NESTS

'TIS spring, warm glows the south,
Chaffinch carries the moss in his mouth
To filbert hedges all day long,
And charms the poet with his beautiful song;
The wind blows bleak o'er the sedgy fen,
But warm the sun shines by the little wood,
Where the old cow at her leisure chews her cud.

1860

NOTES ON THE TEXT

THE text of Section I of this edition is based on that of the 1935 two volumes, *The Poems of John Clare* (Dent). Corrections of, additions to, or readings variant from, the 1935 text are listed below.

Note

SECTION I

1. *The Village Minstrel*, l. 291. *Where* for *were*.

2. *The Enthusiast. A Daydream. The Enthusiast* added from MS. CXXI Peterborough to title.

SECTION II

The text for this section is based, where possible (as in *Child Harold*), on Clare's manuscripts. But for most of the late poems manuscripts are not available. In those cases texts are based on Knight's transcripts which came to light in 1948. Principal variations are noted below.

3. *The Nightingale's Nest*, l. 74. *cuckoo*, not *orchis*.

4. *Child Harold*. In this stanza, the eleven following, the song 'Say what is love' and the ballad 'The blackbird has built in the pasture agen', Clare has used initial capital letters for each work. Such use of captials, like his 'consonant code', are signs of the more troubled periods of his madness. We have omitted the capitals. Clare himself goes back suddenly to ordinary writing in stanza 3 of the ballad 'The rose of the world' but reverts to capitals in the stanza 'The paigles bloom . . .'

5. *Child Harold*. In the notebook (Northampton MS. 110) dated November 1845, there are some nine-line stanzas that, in their mood and content—of struggle toward reconciliation with life and its ills—seem to belong with the *Child Harold* period of composition. On the other hand, other stanzas in this notebook reach out, in both matter and tone, toward Clare's next long poem, *A Rhapsody*. Below are the three stanzas akin to those of *Child Harold*:

> 'Infants are but cradles for the grave
> & death the nurse as soon as life begins
> Time keeps account books for him & they save
> Expenses for his funeral out of sins
> The stone is not put down—but when death wins

Churchyards are chronicles were all sleep well
The gravestones there as after-lives live in
Go search the Scriptures they will plainly tell
That God made heaven——Man himself the hell

'There is a chasm in the heart of man
That nothing fathoms like a gulph at sea
A depth of darkness lines may never span
A shade unsunned in dark eternity
Thoughts without shadow——that eye can see
Or thought imagine tis unknown to fame
Like day at midnight such its youth to me
At ten years old it boyhoods acorn came
Now manhoods forty past tis just the same

'The present is the funeral of the past
& man the living sepulchre of life
Still in the past he lives——O would it last
In its own dreams of beauty where the strife
Of passion died——yet trouble rife
Dwells on its sweetest music tones & harsh all round
That cord that used to sound the name of wife
On life's jarred music now emits no sound
& sweetheart melodys youth lose are nowhere to be found.

6. *Spring Comes*, l. 9. [no] supplied from Clare's own MS.

7. *The Pale Sun*, l. 8. *these* not *there*.

8. l. 16. *fall* not *full*.

9. *The Sleep of Spring*, l. 10. *my former* not *to perfect*.

10. l. 17. *fields* not *field*.

11. l. 35. *dales* not *vale*.

12. l. 37. *There toil itself was even play* not *There even toil itself was play*.

13. *Poets Love Nature*, l. 2. *The* not *Though*.

14. l. 6. *Her gifts like heaven's own love* not *Like heaven's own love her gifts*.

15. l. 10. *And bloom through regions here below* added from MS.

16. *Love Lies Beyond the Tomb*, l. 10. *even's* not *morning's*.

17. l. 16. Knight has *wind* for *mind*.

18. l. 18. *beautifully sweet* not *beautiful and sweet*.

19. l. 20. *When* not *where*.

20. *O Love is so decieving*. From MS. 10, Northampton, in Clare's own hand.

21. *I'll come to thee at eventide*. Also in Clare's own handwriting (MS. 9).

22. *Haymaking.* Taylor's copyist transcribes this in 'fourteener' stanzas, as if he saw a different MS. from the one Knight transcribed.

23. *Mary. It is the evening hour.* l. 5. *just* not *prest.*

24. l. 9. *stories* not *stores.*

25. *Stanzas. Black absence hides,* l. 1. possibly *bides,* which makes better sense.

26. *An Invite to Eternity. An Invite* not *Invitation.*

27. l. 1. *Wilt* not *Say, wilt.*

28. l. 7. *life nor light* not *light nor life.*

29. l. 18. *death of life* not *death-in-life.*

30. l. 25. *And look—nor* not *Nor look nor.*

31. l. 26. *mixed* not *marred.*

32. l. 27. *with the dead* not *and the dead.*

33. *I Am.* There are two lines of descent for the text of the first eighteen lines of *I Am*:

Lost original (written between 1844 and 1846)

Bedford Times
(Jan. 1848)

Knight's transcripts
(Knight's own hand
between 1844 and 1850)

Peterborough transcript
and
Northampton second transcript
Cherry (1873)
Symons (1908)
Blunden (1920)
Tibble (1935)

(acquired by the
Northampton Library
1948)
(Grigson (1950)

The text here now follows Knight.

34. l. 4. *oblivion's* not *oblivious.*

35. ll. 5 and 6. Thus Knight; though he gives *vapours lost.* We have given *tost* rather than repeat *lost,* since there can be no authority at present for what Clare wrote.

36. l. 9. *or* not *nor.*

37. l. 11. *love* not *loved.*

38. *Sonnet. I Am.* Knight's title. In line 3 Knight has *dam* not *dram.*

39. *A Vision. A Vision* not *I Lost the Love of Heaven.*

40. l. 12. *fame* not *flame.*

41. *Drinking Song.* Taylor's copyist makes this 'fourteener' measure.

42. *Autumn,* l. 4. *leaf* not *leaves.*

43. l. 5. *it* not *they.*

44. l. 22. *Fall* not *Drop.*

45. *The Autumn Wind's,* l. 17. *clouds like smoke slow sail* not *clouds of smoke they sail.*

46. l. 18. *like the human tread* not *from their mossy bed.*

47. l. 24. *Or stranger.*

48. l. 25. *it turns to gray* not *is turned to grey.*

49. l. 26. *As leaves lift up their undersides* not *And crowds of leaves do by it ride.*

50. l. 27. *birch it* not *birch-tree.*

51. l. 28. *To rippling billows petrified* not *in concert with the rippling tide.*

52. l. 37. *swound* is far more likely to be what Clare wrote and Knight's word is not clearly decipherable.

53. *To Miss B.,* l. 32. [*not*] supplied. Knight has *love was wi' man,* a slip surely.

54. *Misfortune,* l. 10. [*for*] supplied instead of Knight's *frae.*

55. l. 22. Knight has *waur than passage puir.* Taylor's copyist has *waur than parritch puir,* i.e. 'worse than poor folk who live on parish relief' or 'worse than poor folk who live on porridge'?

56. *Love of Nature,* l. 5. *harp* not *heart.*

57. *Little Trotty Wagtail,* l. 2. *near* not *ne'er.*

58. *Clock-a-clay,* l. 1. *cowslips peeps* not *cowslip pips.*

59. l. 7. *forests quake* not *forest quakes.*

60. l. 11. Knight has *purtering*; far more likely Clare wrote *puthering,* here offered.

61. l. 19. *My home it shakes* not *My home shakes.*

62. l. 20. *top't wi'* not *topped with.*

63. l. 23. *Here still I live* not *Here I live.*

64. *The Invitation,* l. 1. *Come hither, my fair one* (Knight) not *Come hither my dear one.*

65. l. 3. *pilewort and daisies in light and gold blazes* not *on pilewort and daisies the eye fondly gazes.*

66. l. 5. *Come in* not *Come with*; *silk and satin* not *silks and satins.*

67. l. 6. *green* not *grey.*

68. l. 7. *my dear* not *dear*; *flag* not *flags.*

69. l. 8. *bow up and down* not *bowing low down.*

70. l. 11. *On* not *To.*

71. l. 13. *speedwell* not *violet*.

72. *Clare to his Wife.* Knight's title.

73. l. 3. *Young Patty* not *Patty*.

74. l. 6. *wild roses* not *roses*.

75. l. 19. *wi' scorchin'* not *with brooding*.

76. l. 21. *cheeped on the whitethorn* not *chirruped on the thorn*.

77. l. 31. *live* not *love*.

78. *Where She Told her Love,* l. 10. *the dearest* not *made dearer*.

79. l. 20. *a stone* not *to stone*.

80. *The Dying Child. Sick* is pencilled above *Dying* in Knight.

81. l. 10. *little heart* not *heart*.

82. l. 23. *made* not *caused*.

83. ll. 24–5. *Nor any blossoms got : All* not *He now no blossoms got : They*.

84. l. 27. *was* not *were*.

85. *Death,* ll. 3–4. *coffin lids, Sadder than tears on grief's eyelids* not *coffin hid, Sadder than tears on grief's eyelid*.

86. l. 7. *tears of sorrow* not *tears and sorrow*.

87. *First Love,* l. 10. *took my eyesight quite away* not *took my sight away*.

88. l. 24. *Not love's appeals* not *And love's appeal*.

89. *Adieu,* ll. 5–7.

> Dews are on the braken
> Which the playful winds are shaking
> Sweet songs the birds are making

not

> The cows their thirst were slaking
> Trees the playful winds were shaking
> Sweet songs the birds were making

90. l. 20. *Chiming* not *Humming*.

91. l. 21. *blue-wing'd* not *red-winged*.

92. *The Peasant Poet,* l. 7. *Rack* could conceivably be *rock*; but *rack* makes better sense.

93. *My loved one my Own,* l. 3. Knight's transcript (Edwin Wing's (?) writing) has '*waiseys*. Did Wing find the word a puzzle but forget to close his raised commas? Taylor's copyist guessed *daiseys* but crossed his or her guess out. A suggestion is that *waiseys* is a noun from adj. *wasie* or *wazie* (Wright, vol. vi, p. 394), meaning 'gay', 'lively', 'sensible'. Such a word Clare knew from Beattie: 'The ploughmen, now their labour o'er . . . Right *wazie* waxed and full of fun' (Beattie: *Arnha'* (c. 1820)).

94. *The Dark Days of Autumn*. Unfinished.

95. l. 11. Knight's transcript has *instance*.

96. l. 12. Gap in MS. and transcripts.

97. *Fragment*. In the Peterborough transcript only, and in Clare's own writing.

98. '*Come the back way dear*'. Peterborough entitles this *Now Granny's gone to bed*.

99. *Song. I Hid my Love. I Hid my Love* not *Secret Love*.

100. l. 1. *while* not *till*.

101. l. 20. *buzz* not *bass*. Knight's transcript has *buss*.

102. *Born upon an Angel's Breast. Born upon an Angel's Breast* not *Love Cannot Die*.

103. l. 20. *even in its smart* not *in its very smart*.

104. *Wilt thou think o' me*. Knight's transcript has the first stanza of this ballad in semi-code, similar to the consonant-code that Clare used in the 'Halfpenny Ballads' MS. book: thus

> Now the spring's coming and wild b's 'r humming
> Mary think of me
> When leaves come to the wild wind
> So loved b' th' 'n childhd
> O thn remembr m
> Thn think who lvd th derst
> And clmd th kss snerst
> Which Mr still ws m
> O Mr n sprng wthr
> Lts bth go thr tgthr
> And still remembr m
> Where places are greenest
> And summer's serenest
> Wilt thou think o' me

105. *Song for Miss B——*. This ballad, not in the second volume of Knight's or in the Taylor transcripts, has the following note, in the handwriting of the Peterborough copyist: 'Copied from the original in possession of Mr Henry Harris.' There is a note from Clare:

DEAR MISS

I beg your acceptance of the enclosed ballad as the best I could make. The spring may bring better days, and better opportunitys to write a better song,

Yours truly

JOHN CLARE.

106.   l. 14. Noun from adj. *hasty* or *heasty*? (Wright, vol. iii, p. 80).
See Glossary. *vastiness* and *haziness* are both possible as C.'s
intended meaning; but what the Taylor copyist wrote is clearly
hastiness.

107.   *Written in Prison*, l. 14. *goal* not *rest*.

108.   *The Daisy*. This poem, not in Knight's transcripts, is from the
Peterborough copyist and carries a note: 'Copied from the original
in possession of Mr G. Packer.'

109.   l. 9. *form* not *from*.

110.   *To John Clare*. This title is Clare's own from his draft in the Peterborough MSS.

111.   *The Green Lane*. *The Green Lane* not *On a Lane in Spring*.

GLOSSARY

(Chiefly from Clare's own gloss for *Poems Descriptive of Rural Life and Scenery* and from the information which he himself gave for A. E. Baker's *Glossary of Northamptonshire Words and Phrases*.) Entries for which Clare is the chief or only authority are marked †.

Agen, beside, near.

Air-bell, wild hyacinth (see: *Hair-bell, harebell*).

Ariff (*eriff, erriff, harif*—Wright), goosegrass, cleavers.

Arum, cuckoo-pint, lords-and-ladies (see: *Cuckoo-flower*).

Ayont, beyond.

Baffles, gaiters.

Balk, bauk, baulk, narrow strip of grassland used, before hedges, to divide, individually owned strips in the old, open fields.

Bandy, game similar to hockey.

Bang, to rush violently.

Bantered, taunted.

Batter, to labour; or to walk at a great rate.

Battled, mud-bespattered.

Beaking, basking.

Bedlam-cowslip, *Primula variabilis*.

Beetling, striking with a heavy wooden mallet or beetle.

Bents, grass stalks.

Besprent, besprinkled.

Bever, refreshment.

Bevering, drinking, usually by hay-makers or harvesters in the fields.

Bield neuk, shed in the corner of a field.

Bigg, a coarse kind of barley.

Bitter-sweet, woody nightshade.

Blathering, clamouring.

Blea, bleak.

Bleb, a drop; vb.: to cover with drops.

Bloodwall, wallflower.

Bluecap, blue tit.

Blue-cap, blue cornflower, *Centaurea cyanus*.

Bog-bean, marsh trefoil.

† *Booning* (hours), times for refreshment during field-work.

Bottle, bundle of hay, straw or sticks; small keg for beer.

Brere, brier, briar, wild rose bush.

Brig, bridge.

Brother chip, fellow workman.

Brun, freckle.

Brustle, to bustle.

Budget, tinker's wallet.

Bullace, sloe.

Bum, to buzz, *bum-clock*, usually cockchafer; any flying beetle.

Bumbarrel, long-tailed tit.

Burr, to whir.

Burred, haloed (moon).

Butter-bump, bittern.

Cat-gallows, two vertical sticks with a third across the top used in jumping games.

Cat-tail, *Phleum pratense* grass.

Cawdy-mawdy, seagull (see Clare's list of birds).

Chat, wheatear, sedge-warbler, lesser whitethroat: any bird that makes the note *chat*.

Chelp, to chirp; to chatter, gossip.

Chickering, chirping of cricket or grasshopper.

Chitter, to twitter.

Chock, or *chuck*, game with marbles.

Chuffed, swollen.

Chumble, to nibble.

Churn, churn-owl, fern-owl, goat-sucker, nightjar.

Churring, whirring, of nightjar.

Clack, chatter.

Clammed, parched with thirst.

Clench, to rivet; to strengthen shoes with 'clinkers'.

Clipping-pinks, or *-posies*, flowers presented to shearers at shearing feasts and sometimes sprinkled with pepper for a joke.

Clock-a-clay, ladybird (see also: *Lady-cow*).

Clodhopper, wheatear.

Closen, small fields.

Cockle, corn-cockle, yellow corn-marigold.

Cock's stride, small distance, used of lengthening day.

Coddled apples, greater willow-herb.

Copple, crest on bird's head.

Corn-bottle, blue cornflower.

Crack, to boast.

Crank, to croak.

Creep up your sleeve, to deceive by coaxing.

Crib, food-rack, or small stall, for cattle.

Crimp, or *crimple*, to ripple, or to wrinkle; also 'crink'.

Crizzle, to roughen or become ridged, as of water beginning to freeze.

Croodling, shrinking from cold.

Crumble, a crumb.

Crump, to make a crackling sound, as frozen snow when trodden on; to crunch with the teeth.

Cuckoo-flower, cuckoo-pint, *Arum maculatum* (see: *Lords-and-ladies*).

Curdle, to ripple until white like curd.

Dither, to shiver with cold.

Dizen, to dress showily.

Dotterel, a cut or pollarded tree.

†*Dropple*, drop.

†*Drowk*, to droop, faint with drouth; also adj.

Duck-neath-water, May Day game in which players run, two by two, under a handkerchief held aloft between two other players.

Ducks and drakes, ancient game of throwing flat stones so that they skim the surface of the water.

†*Edding*, grass left for turning plough and horses at edges of ploughed fields.

Eking, stretching, spinning out.

Eldern, elderberry tree.

Elting, moist, damp, of soil new ploughed.

Feather-grass, meadow soft-grass.

Felfare, fieldfare.

Fen-sparrow, reed-bunting.

Fern-owl, nightjar (see: *Churn*).

Fetch, or *fitch*, any of the flowering vetches.

Finweed, rest-harrow.

Firdeal, or *firdale*, any fir tree that could be used for deals or planks.

Firetail, redstart.

Foulroyce, foul-rush, red-dogwood.

Freck, or *freak*, to spot, dapple.

Furmety, baked, or 'cree-ed' wheat, boiled in milk, with sugar and plums, and thickened with flour and eggs for Christmas fare.

Firze-lark, pipit.

Fuzz-ball, puff-ball, fungus.

Gilafer, *gillyflower*, *gilliflower*, wall-flower (see: *Bloodwall*).

Gleg, to peep at, to look askance at.

Glib, smooth, slippery, of ice.

†*Glimp*, *of the evening*, grey of twilight.

†*Glimpt*, *past part*, made from 'glimp'; having a touch of dusk.

Glize, to stare.

Glower, to look angrily at; to look gloomy, of the weather.

Goat's-beard, old man's beard, *Clematis vitalba*.

Goss, gorse.

Grain, a main branch of a tree.

Grounds, fields.

Grubbling, grasping, greedy.

Gulled, *gulling*, washed out, of a hole by water.

Gulsh, to drink voraciously; to fall and cut into the ground, of a tree; to gush, of water.

Hairbell, harebell, *Campanula rotundifolia*.

Hapt, covered.

Hastiness, or *heastiness* from adj. *hasty* or *heasty*, threatening, of rain.

Haum, haulm, head of barley.

Headache, scarlet corn-poppy.

Heronshaw, heron.

High-lows, laced boots with thick soles to raise them above the wet.

Hing, hang.

Hirpling, moving unevenly and askew, of a hare; limping, crouching, as from cold.

Horse-blob, marsh-marigold (see also: *Mare-blob*, *mere-blob*.

Horse-tail, *Equisetum*.

Hurkle, to crouch.

Ironweed, black knapweed (see also: *Knobweed*).

†*Jilt*, to jerk or throw underhand or backhand.

John-go-to-bed-at-noon, scarlet pimpernel.

†*Joll*, to walk lumberingly, to roll when walking.

Keck, hemlock, or chervil.

Knap, to crop, or bite, of grass.

Knobweed, knapweed, knotweed.

Knopple, flower-head.

Lad's-love, traveller's joy.

Lady-cow, ladybird (see also: *Clock-a-clay*).

Lady's laces, ribbon-grass.

Lady's smock, bitter cress, Shakespeare's 'Lady-smocks all silver white'.

Lambtoe, kidney vetch, also lady's finger, or bird's-foot refoil.

Lap, to wrap.

†*Lisper*, to lisp.

Long purples, purple loosestrife (or purple bugle?).

Looby, clown, lout.

Lords-and-ladies, cuckoo-pint, *Arum maculatum*.

Love-knot, charm made from blades of oat or wheat.

Lowk, to beat, thresh.

Lown, peasant.

Lug, to pull or drag.

Lump, to thresh.

Lunge, to lounge; or to hide.

Mare-blob, also *mere-blob*, marsh-marigold (see also: *Horse-blob*).

†*Midgeon*, gnats.

Miller's-thumb, small freshwater fish.

Moiled, weary with toil.

†*Moozing*, dozing.

Moping, dreamy, vacant.

Mort, *morts*, much, many, a great number; *mort to do*, great concern.

Mouldiwarp, mole.

†*Mozzling*, *mozzly*, mingled, of colours.

Muircock, name usually given to male ptarmigan, a bird not common in the Fens even in Clare's day (see Clare's list of birds); more likely Clare meant the male water-hen.

Nappy, ale.

†*Nauntle*, to raise, hold erect.

†*Nauntly*, jaunty.

Nimble, to move nimbly and quickly.

Nine-peg Morris, game played with stones, moved as in draughts, on squares cut in turf.

Noah's Ark, cloud in shape of a boat, supposed to portend floods.

Nuzzling, caressing, nestling.

Oddling, solitary.

Old Ball, name for a cart-horse.

Old man's beard, traveller's joy (see also: *Lad's love*).

Pad, a path.

Palm grass, reed meadow-grass, *Poa aquatica*.

Partraik, partridge.

Patty kay, hepatica.

Peep, or *pip*, single blossom in a flower-head.

Pettichap, either chiff-chaff or willow-warbler.

Pinder, villager whose job it was to impound strayed cattle.

†*Pingle*, clump of trees smaller than a spinney; enclosure or croft.

Pismire, earwig, or maybe ant.

Plashy, wet.

†*Pleaching*, bleaching.

†*Pleachy*, sun-dried, bleached.

Plough-Monday, festival of the Monday after Twelfth Day when husbandmen resumed labour.

Plump, forthright.

†*Pooty*, girdled snail shell.

†*Prime*, to preen.

Princifeather, lilac, or maybe laburnum.

Printings, lighter green markings where swaths of hay have lain.

Puddock, kite, or forked-tailed buzzard.

Pudge, puddle.

Puther, to reek, puff, of smoke or dust.

Quickset, hedge cut and laid for regrowing.

†*Quirk*, to search about.

†*Quirking*, nimble.

Ramp, to grow luxuriantly.

Ramping, coarsely growing.

Rauk, *rawk*, mist, fog.

Redcap, goldfinch.

Riddle, or *ruddle*, red ochre for marking sheep.

Riding, greensward road intersecting a wood.

Rig, joke, trick; ridge, in ploughed land or pasture.

Rocket, corn marigold.

Roil, to climb and tumble; to become turbid, of water.

Runnel, stream, open drain.

Sawn, saunter.

Scranny, wild, crazy.

Sedge-bird, sedge warbler.

Seemly, seemingly.

†*Seethe*, to soak, of dew or water.

Shagged, shaggy-haired.

Shanny, shy.

Shool, to shuffle.

Sile, to sink to the bottom.

Skewing, looking askance.

Slive, to slip past.

Sloomy, slow, dreamy, gloomy.

Slove, past tense of 'to slive'.

Soak, to drink heavily.

Soodle, to linger, saunter.

Sphinx, hornet sphinx moth.

Spindle, vb., to shoot up.

Sputter, to splutter.

†*Squirking*, squeaking.

Stalled, stuck fast.

Starnel, starling.

Statute, hiring Fair, before Michaelmas, for the purpose of hiring husbandmen and domestic servants.

Stingo, strong ale.

Stirtle, to start.

Stool, cluster of stems growing from a cut trunk of a tree.

Stoven, stump of a tree, either growing, or put in ground for post.

Stowk, shock of corn made of sheaves.

Streak, to stretch.

Struttle, gudgeon, stickleback, or any small freshwater fish.

Stulp, tree stump.

Sueing, or *sughing*, soughing or sighing of wind.

Suther, to rush, or moan, of wind; to whir, of birds' wings.

Swail, *swale*, shade.

Swaly, cool, shady.

Swap, or *swop*, vb. and n., to swoop, of pigeons usually; the noisy clap of their wings when pigeons alight.

Swee, to sway, swing.

Swift, newt; small lizard maybe.

Swingle, flail.

Swound, vb., to faint, swoon.

Taw, marble; *taws*, game of marbles.

Tedded, spread out to dry, of grass.

Tent, to tend, of cattle, sheep, goats or geese on the common lands.

Totter-grass, quaking-grass.

Tray, feeding-trough.

Trundle, path, course.

Tunkey, short and curly; A. E. Baker says a chunkey pig was often of Chinese breed.

Twitch, spear-grass, couch-grass.

Twitter, to tremble.

Tyke, churl.

†*Unbrunt*, unscathed (?).

Waffling, yapping.

Warp, to entwine, weave.

Water-blob, marsh-marigold.

Whemble, connected with vb. 'whemmle'; to turn upside-down.

Whew, to cry, of the plover; also n., to whirl, rush through the air.

Whopstraw, countryman (a term of contempt).

Wilding, crab-apple.

Wildling, wild rose.

Wimple, to ripple.

Witchen, mountain ash.

Wood-seer, insect that makes a knot of froth on leaves or flowers; one of the shepherd's weather-glasses, Clare says; the frog-hopper.

Writing-lark, yellow-hammer.

Yoe, ewe.

Younker, youngster.

INDEX OF FIRST LINES